SECONDARY PRINCIPAL'S SURVIVAL GUIDE

Practical Techniques & Materials for Successful School Administration

Robert D. Ramsey

Prentice Hall
Englewood Cliffs, New Jersey

Prentice-Hall International (UK) Limited, *London*
Prentice-Hall of Australia Pty. Limited, *Sydney*
Prentice-Hall Canada, Inc., *Toronto*
Prentice-Hall Hispanoamericana, S.A., *Mexico*
Prentice-Hall of India Private Limited, *New Delhi*
Prentice-Hall of Japan, Inc., *Tokyo*
Simon & Schuster Asia Pte. Ltd., *Singapore*
Editora Prentice-Hall do Brasil, *Rio de Janeiro*

10 9 8 7 6 5 4 3 2 1

Library of Congress Cataloging-in-Publication Data

Ramsey, Robert D.
    Secondary principal's survival guide : practical techniques & materials for successful school administration / Robert D. Ramsey
        p. 272. cm.
    Includes index.
    ISBN 0-13-799388-9
    1. High schools—United States—Administration—Handbooks, manuals, etc. 2. High school principals—United States—Handbooks, manuals, etc. 3. School management and organization—United States—Handbooks, manuals, etc. I. Title.
    LB2822.2.R36   1992   91-37419
    373.12é00973—dc20   CIP

PRENTICE HALL
Business Information & Publishing Division
Englewood Cliffs, NJ 07632
Simon & Schuster. A Paramount Communications Company

Printed in the United States of America

Dedication

To my mentors:

Oscar Haugh
Owen Henson
Carl Knox
Mike Hickey

I hope that some of their gifts of wisdom, integrity and intuitive
leadership are reflected in this text.

Acknowledgements

It takes many talents to produce a book. In this case, I want to acknowledge the specific and special talents of Elaine Lerdall and Sue Thomas who were instrumental in producing numerous drafts and the final manuscript.

R.D.R.

About the Author

Robert D. Ramsey currently serves as Associate Superintendent of the award-winning St. Louis Park (MN) Public Schools. His professional preparation includes B.S., M.S. and Ed.D. degrees from the University of Kansas and his front-line experience spans 35 years as a teacher, counselor, supervisor of social studies, curriculum director, personnel administratior, assistant superintendent and acting superintendent.

Dr. Ramsey has demonstrated a special, career-long interest in secondary education. He was instrumental in initiating an innovative schools-within-a-school program at Topeka (KS) West High School in the 1960's and in shaping a "national school of excellence" at St. Louis Park in the 1980's. In three school districts in two states, he has assisted, supervised and mentored some of the best secondary principals in the nation.

In addition to contributing numerous articles to leading education journals, Dr. Ramsey is author of the *Educator's Discipline Handbook* (Parker Publishing Company, 1981) and *Management Techniques for Solving School Personnel Problems* (Parker Publishing Company, 1984).

About This Resource

The secondary school principal holds one of the most difficult and demanding positions in American education. Senior high, junior high and middle school principals throughout the country are expected to provide inspiring educational leadership for a population of rapidly changing learners, implement reforms to meet escalating expectations from a critical and cost-conscious public, and provide creative supervision for a new breed of teaching staff. They must maintain a delicate balance between visionary leadership and managerial administration.

The *Secondary Principal's Survival Guide* is a roll-up-your-sleeves resource that details practical tools, techniques and time-savers you can use to solve the problems you face as a school leader. Conveniently organized for quick reference, the *Guide* is packed with real-world examples and successful, school-tested strategies for handling the many challenges encountered by both new and veteran administrators.

You will find information and techniques you can put to work in your job *today* in key sections like:

- Leadership Vs. Traditional Management
- How to Get Results by Nurturing the School's Climate
- What to Look for in the Staff of the Future
- Working with Staff Members Who Have an Attitude Problem
- Supervising Clerical and Custodial Personnel
- How to Have a Drug and Alcohol Free School
- New Ways to Handle the Old Problems of Attendance and Truancy
- Using Assessment to Drive Instruction
- Practical Ways to Reduce Paper Work
- Hints on Handling Complaints
- What to Do in Times of Cost Containment
- Guidelines for Crisis Management
- Essentials of Stress Management

The *Secondary Principal's Survival Guide* offers you practical advice on a wide range of difficult topics, from firing incompetent personnel to protecting students and staff from a maniac on the school grounds. It contains secrets of success for school discipline, budgeting, staff development, administrative politics, and more. Best of all, the tips, information and examples in the *Guide* were drawn from actual current experiences in successful schools across the country—schools in which principals not only survive, but excel!

Robert D. Ramsey

Table of Contents

Chapter 4. Managing Today's Adolescent Learners

Chapter 8. Managing Crises

Chapter 9. Managing Yourself As A School Leader

Final Word: Managing Tomorrow

Chapter 1

Leading Today's Secondary School: An Overview

America's schools tend to be bound by institutional inertia and a tenacious resistance to reform. The popular perception is that changing public education is like walking through a cemetery at night—in the darkness, people are certain they see movement, but in the cold light of day, nothing has really stirred.

Nevertheless, today's schools have undergone enormous transformations in the last few decades. Almost in spite of themselves, the nation's educational institutions have been compelled to respond to repeated and wrenching alterations in the structure of society. Schools at all levels serve a different clientele and are served by a new breed of professional staff (see Chapter 3).

More important, the nature and needs of today's student learners are radically different from those in the past. The inmates may not be running the institution, but emerging student values, needs, and expectations are driving all public schools in new directions. Where reformers have failed in efforts to reshape education, the learners themselves have and are changing schools and school leadership.

This chapter defines the different context in which today's secondary principals operate and pinpoints the specific new roles and skills required for survival and success.

TODAY'S CHANGED AND CHANGING LEARNER

Educators everywhere testify that there is something new and different about today's middle, junior, and senior high school students. Evidence of change lies in:

- growing disaffection
- rampant substance use and abuse
- surging suicide rates
- establishment of a growing "gang culture" among young people

1

For America's youth, these are the best of times and the worst of times. By world standards, many of our young people have an embarrassment of riches, mind-boggling opportunities, and unfettered freedoms. Others are continually suppressed by the harsh realities of discrimination and economic disparity. Both advantaged and disadvantaged youth, however, suffer from accelerating societal pressures, confusion with society's polarization of values, and feelings of profound loneliness in a crowded land.

What's different for and about today's teen and preteen learners is almost everything—their fears, concerns, and dreams constitute a new agenda of youth issues:

Today's Agenda for American Youth

A. *Family issues*

  1. Single parents
  2. Working parents
  3. Divorced parents
  4. Blended families
  5. Reduced family time ("quality time")
  6. Less energy and interest in parenting

B. *Social issues*

  1. Threats of war
  2. Economic instability
  3. Environmental concerns
  4. Racial tensions
  5. Unemployment
  6. Cost of higher education

C. *Health and safety issues*

  1. AIDS and sexually transmitted diseases
  2. Gangs
  3. Violence
  4. Addiction/dependency
  5. Teen pregnancy

D. *Personal issues*

  1. Insecurity
  2. Lack of trust in relationships
  3. Pessimism about success
  4. Peer pressure
  5. Sexual concerns

In many ways, the intrinsic nature of young people has probably not been fundamentally altered. Nevertheless, in coping and adapting to a society in transition and a new agenda of youth issues, students are bringing dramatically changed and changing needs into every classroom every day.

To meet those new needs, secondary schools are increasingly being called on to:

- Personalize education
- Nurture student self-esteem
- Find ways to fit in many varieties of "family"
- Promote/model human values

A NEW ROLE FOR SECONDARY SCHOOL ADMINISTRATORS

The job of the secondary principal has always been and continues to be important, demanding, and crucial to the success of the school. Many of the functions and elements of leadership required of school leaders in the past remain relevant and essential today. In addition, however, new dimensions are being demanded, and a new focus is forming for the leaders of the modern "school in flux."

What hasn't changed about the principal's role are the following features, which have always distinguished this leadership role from other positions of authority within education and in other organizational settings:

- The principal is still the key to effective schooling.
- The principalship, particularly at the secondary levels, remains one of the toughest jobs in the business. (Principals need to admit this to themselves and accept it as a condition of employment. There is no easy way to be an effective principal.)
- The principalship is different from many leadership positions in that it requires daily decision making in the midst of all the constituencies involved. Principals operate in constant crossfire and do not have the luxury of distancing themselves for the purposes of remote problem solving.
- The secondary principal plays to more audiences, serves a broader array of constituents and exercises a wider span of control than do his or her counterparts at the elementary level.
- The secondary principal's decisions affect more segments of the community than do those of any other school official except the superintendent.
- The principal continues to function as the symbolic and ceremonial head of the school.
- The principal is still expected to maintain discipline and manage the building, the budget, and the buses.

All these continuing roles might seem to constitute a full-time job. But today's principal must do and be more.

Secondary schools have become increasingly complex communities, mirroring the myriad elements and issues that make up our society. This complexity, coupled with the new agenda of youth issues, has irrevocably changed the principalship. Successful principals are finding it necessary to establish new priorities, develop new skills, and assume a number of unprecedented leadership roles within the school. As described by Les Bork, principal of St. Louis Park Junior High School (a National School of Excellence), the job of the principal in its most simplistic terms is now threefold:

1. Define direction.
2. Energize the building.
3. Hire the right people.

Other observers and practitioners define a much more complicated collection of functions and responsibilities for effective principals. What are the most pressing new roles which secondary administrators must now perform in order to lead and succeed in the modern school setting?

Emerging Roles for Secondary Principals

Instructional Leader: Although providing leadership for the instructional program has always been in the mix of expectations for the principals, this role is now rapidly assuming preeminent priority status. The distinction between A+ principals and also-rans is the value they place on their role as instructional leader. This role includes any and every function that improves conditions that encourage student learning. (The next portion of this chapter distinguishes between old-style *management* of curriculum and instruction and new-style true instructional *leadership*.)

Morale Builder: Like all effective leaders, principals are responsible for the atmosphere in which they lead. Attending to morale and school climate may be the most important single function exercised by principals who want to make a difference. (See Chapter 2, Managing the Dream.)

Champion of Excellence: Successful principals today constantly convey an unflinching commitment to absolute excellence in all educational programs. In the business world, companies that adopt a goal of "no more than 2 percent defects" often get almost exactly 2 percent defective merchandise. Contrarily, companies with a "zero-defect" policy come closer to perfection. This lesson applies to schools as well as to private enterprise. Everyone in the school community should know full well that the principal is an unequivocal advocate for excellence and that anything less is unacceptable.

Through this role, the principal can establish a self-fulfilling prophecy of success for the school.

"Servant Leader": One new view of school leadership is the concept of "leader as servant." This notion implies that a prime responsibility of the principal is to serve the needs of teachers and others who work on the front line of delivery for students. The principal's goal should be to do anything possible to ensure that every staff member is successful. This involves serving as a resource-broker and orchestrating all the affairs of the school to support the efforts of instructional personnel.

For some principals who are accustomed to viewing staff as subordinates who serve at the beck and call of the "leader," this is a dramatic reversal of roles. Such principals often obstruct, rather than promote and facilitate, learning. Most effective principals, however, quickly figure out that by finding creative ways to meet the needs of staff members, they maximize the possibility that student needs will be met.

Coach: The organizational dynamics of the modern school and emergence of a new breed of professional (see Chapter 3) make it virtually impossible for principals to exercise leadership by fiat, edict, or directive. Top-down direction no longer works (if it ever did). Effective management today demands less controlling and more "resourcing."

Skillful principals realize that empowerment, coaxing, influencing, and negotiating are critical elements in school leadership. The best of staffs can benefit from modeling and mentoring ("Even champions need coaches"). Good principals embrace and build on their role as "coach."

Strategic Planner: In easier times, many principals saw their job as one of merely carrying out plans established by others at the district level. The complexity of today's schools, however, requires that principals reach a new level of leadership by applying both short- and long-range planning strategies to the operation of the school.

Lack of planning is a surefire recipe for failure. The best schools have a clear-cut plan and sense of both purpose and direction. This necessitates that school leaders engage the total school community in continuous planning and re-planning. As schools become more autonomous, the principal's role in strategic planning becomes markedly more important (see Chapter 2).

Prioritizer: More than anyone else on the staff, it is the principal's role to sort out a multiplicity of diverse and diffuse issues and establish clear-cut priorities for the organization. The school cannot be all things to all people, but it can and should be some things that count in the lives of all students. One of the fundamental new roles of the school's chief executive is to identify and "breathe life" into those few things that matter most.

As just detailed, the role of the secondary principal has become a blend of traditional job functions and newly defined leadership responsibilities. The job description that follows reflects this mix of old and new roles:

Job Title: Secondary School Principal
Responsibilities:

1. Provide strong instructional leadership in the development, implementation, coordination, and evaluation of a balanced educational program, including all support services and cocurricular activities.

2. Assume responsibility for establishing a positive schoolwide climate that promotes effective learning and nurtures student and staff self-esteem.

3. Provide leadership in defining the vision/mission of the school and developing appropriate strategic plans to support the school's purpose.

4. Provide appropriate staff development programs at the building level, including orientation of new staff members.

5. Work with appropriate district administrators in the recruitment, selection, and assignment of personnel.

6. Assume overall responsibility for the supervision and evaluation of the performance of all school personnel.

7. Assume responsibility for the formulation, implementation, and evaluation of school procedures, rules, and regulations.

8. Assume ultimate responsibility for student discipline.

9. Foster a climate of positive school-community relations, provide information to the community about school programs, and involve the community and its resources in the educational program.

In many ways, the mixture of old and new roles for principals reflects a dichotomy between leadership versus management functions. Many of the traditional expectations for school leaders might be categorized as management-type activities, while most of the new roles are clearly higher-level leadership responsibilities.

LEADERSHIP VERSUS TRADITIONAL MANAGEMENT

Principals who plan to stay around long enough to see some positive payoff for their efforts must be both effective managers and visionary leaders. This is not a matter of choice. Such a dual role is required to meet the expectations that communities, school boards, and superintendents have for principals today. Heading up the school is no longer a matter of leadership or management, but a challenge to provide both. For those educators who may say that it can't be done—it's too big a job—the response is simply, "Yes, it can be done and is being done by the best secondary school principals throughout the country." As the "chief executive officer" (CEO) of the school, you must function both as manager and leader. More and more principals, however, realize that they must increasingly emphasize the leadership side of the equation.

The Difference Between Managers and Leaders

Managers	Leaders
• React (handle the crisis of the moment—damage control)	• Proact (anticipate problems—practice prevention)
• Deal with problems	• Set goals
• Attend to tangibles (the "stuff" of running a building)	• Address intangibles (goals, values, ideas, etc.)
• Allocate existing resources	• Create or find new resources
• Focus on "here and now"	• Focus on the future
• Cope with the system	• Change the system
• Follow the district's road map	• Define new places to go
• Make rules	• Create dreams

Obviously there is considerable overlap between leadership and management functions. Sometimes, in fact, creative management is the best leadership possible under the circumstances at hand.

For some principals, distinguishing the difference between leadership and management and understanding what true leadership entails is extremely difficult. If leadership isn't staying on top of the daily issues and incidents within the building, what is it?

Five Action Axioms of Leadership

1. *Leadership is about vision.* Winning individuals and organizations both start with and are driven toward a dream (a vision of success). Such dreams are the stuff with which leaders build the future. Leadership means setting goals and getting others to commit to them. A priority role of the leader is to help (force, if necessary) the organization to identify and clarify its mission, direction, and values. This is what effective principals do for successful schools.

2. *Leadership is about health.* True leaders are obsessed with the health of the groups and institutions they lead. To lead is to be relentless in diagnosing signs of sickness, rooting out diseased spots, and fending off any pressures that might damage growth and vitality. The leader's first priority is to keep the organization whole, moving, and doing what it's supposed to do. This applies to schools as much as to corporations

or other entities. This means keeping in touch with community expectations, making curriculum evaluation a way of life, constantly improving the operational systems of the school, and never backing away from tough personnel issues.

3. *Leadership is about inclusion.* All leaders must work through others and realize that every group draws its strength from *all* the parties involved. There are no leaders without followers, and there are no unimportant followers. The best leaders attend to all individuals and groups within the organization, stress involvement, build inclusive teams, and see success as a group achievement. The picture of an effective organization is a circle big enough to include everyone. For schools and school leaders, this means decentralized decision making, shared power, and an accent on openness. Inclusion in schools can run the gamut from forming advisory councils to instituting a full-blown site-management program.

4. *Leadership is about ethics.* Leadership demands integrity in order to achieve credibility. Leaders who want to leave a positive lasting legacy are principled. They keep promises and model authenticity. They don't compromise basic values or violate trust. All leaders make mistakes and suffer imperfections, but the best are never willfully unethical. This is a tough standard to meet, but this is leadership at its finest. People support, follow, and go the extra mile for leaders they trust. The best principals and other school leaders develop such trust over time by behaving honorably and by painstakingly paying attention to the perception of ethical behavior. In schools, ethical leadership begins by respecting confidentiality, refusing to whitewash mistakes, and avoiding credit for the accomplishments of others.

5. *Leadership is about politics.* Dictionaries have varied definitions for the term "politics":

   • the art of the possible

   • the total complex of relations between people in society

   • competition between competing interest groups or individuals for power or leadership in a group

Regardless of definition, all human organizations, including schools, are political entities and successful leaders use the political process to achieve desired ends. This requires understanding power structures and learning how to negotiate and when to draw the line. Results come from pushing the limits of reality, not from ignoring them. Schools are a unique construct of internal and external political forces including staff factions, student groups, district personnel, parents, the school board, state legislators, community members, and more. Principals, like leaders in all fields, must learn to "read" the political power swings within the organization and to unite and integrate diverse political forces behind common goals. To succeed and survive in school politics, your best course as principal is to align yourself with issues rather than personalities and resist compromising principle for personal gain.

Based on these axioms, leadership clearly deals with issues, ideas, and relationships, whereas management centers more on matters of materials, time, and space (you lead people and manage things). A critical issue for most principals is how to find time for both leadership and management responsibilities. Handling both is difficult but "doable." The secret lies in self-discipline and setting priorities.

Reams of research findings have identified workable techniques that overloaded leaders in all fields can use to save time and make time for both leadership and management functions. Consider the following 20 most common strategies that appear in almost all research studies on time management:

The 20 Most Common "Time Management" Tips for Leaders

1. Work on the big things (prioritize, prioritize, prioritize).
2. Match your effort to the importance of the tasks—practice selective perfectionism. (It doesn't take a tidal wave to extinguish a spark.) You don't want to spend the same time on a routine report to a state agency as you do on a major presentation to the school board.
3. Block out time for leadership. (Schedule meetings with yourself.)
4. Delegate whenever and wherever appropriate (share the power and the fun).
5. Put organizational and personal goals in *writing*.
6. Practice "benign neglect;" ignore issues that will likely be readily resolved by others or by the passage of time.
7. Bite the bullet (just do it). Beat the demon procrastination.
8. "Chunk" large tasks; tackle a piece at a time.
9. Pass the buck back. Don't take on everyone else's problems.
10. Organize *every day*. Be sensitive to your own unique time use patterns and organize activities around your peak periods.
11. Modify your open-door policy by controlling who enters your office and how long they stay. (Adopt a "door ajar" policy when appropriate.)
12. Make good use of your secretary as a buffer to control your calendar.
13. Use tickler files as reminders of recurring activities, deadlines, and so on.
14. Tame the paper tiger. Minimize the number of times you handle any piece of paper—act on it, delegate it to someone else, file it for future reference, or scrap it the first time you see it. Don't set papers aside and keep coming back to them repeatedly before deciding what to do with them.
15. Streamline/limit meetings. Most regularly scheduled, routine meet-

ings become dysfunctional. Hold meetings only when you have to, and then follow a tight agenda.

16. Set a specific time each day to return telephone calls.

17. Use "downtime" (waiting time, on-hold time, etc.) to read and plan.

18. Use technology (computers, word processors, voice mail, fax machines, dictating devices, etc.) to maximize efficient time use.

19. Find a hideaway away from your office to work on projects requiring extended uninterrupted periods.

20. Reward yourself for completing onerous tasks. Treat yourself to observing or participating in something you like to do at school or enjoying one of your favorite pastimes outside of work.

This section has drawn the boundaries around the leadership and management functions that must be performed by all secondary principals and pointed out tested ways to have the time to meet both areas of responsibility and accountability.

A NEW VIEW OF THE SCHOOL'S LEADERSHIP TEAMS

Leadership in groups of any size, particularly in the complex organization of a secondary school, can no longer be the prerogative of a single "point person." One way to face multiple challenges and problems is to engage multiple problem-solvers and decision-makers. Just as migratory birds rotate leaders in flight and, thus, fly faster and farther than they could singly, schools may take off and soar by learning to share leadership roles in a variety of unconventional arrangements.

As principal, you are ultimately responsible for what happens and doesn't happen in the school, where the school is headed, and where the school ends up. However, there can and should be varying levels of leadership responsibilities throughout the organization.

The watchwords for successful school management and instructional leadership include:

- Empowerment
- Shared management
- Collegial leadership
- Participatory decision making
- Teamwork/team building
- Decentralized decision making

The principal has many hands to call on to help in goal setting, decision making, and conflict resolution within the school. The roster of resources includes assistant principals, administrative aides and interns, department chairs (see Chapter 4), teachers, parents, student leaders, district administrative personnel, consultants, outside agencies, and professional associations.

The trick is to relinquish measured authority in meaningful ways without resorting to chaos or governing solely by plebiscite. This requires that school leaders truly become willing to "let go" and to forsake ego—de-emphasize the *me* and stress the *we* within the organization. Power and responsibility must be honestly delegated, coupled with authority, accountability, and commitment to live with compromise and group decisions. The necessary ingredients for developing a viable and valid school leadership team are depicted as follows:

Steps to a Successful Leadership Team

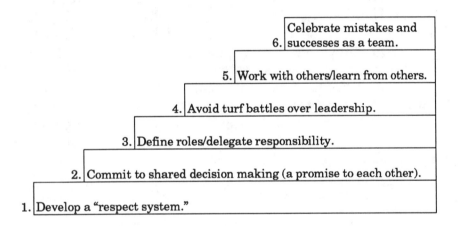

6. Celebrate mistakes and successes as a team.
5. Work with others/learn from others.
4. Avoid turf battles over leadership.
3. Define roles/delegate responsibility.
2. Commit to shared decision making (a promise to each other).
1. Develop a "respect system."

The move toward multiple management, shared power, and authentic leadership teams in schools has been supported and reinforced by a number of reform efforts at the state and local level throughout the nation. Following are concrete examples of the different forms that team leadership has taken and ways that shared power can really work:

Career Ladders for Teachers: In rethinking the organization and structure of American schools, increasing attention is being paid to providing "career ladders" for professional teachers. The intent of such programs is:

1. To tap the talents of the best teachers and extend their skills to more students and colleagues
2. To provide opportunities for career advancement for outstanding teachers
3. To realign school resources to foster better instructional leadership, staff development, school management, and student learning

Most career ladder arrangements establish a tier of teacher roles in which professionals with unusual expertise can become "master" or "lead" teachers with responsibility for helping plan, shape, and implement the instructional program. Often, lead teachers receive extra compensation and/or released time from regular classroom assignments to assist in training other teachers or intervening with teachers who need help.

Where such an organization exists or can be created, the principal has a brand new set of allies and resources for the leadership team at the school. Although some may see the trend toward career ladders as an erosion of administrative power, most principals welcome the additional leadership assistance.

Department Heads Revisited: Many secondary schools have always had some provision for subject area department heads or chairs. In the majority of cases, however, the role of the department chairperson has been relatively perfunctory and limited primarily to scheduling classes, ordering supplies, inventory control, arranging field trips, and paper shuffling.

With today's new demands and expectations on already strained resources, many principals are looking for means to revitalize the role of department heads, to enhance their leadership functions, and to engage them as meaningful partners in the conduct of the school.

The job description that follow illustrates how the role of department heads can be redefined to incorporate them as active participants in school leadership.

Job Title: Department Chair
Responsibilities:

1. Act as liaison between the building principal and staff and students in the assigned areas.
2. Work with the principal to plan cooperatively and evaluate teaching and instructional procedures.
3. Assist in the planning, implementation, and evaluation of the curriculum.
4. Stimulate the implementation of new instructional methods by teachers.
5. Assist in screening, interviewing, and selection of new staff members.
6. Prepare and propose appropriate department budgets.
7. Coordinate accurate ordering and inventorying of textbooks, instructional supplies, and capital equipment.
8. Provide leadership in planning and implementing appropriate staff development programs.
9. Assist building supervision in the principal's absence.
10. Assist the principal in determining teaching and room assignments.
11. Assess the curriculum to assure its consistency with district educational philosophy and goals.
12. Propose curriculum development projects and assist in overall supervision of the curriculum.
13. Encourage creativity and innovation that will result in enriched learning for students.

Chapter 4 contains additions suggestions for making effective use of department heads as leaders in the school.

Parent Advisory Councils: Across the country, parents are rapidly emerging as a legitimate force in the leadership of the school. Many schools have moved beyond the traditional perspective of parental involvement as fundraising, forming booster clubs, and so on, and have established formal parent advisory councils (PACs) to assist the principal in charting new directions for the school. Such councils can be a valued and valuable resource for the school leader by providing input, advice, and support for new programs, goals, and reforms.

A special section in Chapter 6, "Guidelines for Successful Parent Advisory Councils," spells out detailed strategies for using parents to help lead the school and for involving them directly in the power structure of the organization.

Site-Based Management: Some schools have taken the concept of parent involvement in school leadership a quantum leap beyond the Parent Advisory Council by establishing a full-blown site-management system. Ordinarily, such a system fosters decentralized decision making that is carried out by a school site-management council comprised of administrators, teachers, parents, students, and other community members.

The purpose of site management is to give all members of the school community a greater stake in the educational process, operation, and management of the school. Under site management, there can be a variety of approaches to delegating decision-making authority for curriculum, staffing, budgeting, materials, and facilities. Regardless of the exact form a site management program takes, it is important that the principal remain the accountable party in all matters of operation, objectives, and school policy. Experiences in New York and Chicago during the 1980s demonstrate the disarray that can result when citizen councils operate without accountability.

The Site Council Mission Statement and Responsibility Flow Chart that follow explain the "how" and "why" of site management.

Site Council Mission Statement

The mission of the site council is to provide a
shared decision-making process toward better
education for students and a better educational
environment for the school through decentralized,
democratic stakeholder partnerships.

Obviously, the site-management approach represents a radically different management milieu which embodies all the essential elements of

Site Council Responsibility Flow Chart

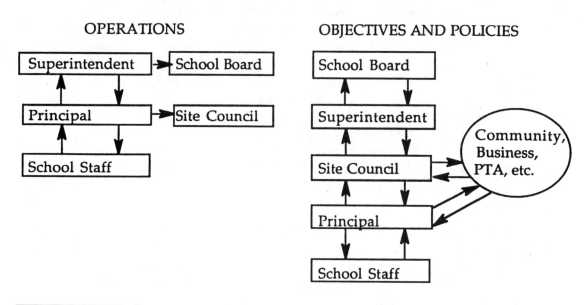

OPERATIONS

OBJECTIVES AND POLICIES

shared leadership. Although there may be many variations on the theme, site-management constitutes a viable model of participatory decision making now and for the future.

Parent Choice: Another manifestation of parent influence on school leadership is the rapid expansion of parental choice in the educational process. In many places, parents may now indicate preferences and make choices of teachers, schools and even school districts (including the option of attending nonpublic schools). This phenomenon seems destined to grow.

The more choices that are offered to and made by parents, the greater role they have in guiding and influencing educational programs and school philosophy. The choice movement automatically places parents in the mix of school policy making. Principals are well advised to welcome choice, recognize it as a new dimension affecting decision making, and use it as a positive force for the leadership of the school. Chapter 6 contains detailed approaches to channeling choice and making it work for the betterment of school programs.

Business Partnerships: More and more schools are forming partnerships and alliances with businesses in the community. These linkages include several types of cooperative ventures, such as:

• Adopt-a-school program

- Corporate sponsorships
- Mentoring programs
- Executive exchanges
- Career "shadowing" programs
- Shared personnel and facility arrangements

Regardless of form, partnerships give the business community a new voice in school affairs. Politically savvy principals are rapidly learning to accept and capitalize on the expertise and real-world guidance that the corporate community can contribute to school management.

This chapter has provided an overview and orientation to managing today's secondary school. The rest of the text embellishes on means to help you survive and succeed as a productive principal. Chapter 2 focuses on the first critical step—nurturing the dream that drives the school and the "culture" that can make the dream become reality.

Chapter 2

Managing the Dream

The best schools—the best organizations of any kind—are dream driven. This dream is the shared image of what the school is all about, what it stands for, what it values, where it's going, and what is *really* important.

This vision breathes life into the organization. It focuses team efforts and provides busy professionals with a reason to come to work every morning with exuberance and enthusiasm. The dream is the rallying point for everyone in the organization—it's the brass ring that the school is grabbing for. The vision and purpose add meaning to what teachers, administrators, clerks, custodians, and other staff members do on a daily basis.

The principal is the caretaker of the vision. There is little you can do that is more important than attending to the vision, morale, climate and culture of your particular school. Good leaders sell dreams and help people realize them. In managing the dream of the school, the principal is the primary catalyst who can:

- Make it real
- Make it happen
- Make it better
- Make it last

The culture or "personality" of the school is what you have to work with to define, nurture, and achieve the school's dreams.

WHY THE CULTURE OF THE SCHOOL IS CRUCIAL TO SUCCESS

When people talk about a specific school, they usually refer to the building, the curriculum, the staff and the athletic teams. But what the school really is, is its unique character—its environment of unwritten norms and expectations—in other words, its culture.

Some schools are businesslike and serious. Some are fun. Some are institutions that place a premium on performance and productivity. Others are places built around caring human relationships. The best schools are all of the foregoing. No organization can be better than how people in it feel about it. Some aspects of culture grow unconsciously; but much of it is

17

planned. Successful organizations take the importance of culture seriously because a positive culture makes good things happen. This is why cultivating the culture is a major function of effective school leaders.

Creating a culture of caring and commitment has to start on the inside—with all the employees of the organization—and is developed through pride, celebration, recognition, ownership, authentic communication, and staff development. The ultimate goal is improved staff morale. If staff members are enthusiastic and take pride in their work, everyone wins—students, the community, and the employees themselves.

Here are eight reasons why the school's culture must be high on every principal's action agenda:

Why Culture Is Important to an Organization

- It sets the standard of performance and productivity and conditions participants to meet certain expectations.
- It defines what "quality" is and determines the quality of life within the organization.
- It provides meaning and fosters fulfillment.
- It spells the difference between a mere group of employees and a winning team.
- It can make commitment a cultural imperative.
- It creates the synergy that transforms the whole into something greater than all the individual parts.
- It's what makes the organization "up close and personal." It defines how people treat and get along with each other.
- It sends a message about the place and the people in it.

In the schools that work best, there is a culture rooted in a prevailing mood of cooperation and human concern interfaced with visible evidence of mutual support and trust. This should be the goal of every secondary school principal. Other essentials of an effective organizational culture include the following:

- Quality is a habit.
- People feel good about themselves and are motivated.
- There is a feeling of family within the organization.
- Most people are customer conscious.
- Collegialism and enthusiasm permeate the organization.
- Workers determine the patterns of work.
- Power is plural.
- The environment is fluid. People accept and even embrace change.
- Members are proud and confident.

- Participatory planning prevails.
- The organization provides a growth environment for everyone.
- A feeling of trust, sharing, and caring is evident.
- The organization has its priorities straight.
- Employees have a sense of ownership.
- The culture arouses and nurtures hope in everyone involved.
- The culture is a support base. People share problems, help each other, and back each other up.
- There is an atmosphere of self-renewal.
- The organization values ethical responsibility.
- People have fun at work.

When it comes to nurturing and attending the culture of the school, you must come ready to play every day. It requires ongoing, overt attention.

HOW TO GET RESULTS BY NURTURING THE SCHOOL'S CULTURE

An effective school has to be much more than merely a place where happy people have fun working together comfortably. Good schools have to produce quality teaching, learning, growth, development, and positive change. Fortunately, the two scenarios are not mutually exclusive. The best results come from schools with a culture that helps people produce, as well as to feel accepted, valued, recognized, and rewarded. This is why wise principals invest time, energy, and effort into caring for the culture of the organization—it pays off in improved performance.

Where the school's climate or culture is concerned, there can't be too much leadership. Some schools may have too many pseudo-leaders, self-appointed leaders or would-be leaders, but they can't have an excess of true leadership directed toward promoting healthy relationships and a positive climate.

The good news is that it is not that difficult (see the accompanying "The Ease (E's) of an Effective Culture". The bad news is that not many administrators realize the power and importance of the culture of the school.

The Ease (E's) of an Effective Culture	
Empowerment	Energy
Encouragement	Entrustment
Enthusiasm	Entitlement
Excitement	Exuberance

The first step in getting results by nurturing the school's culture is to work with the staff to diagnose the organization. The entire staff should periodically engage in a reflective and introspective process of inquiry regarding the beliefs and behaviors within the organization—what is working and what isn't for the human beings who have to show up every day and produce. (A later section of this chapter offers tips on conducting an in-house morale survey.)

Where there are problems or dysfunctional relationships, you must lead the way in helping the staff to look at things differently and to revisit the human basis for the school. The focus should be on doing things today that will help assure success tomorrow.

The single most important action that principals can take to improve the school's culture is to model caring and sharing behavior actively as illustrated here:

A Principal's Model for Caring/Sharing
• Be open and honest.
• Listen to people's problems (personal and professional).
• Demonstrate self-disclosure.
• Handle people first, paper second.
• Provide time for change.
• Stick to your word.
• Respond to complaints.
• Accept criticism.
• Provide recognition.
• Share success.
• Try to improve working conditions.
• Avoid playing favorites.

There are a number of other initiatives that school leaders can undertake to encourage a culture that works for, not against, school goals. The best of these strategies are itemized as follows:

- Abandon top-down management. (Free people to produce on their own in their own way.)
- Assign responsibility for morale to the group itself.
- Act as a buffer and advocate for the staff.
- Encourage healthy relationships and reward cooperation.
- Value vitality and validate good performance with personalized praise.
- Appreciate difference and integrate individual personalities.
- Provide tangible support for staff efforts (materials, supplies, time, etc.).
- Work with one person at a time whenever possible.
- Arrange opportunities for people to get away together.
- Help people to stretch their individual styles in order to work with others.

THE SECRET OF CHAMPIONSHIP PERFORMANCE

The easiest ways to achieve an effective culture are either to inherit one or to hire all superstars who are caring, competent, and committed. In the real world, however, you have to work with what you've got, which is usually a duke's mixture of talent, intensity, loyalty, and connectedness. What you should strive for is an environment that frees and stretches ordinary people to become overachievers and to perform at a championship level. The secret of championship performance is to bring out the best in others, to deny anyone the opportunity to fail, and to know when to leave people alone. Successful leaders in any kind of organization do this by:

- Clarifying and dramatizing goals
- Demonstrating initiative for action, not reaction
- Team building
- Developing trust
- Sponsoring, supporting, and cheerleading
- Sharing and shaping values
- Generating pride
- Sharing successes (allowing no room for prima donnas)
- Give everyone in the organization a feeling of personal significance

USING BELIEF STATEMENTS TO FOCUS TEAM EFFORTS

An organization becomes what it believes. The vision and the culture of any group are rooted in its prevailing set of commonly held beliefs. Everyone in the organization must know what the organization believes. People can't commit or connect if they don't know what the organization stands for. "I don't know what we believe" is the most damning indictment of any institution—particularly a school.

Every principal has an obligation to help shape and articulate the belief system of the school. Many school and school districts have sharpened their vision and vigor by developing a clearly defined set of belief statements. Such statements should be brief and specific. To be effective, belief statements must be authentic representations of what the organization and its constituencies truly value. The best statements of belief are defined by consensus and come from the hearts of those who make up the organization. (See sample provided).

The most common means of reaching consensus on belief statements is to use a "force-choice" approach whereby all suggestions are listed and, then, systematically reduced or eliminated by requiring all parties to

In This We Believe . . .

- **Success**

  All people can learn and their learning should be lifelong. Everyone should experience success and be truly recognized. Our goal is for everyone to be the best they can be.

- **Service**

  The whole community is our customer and our sole purpose is to serve them. Thus, we value parental and community involvement. Getting along with people is one of the important talents we bring to our profession.

- **Empowerment**

  Empowering people within their area of responsibility, encouraging risk taking, practicing participatory decision making, and fostering learning opportunities are fundamental to the growth of all students and staff.

- **Culture**

  The culture of the organization is an important and powerful variable that should be nurtured and celebrated in order for our school to be a healthy, happy, and productive place to live and learn.

- **Team work**

  We are each other's greatest strength and are all accountable for organizational outcomes. Collaboration, congeniality, open communication, caring, listening, and loyalty are essential to success of our team.

- **Evaluation**

  Evaluation should drive instruction to meet individual student needs. Effective evaluation and the proper use of results enables us to reallocate limited resources to accomplish desired goals.

- **The Future**

  The future is ours to create. It is our responsibility to model this belief for our students, our community, and ourselves.

. . . for excellence in teaching, learning, and growing in our school.

indicate their highest priorities until a final and workable list is achieved. Another popular consensus-reaching technique is to use an "affinity diagram" that organizes all suggestions into clusters based on similarities and common themes, and then, selecting the most representative idea from each cluster.

Once established, the belief statements of the school should be widely publicized internally and externally through a variety of means such as posting in all classrooms and offices, featuring in school publications, and distributing billfold-size cards to students, staff, and community members. In this way, the belief statements focus team efforts on what is important and serve as a constant reminder of what counts in the school.

The next step is to get staff members to act their beliefs. This is most likely to happen in a culture where morale is high and people are unafraid to demonstrate the strength of their convictions.

TESTED TECHNIQUES FOR BOOSTING STUDENT AND STAFF MORALE

As principal, you set the feeling tone for the school and model what is important in school relationships. Part of your responsibility in fostering a positive school climate is to promote growth opportunities for everyone in the organization that include self-development activities, as well as instructional improvement programs. (See list of personal development programs that follows.)

Personal Development Programs for School Personnel

- Faculty aerobics
- Stop smoking clinics
- Self defense
- Humor and your health
- Weight watchers at work
- Being a better health care consumer
- Building a leisure identity
- Body talk—the hidden language
- Grief relief
- Work smarter, not harder
- Assertive communications
- Organizing files
- Stress management
- Planning your own wellness program

Part of your role as principal is to be the primary mover in morale management. The best way to know where to start is to diagnose the existing school climate through observation, staff focus groups, exit interviews, and/or a more formal study.

A structured morale survey may be targeted toward an entire school district or to a specific school or department. In any case, the aim is to assess the existing climate of attitudes, feelings, and perceptions as the basis for forming specific improvement plans. A formal morale study can be a valuable tool for helping you to understand and influence group dynamics within the school. The following guidelines have proved valuable to many school leaders:

Guidelines for Structured Staff Morale Study

1. The purpose should be clear to all potential respondents.
2. Everyone involved should understand that there are no right or wrong answers. What is asked for is personal perception and opinion based on knowledge and experience within the organization.
3. Survey respondents must remain anonymous.
4. The survey should involve *all* categories of personnel.
5. The survey instrument should be designed around "forced choice." Do not permit respondents any "weasel room" to opt out of answering items or to duck difficult issues.
6. Survey items should be carefully crafted and explicit (see sample survey provided). Validity of responses is increased if the same issue is tested in a variety of ways.
7. The survey should include an open-ended comment section for areas that may have been missed or slighted.
8. Results should be reported fairly, honestly, and accurately to all respondents and other affected parties.
9. Follow-up and follow-through are essential. The school leader must act on the results in a visible way.

Morale Survey Questions

Key: SA–Strongly agree
      TA–Tend to agree
      TD–Tend to disagree
      SD–Strongly disagree

Questions	SA	TA	TD	SD
1. My principal tries to get my ideas.				
2. Administrative decisions seem fair.				
3. I am treated like a professional.				
4. There is too much friction between groups.				
5. Administration does not respond to needs.				
6. I generally support building policy.				
7. School rules make sense.				
8. My performance is judged fairly.				
9. We are kept adequately informed.				
10. I don't know much about my fellow workers.				

Once you have a clear and accurate sense of the state of morale within the school, you must take some action. This means both building on strengths and shoring up weaknesses. Where problems exist, the solution often lies in relatively simple, but direct, corrective measures. The following are some common small morale boosters that can make big differences in school climate:

- Remembering and recognizing birthdays
- Keeping out bothersome sales representatives
- Providing notary public services on site
- Developing a systematic process for handling complaints
- Using the intercom sparingly
- Championing teacher privacy (buffeting the staff from interruptions, providing space for private phone use, etc.)
- Making telephones accessible for staff use
- Easing parking problems
- Buffeting staff from interruptions
- Sponsoring special activities that showcase staff talent and foster team-building (faculty art shows, bowling league, golf tournaments, volley ball teams, etc.)

In every effort (big or small) to boost morale, the goal is always to make the organization the healthiest place it can be. Positive morale is the first condition for success in attaining institutional goals. One prerequisite for high morale is a sense of pride, and pride feeds on recognition.

HOW TO USE RECOGNITION TO GUARANTEE SUCCESS

Recognition is the kind of incentive that pulls, rather than pushes, people toward their personal best and toward attaining organizational goals. Effective leaders understand the power and importance of appropriate and deserved recognition in motivating individuals and bolstering group morale. Applause and praise are free and should be used freely.

Recognition is most effective when it is authentic, earned, and results from catching people doing better than their previous performance, better than others; and/or better than expected.

The basic rule of recognition giving is to pick the appropriate occasion and format for conveying appreciation, gratitude and honors. Recognition may be private or public, tangible, or intangible. Opportunities for giving praise are boundless. Following is a sample of suggestions for recognizing deserving staff members that have worked in many schools.

Recognition Techniques

- Simple "Thanks for being a Real Pro" notes. (Recognition often means more if it's in writing, especially handwriting.)
- Handshakes, hugs, and pats on the back.
- A+ awards/certificates, given to employees for excellence and extra effort. (See the nomination form following.)
- Class act awards, given for demonstrated outstanding teaching. (See the nomination form following.)
- Kudos and recognition in building and district publications.
- Bulletin board achievement displays.
- Retirement parties.
- Recognition gifts—clocks, desk sets, plaques, and so on.
- Articles in the employee's hometown newspaper.
- School board spotlight honoring achievers at public school board meetings.
- Memorials to honor deceased colleagues (e.g., a memorial garden on school grounds).
- Recognition banquet(s) for staff, for volunteers, for substitute teachers, for community education contributors, an so on.
- Service pins.
- A "Reflections" booklet highlighting the career of retiring personnel.
- Miniawards to show collegial support and recognition. (See "Praise for Peers Pizza" announcement.)

A+ Award Nomination

This award is to recognize employees who are doing their share—and then giving that "extra A+ effort." Please use this form to nominate anyone you feel deserves special recognition. Some of the qualifications we're looking for are the following: communicates effectively, represents the district well, is self-motivated and helpful, consistently gives "100 percent plus" effort, and seeks ways to improve the district.

Employee's name: _____ Building: _____

Consistently goes beyond job expectations: _____

_____

_____

Is a positive representative of the district: _____

_____

_____

Is innovative and seeks new ideas and methods: _____

_____

_____

Is self motivated: _____

_____

_____

Shows involvement in total district concerns: _____

_____

_____

Other reasons this employee is outstanding: _____

_____

_____

Name _____ Date _____

_____ Check if you wish to remain anonymous.

CLASS ACT AWARD RECOMMENDATION

Please consider _____
name

_____ as a recipient of the Class Act
building
Award.

I AM RECOMMENDING THE ABOVE PERSON BECAUSE:

List at least four specific reasons for this nomination.

List specific examples of achievements or services.

This information will be used in the presentation of the Award and included in district publication.

Recommended by: _____ _____
Date

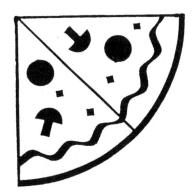

Praise Peers for Pizza!

You know people who deliver for learners everyday . . . Let us deliver pizza to them!

We all like praise and most of us like pizza.

Here's your chance to give a colleague a boost with a little bit of both!

To affirm your colleagues, enter them in the Praise Peers for Pizza drawing. Write a brief statement telling how each one has helped you, a student, or the district in some way. Send the form below to Judi Mollerus in the district office.

At the end of each month from January through May, the SD2 committee will draw four names. Winners will receive a coupon for a large, two-topping pizza from Cheeta Pizza delivered to school on the day of their choice. As many entries as possible (not just the winners) will be published in Staff letter to let the whole district know about these positive contributions.

- -

Nomination Form

Name of person praised: _____

Building: _____

Position: _____

Your name: _____

Praise statement: _____

_____

_____

Return to Judi Mollerus in the district office.

Whatever form it takes, recognition should be designed to reward performance, to affirm commitment and effort, and to show that the organization and the people in it care about quality and excellence. Leaders need to accept and appreciate these staff members who meet expectations and make the organization function on a daily basis, but they must also give special recognition to the "doers" whose performance advances the entire organization a notch or two toward fulfilling its dream.

USING SCHOOL STORIES, HEROES, AND CELEBRATIONS TO BUILD COOPERATION

Teams that come out on top share a heritage of tradition. This is what distinguishes them from just another assortment of individuals who show up at the same time and place for work each day. Winning teams have built a history together. They share stories of "legendary" heroes and epic events from the past. These stories foster pride and help people feel part of a distinctive organization. They draw people together and give the group its own mystique. Sharing a common heritage promotes loyalty, rapport, and camaraderie. This is how the culture of the organization is preserved, maintained, reinforced, and conveyed to newcomers.

Institutional tales make the organization seem larger than life and give its members a feeling of history (where we've been) and a sense of survival. They also provide the source of humor and fun which enables the organization to laugh at itself.

Every school has stories, like the ones about:

- The iron maiden principal whose approach was forewarned by banging on the pipes that ran throughout the building.

- The principal who embarrassedly received a speeding ticket in the parking lot while the student body observed from the library windows above.

- The "depression" when budget cutting meant counting paper clips and hoarding rubber bands.

- The school board chair who delivered a commencement address with his shirttail sticking out of the fly of his pants.

These stories form a powerful anecdotal history of the organization and help establish its identity and exemplify its beliefs. "Remember the time that . . ." is a testimony to the endurance of the organization and its culture. Astute principals recognize the bonding power of stories.

One of the success secrets of the best principals is that these individuals do everything they can to preserve, promote, and perpetuate the school's legends, stories, and heroes. More importantly, they seize every opportunity to celebrate the school's history and culture. Organizations that celebrate, laugh, and raise the banners are organizations of spirit, energy, and pride. Celebration releases tension, encourages innovation, and bands people together. In schools where excellence and excitement prevail, every staff gathering has an element of celebration.

Schools celebrates in different ways, such as:

- Adopting themes which serve as a rallying point to express pride in the organization
- Using T-shirts, caps, and so on, as symbols of pride
- Holding special "Pride Week" activities during the year (see later section of this chapter)
- Sponsoring welcome activities, newcomer receptions, staff socials, and so on
- Appointing a special staff celebration committee to plan ways to show pride in themselves and in the institution

The more the school staff celebrates together, the more it usually has to celebrate about.

Valuing past traditions of excellence adds extra impetus and momentum to school celebrations. Almost every secondary school has some history it can look back on with pride. When such traditions are preserved, nurtured, and celebrated, staff members gain a renewed sense of worth and purpose. Respect for past accomplishments can often move and motivate (even obligate) current staff to perpetuate the dream through new achievement and added honors.

No school can survive on past records alone, but any school can benefit from learning what worked in the past and why and applying those lessons to the future. Principals miss a good bet if they squander the richness of the school's tradition, instead of capitalizing on it as an investment that can continue to pay dividends for years to come. There are many ways that you can use the past as a prelude to continued success. Following are some of the most popular means of celebrating tradition as a source of pride for today and energy for tomorrow:

- Form an alumni association as a resource for maintaining ties with former graduates, keeping alive past visions and victories, and establishing a base of support when the school needs help (bond issues, referendum campaigns, etc.).
- Encourage/support class reunions and efforts by former classes to perpetuate their identity.
- Honor successful former graduates at homecoming and commencement time.
- Sponsor intergenerational activities involving past and present staff

members. This lets current faculty and others learn from previous staff members and feed on their pride.

- Make the most of special historical events such as anniversaries, centennial celebrations, and so on. (See announcements following.)
- Develop displays (a minimuseum) of historical pictures, awards, and artifacts associated with the school.
- Maintain and feature a complete collection of past yearbooks.
- Make a habit of valuing retirees and other "old timers."
- Use quizzes on school history as part of annual pride week celebrations.
- Have students interview important figures from the past to develop oral histories of the school.
- Use video yearbooks to maintain a living history of school events and achievements.

In schools, as in other organizations, most current successes are rooted in past performances. Thus, every school should celebrate its history and tradition, along with its current attainments. Some principals have found that it even pays to celebrate mistakes as well as victories.

WINNING WAYS TO CELEBRATE MISTAKES

Fearful organizations tend to deny, ignore, and/or belittle mistakes and failed efforts. We all know weak principals who excel at sweeping aborted projects under the rug. Vital organizations, however, admit and accept mistakes as necessary steps in discovering what doesn't work and upping the odds for future success.

It takes guts to own up to mistakes. Where the culture is secure, principals and staff realize that mistakes are neither final nor fatal failures, but, rather, serve as opportunities to learn how to advance the vision of the school. Mistakes are the common denominator shared by all organizations. What's different about winners and losers is how they handle efforts that fall short. The best realize that recognizing mistakes validates the humanness of the organization. Mistakes are a necessary foundation for improvement. The trick is to learn something from each error and avoid repeating them needlessly.

Being able to acknowledge, celebrate, and laugh at mistakes dramatizes acceptance of risk taking. It signifies openness and is a significant tribute to the trust level within the organization. Best of all, mistakes are a rich source of fun for everyone on the staff.

One good way to put mistakes in perspective is to present those responsible with a goofy award ("Worst Idea of the Year," "Honorary Ziggy Award," etc.) Some schools have also enjoyed posting cartoons depicting major goofs or making videotapes of mistakes, similar to TV video bloopers. (You need to be sure, however, that whoever is involved appreciates the

St. Louis Park High School's Centennial Celebration

Join past and present Staff members,
Alumni, and Community Members
in celebrating Park High's past 100 years.

- Kick-off the festivities with the **Homecoming Football Game** Friday, Oct. 5 at 7:30 p.m.

- Attend the **Open House** Saturday, Oct. 6 from 1:30 p.m. to 5 p.m. Visit with former teachers and classmates, view displays and participate in the program at 4 p.m.

The school bell was for many years a fixture in front of St. Louis Park High School. It was originally in Lincoln school and currently is mounted in the circle of the senior high.

Below: The St. Louis Park High School football team of 1926. The Orioles athletic tradition includes charter membership in the Lake Conference.

St. Louis Park High School's
Centennial Celebration

Join past and present staff members,
alumni, and community members
in celebrating Park High's past 100 years.

Kick off the festivities with the

Homecoming Football Game

Friday, October 5, at 7:30 PM

Visit with former teachers and classmates
View displays
Participate in the program at the

Open House

Saturday, October 6

1:30 to 5 PM

Program at 4 PM

humor.) Whatever twist is given to celebrating mistakes, it is always better to laugh than to cry over efforts gone awry.

An excellent opportunity to celebrate both mistakes and successes is to stage an annual Pride Week celebration as described in the next section.

NUTS AND BOLTS OF A SUCCESSFUL PRIDE WEEK

While celebration should be commonplace throughout the year, setting aside a special week to highlight accomplishments and to enjoy each other can be a major morale booster. Many schools plan such "pride weeks" or "spirit weeks" during January or February to break up the doldrums of a long winter. To be successful, a schoolwide pride week should feature a series of special events and socializing activities involving staff, students, and parents. The week provides a unique opportunity to publicize successes and to refocus staff attention toward what's important. The best such projects are planned long in advance by a broad-based committee made up of representatives of all segments of the staff. In some schools, student groups plan activities of their own to parallel the staff's weeklong celebration of pride. The purpose is to have fun, share successes, give credit where credit is due—and have more fun together!

The accompanying list illustrates sample activities for a successful pride week:

- Burying a time capsule
- Slogans/essay contests
- Scavenger hunts
- Door prizes
- Balloons on all classroom doors
- Principal/staff exchanges with other schools
- Staff appreciation note exchanges
- School board treats for the staff
- Pencil day—all students receive a school pencil
- Litter cleanup campaigns
- School colors days
- "Sweets" day
- New Year's resolution for the school contest
- Displays of student work throughout the community
- Concerts
- Bingo parties
- Hoola-hoop contests

- Talent shows
- Tug-of-war contests
- Silly games and races
- Class competitions (seniors versus juniors, etc.)
- Charity drives
- Baby picture contest
- Student-staff volleyball competitions
- Historical displays
- "Worst Joke of the Day" contest
- Ice cream socials
- Yearbook displays
- Staff greet students at school entrances each morning
- Bumper sticker contests
- 1950s dress-up day—best costume contest at lunch
- "Pig-out" party
- Treasure hunts
- "Goof off" day (wear goofy clothes, be goofy)
- Ice sculpture contests
- Lip-synching contests

The possibilities for celebration and excitement are as limitless as the creativity of the people involved. Where possible, extending the celebration into the community by involving city officials, the public library, and local merchants provides added fun and fanfare for the school. Pride week celebrations help bind people together, build new traditions, and pump new blood into the culture of the school.

While special events like pride week add zest to the organization, it is the step-by-step, day-to-day activities that ultimately make long range dreams come true. An important way for school leaders to keep in tune with daily programs is to practice "managing while walking around" (MWWA).

APPLYING MWWA TO SCHOOL ADMINISTRATION

Success is not a fixed point. It has no closure. Likewise, managing the dream of the school requires daily attention on the part of the principal. In schools that work best, the leader stays in touch with all students and staff and with what is *really* going on in the organization. Face-to-face feedback, support, clarification, and reinforcement are prerequisites to achieving meaningful goals. Good principals don't lead from behind a desk or at the other end of the intercom. They go where the action is.

In the corporate world, the most respected chief executive officers "manage by walking around." They are out and about maintaining close contact with staff and customers alike. They don't just read about the company gains and losses—they touch the flesh of the organization in a personal way. They know the people who make things happen and those people know them. In the complex structure of today's secondary school, MWWA has also become an essential element of effective management.

Being visible isn't easy. It requires time and takes saying "no" to lots of tasks and activities that can get between the leader and the "real world" of the organization. Nevertheless, even the busiest principal can find ways to practice MWWA:

- Schedule "visibility time" each day.
- Use walk-by and drop-in classroom observations.
- "Go public" before and after school. (Get out of the office during the times that traffic is busiest throughout the building.)
- Conduct hallway conferences.
- Eat lunch with students and staff members.
- Take a turn at supervisory assignments.
- Help out with field trips.
- Substitute for a period or two in emergencies.
- Attend a variety of school functions.
- Help chaperon parties.
- Spend time in the teacher's lounge.
- Help load buses.
- Take a turn serving in the lunch line.
- Visit team practices, including minor sports.
- Listen to what's being said in the hallways and on the school grounds.
- Keep a log of contacts with individual staff members. (Don't let too much time pass between personal contacts with every employee.)

Managing the dream of the school is a hands-on activity. MWWA is your best means for keeping the vision on track. One quick test of the health of the organization is to ask students who the principal is. In schools where the principal is more than a name and a voice over the public address system, the dream is usually alive and well.

Part of the purpose of MWWA is "vision screening"—assessing how clearly people perceive the purpose of what they're about and where they're going.

USING CUSTOMERS AND CONSTITUENTS TO CHART FUTURE DIRECTIONS

Visioning is a participatory process, not the sole province of the principal. Everyone intimately associated with the school should be directly involved in defining its dream and shaping its goals. Ownership generates commitment and commitment is the force that transforms dreams to reality. Every constituent should have a say in the vision, a piece of the action, and a chance to contribute. In the school setting, these constituents include, at a minimum, students, staff, and parents. Where the school is the centerpiece of the community, the ultimate customers include all citizens and taxpayers.

It behooves school leaders to tap the ideas of all these involved in the visioning and revisioning process. In every school and community, the principal has ready-made access to all constituencies through a number of existing groups and organizations such as those listed here:

Access to Staff	*Access to Students*
• Regular staff meetings	• Student councils
• Department head meetings	• Student open forums
• Faculty senates	• Leadership councils
• Prep period forums	• National Honor Society

Access to Parents	*Access to Community-at-large*
• PTA	• Civic clubs
• Advisory councils	• Chamber of commerce
• Principal's coffees	• Ad hoc planning committees
• Site-management councils	• Neighborhood meetings

The purpose of soliciting constituent and customer input is to gain the broadest possible perspective, the capitalize on the collective wisdom of the school community and to gather maximum energy and support behind the school's vision and goals. The standard steps for using constituents to help chart future directions for the school include the following:

1. Hold a series of meetings to ask customers and constituents (individually and collectively) to identify strategic issues important to the school's future. (See the accompanying Stakeholders Input Worksheet.)

2. Summarize results by clustering issues and initiatives under central themes to reduce redundancy.

3. Return issue summaries to the same constituents to rank and prioritize. (See the accompanying Issues Ranking Form.)

4. Use identified priorities to draft a tentative vision/mission statement for final review by all input groups.

Stakeholder's Input Worksheet

Please respond to the following questions:

A. Are there school initiatives, programs, or priorities that should be receiving less attention or be dropped? List.

_____

_____

_____

B. What, if any, new results should the school seek to achieve in the next three to five years?

_____

_____

_____

C. Check one. The foregoing suggestions are a result of:

_____ Group consensus _____ Individual recommendation

HOW SCHOOL LEADERS USE THE PROCESS OF VISIONING

When we talk about the dream of the school, we mean the future of the organization—its picture of where the school wants to go and what it wants to be. In times when myriad forces strive to tug the school in many directions, it is more important than ever for *every* school to have some shared vision of the niche it wants to carve out for itself. The vision is simply what the school wants to stand for, what it wants to be known for, and what it wants to be remembered for. The dream of the school is not the principal's vision alone, but it is the principal who bears the brunt of responsibility for keeping the vision constantly in view and on everyone's agenda.

To stay alive, a vision must be challenging, motivating, and clearly perceived. It can serve as a beacon attracting the best efforts of all those serving and served by the organization. Most important, it should be fun, and it should be designed to make things better. Every school should be in a constant state of visioning and revisioning. It is the principal's job to see that this happens.

Once the visioning process is completed, the outcome should not be cast in stone. Visioning is continuous, and revisioning is necessary to accommodate changing times and circumstances. One effective means of revisioning is to hold periodic "reunions" of all those involved in the ongoing process. The purposes of such reunions are to:

1. Share progress
2. Conduct a midcourse needs assessment

Issues Ranking Form

The following issues have surfaced as a result of recent vision planning sessions. The number in parentheses after each issue represents the number of respondents who listed the issues a top priority for consideration.

Highlights: Using the numbers 1–5 (with "1" being most important), rank the five issues *you* believe the schools should adopt as priority planning issues for the future.

Priority Issues

____1. Focus on global awareness and world citizenship. (69)

____2. Increase emphasis on fine arts. (22)

____3. Place greater emphasis on basic skills. (26)

____4. Provide more programs for average learners. (21)

____5. Emphasize environmental issues. (10)

____6. Expand uses of technology. (81)

____7. Touch on how to learn and access information. (80)

____8. Focus on student self-esteem. (110)

____9. Provide school-based day care. (52)

____10. Redefine the school day/school year. (19)

____11. Increase parent involvement. (45)

____12. Emphasize lifelong learning for all ages. (16)

____13. Upgrade/modernize school facilities. (28)

3. Reaffirm major thrusts

4. Identify new issues, ideas and directions

5. Make mid-course corrections as needed

Schools can plod along without any clear vision, but they can't achieve stardom without a common goal to live and strive for. The school's vision validates the organization, legitimizes its existence, and provides the hope necessary to achieve excellence. In the final analysis, one of the most significant things that you can do as school leader is to guide the ongoing visioning process.

NEW APPROACHES TO GOAL SETTING AND STRATEGIC PLANNING

The best part of the dream in any organization is making it happen. Visions don't materialize into reality on their own volition. It requires hard work in mapping out and implementing strategies to achieve desired goals. Strategic planning is part of this process. As schools become more complicated, demands expand, "choice" spawns competition, and decentralized decision making occurs, the chief executive of the school must become a strategic planner.

In simplest terms, a strategic plan is merely a long-range (usually three to five years) action agenda. The essence of strategic planning is analyzing the current state of the school measured against its future vision and finding ways to get from here to there.

To become meaningful, any strategic plan must be driven by the vision or dream of the school. (It's fruitless to spend time designing an elaborate plan for getting nowhere.) Strategic planning is basically a process of setting goals and spelling out what it takes to achieve them. In this sense, the planning process can be a source of revitalization for the entire organization.

Too many school leaders view strategic planning as an onerous, paper and pencil exercise. More and more principals, however, are realizing that strategic planning is a true form of leadership in action. Goals are powerful performance incentives and the goal-setting process is cleansing, healthy, and renewing for all members of the institution.

Because of the critical importance of the planning function, the process has almost been reduced to an exact science. The professional literature is replete with strategic planning models and guides. Following are the basic steps common to the most popular planning prototypes:

Steps in Strategic Planning for Schools

Step 1: *Define the mission*

a. Engage in the mission/revisioning process described earlier.

Step 2: *External scanning*

a. Review and project societal trends and future needs.

    b. Identify external mandates and "sacred cows" that may control or influence the direction of the organization. (See the next section of this chapter.)

    c. Some schools use outside experts (futurists, demographers, etc.) in this phase.

Step 3: *Internal scanning*

    a. Review strengths and weaknesses within the organization.

    b. Pinpoint disparities between "what is" and "what should be" in the future.

Step 4: *Identify goals / set priorities*

    a. Define long range key results and subsets of short-term goals. (See Key Results and Goals following.)

    b. Evaluate and validate each goal. (If something is within reach immediately, it isn't a legitimate goal.)

    c. Rank the goals.

Step 5: *Develop implementation plan*

    a. Define strategies and contingency plans. (See the Learner Impact Statement later in this chapter.)

    b. Conceptualize, sequence, and carry out the strategies necessary to achieve goals.

    c. Identify resources, assign responsibilities, and develop a calendar for accomplishment.

Step 6: *Monitor progress*

    a. Track progress (or lack of it) toward achieving each key result and goal. (See Strategic Plan Progress Chart following.)

Step 7: *Review / renew the plan*

    a. Subject the plan to periodic reality checks and relevance tests. (Mission and goal statements need rephrasing and polishing at intervals to retain their power.)

All parties involved should be included and informed at each step of the planning process.

Key Results and Goals

Key Result 1: Teach students how to learn the skills of accessing information; critical thinking, decision-making and problem-solving.

Goal: To place more emphasis on finding and analyzing information through discussion, simulation, experimentation, independent study and cooperative learning.

Goal: To facilitate learning outside the classroom.

Goal: To integrate critical thinking skills throughout the curriculum.

Key Result 2: Focus on world awareness, global education and global thinking.

Goal: To integrate geography into the curriculum.

Goal: To involve parents in awareness of global issues.

Goal: To emphasize global social, economic, cultural and political issues, resulting in understanding of an interdependent world.

Strategic Plan Progress Chart

Key Results X = New √ = Ongoing	Goals	Year 1	Year 2	Year 3
1. World awareness	a. World geography		X	√
	b. Foreign language	√	√	√
	c. Global education	X	√	√
2. How To Learn	a. Access information	X	√	√
	b. Critical thinking			X
	c. Note taking	√	√	√

Dealing with dreams and visions is pretty heady stuff. Sometimes, planners get carried away and forget that even the most outrageous and avant-garde plans must be rooted in reality if they are to come to life. One area commonly missed in the planning process by many leaders is reckoning with mandates and sacred cows that must be accommodated in any realistic plan for the future.

WHAT PRINCIPALS NEED TO KNOW ABOUT
MANDATES AND SACRED COWS

In corporate management, there is an old saying that "No matter who you are, how big you get, or how high you go, there's always somebody bigger than you who can chew you out and tell you what to do." This same sense of established parameters, outside limits, and realistic constraints should apply to strategic planning in schools.

Most organizations don't operate totally unfettered, and planning doesn't occur in a vacuum. Schools, in particular, are ensnarled in a complex web of formal and informal rules, requirements, and restrictions. Mandates are formal (usually legal) requirements, imposed by external authorities and often enforced by penalties (e.g., loss of state or federal financial aid). Mandates take on many forms, including:

Federal and state laws
State department rules
  and regulations
Negotiated contracts
Joint powers agreements
Regulatory agency standards
  (e.g, OSHA)

City ordinances
School board policy
Court orders and decisions
Attorney general's opinions
District regulations and
  guidelines
Building codes

In short, mandates are things schools and school administrators have to do. (See the examples that follow.)

School Mandates

State required curriculum/learner outcomes
State testing programs
Federal special education legislature
Nondiscrimination statutes
Class-size limitations
Teacher licensure requirements
Data privacy laws
Length of school day and school year
Integration orders
Copyright laws

Sacred cows, on the other hand, are perceived requirements or restrictions that are not officially mandated by any agency or authority, but by the power of public opinion. They are the "givens" that guide the operation of the school. These are things schools must do or must not do because they are highly cherished, valued, or "tabooed" by society. Schools serve the public, and there are some things the public demands and some things the public simply won't permit. Some common examples include:

Sacred Cows in Schools

Driver education training
Aquatics instruction
Summer school
Pupil transportation
Food service
Athletic programs
Community education
Child care provisions
Senior citizens programs

A critical component of effective strategic planning must be to identify, acknowledge, and plan around, if necessary, existing restrictions and requirements. Mandates may be waived, changed, or manipulated, but they cannot be ignored. If a change or exemption is necessary to meet goals and achieve the school's vision, then, the planning process must include strategies for bending the rules or securing appropriate waivers. Even the most visionary principals must be realistic and pragmatic in adapting plans to meet well-entrenched parameters.

DEFINING A MISSION STATEMENT FOR YOUR SCHOOL

A mission statement is simply the dream of the school reduced to writing. It explains *exactly* what the school is about, how it differs from others, and what it hopes to become. It is the "why" of the school. No principal should serve very long in a school without a clear-cut statement of shared mission.

School mission statements take on many shapes and variations. Some are short and direct. Others are more lengthy and ethereal:

School Mission Statements

• The purpose of _____ School, as the cornerstone of a lifelong learning community, is to make all learners academically prepared, self-reliant, curious, thoughtful of others, and capable of using their learning to succeed in life in our interdependent world.

• Successful learning today . . . productive living tomorrow.

• Our mission is to provide a:

C aring
E nvironment for
L ifelong learning that
E nhances self-concept and
B roadens social and scholastic skills by
R esponding to our changing society so that
A ll learners survive and
T hrive with
E xcellence!

The best mission statement is whatever works for the people who drive the organization on a daily basis and are responsible for its outcomes. The important thing for principals is to ensure that the school has a definite mission statement, or, if not, to get one developed as soon as possible.

Mission statements, like those just presented, are common to most strategic plans. The next section describes a new feature that can bring an added dimension to the school's planning process.

USING "LEARNER IMPACT STATEMENTS" IN SCHOOL PLANNING

The format and general outline of building-level strategic plans look a great deal alike. One weakness of many plans, however, is that the key results and goals are often stated in terms of what teachers and others will do *to, for,* and *with* students. This places the plan at an immediate disadvantage when it comes to evaluating results. In most instances, the only measurement can be answering the question, "Did we do all the things we said we were going to do?" The more important questions should be, "So what?" "Did it make a difference for students?" If an elaborate plan is carried out and it makes no difference in what and how students learn and perform, it's junk.

The real focus of any school strategic plan should be on what happens to students. What is missing in most plans is a "learner impact statement." Just as the federal government requires an environmental impact statement before major projects are undertaken, schools need to define the precise impact on the learner for every new program or goal under consideration.

Adding learner impact statements to the school's long-range plan has helped some principals sharpen the focus of their planning, provide a reality check, and put some bite in the exercise of applying theory to practice.

The learner impact statement supplies a heretofore missing piece in the planning process. A learner impact statement assumes that any change must be justified solely in terms of a greater positive impact on learners. It also establishes a system for measuring and reporting this impact.

Learner impact statements describe and define the specific effect that the school's efforts will have on the learners involved. In short, it delineates the precise benefits to the target population gained from the achievement of each goal in the building's strategic plan. The multi-page "Strategic Plan: Learner Impact Statement Form" included here shows how it works.

STRATEGIC PLAN: LEARNER IMPACT STATEMENT FORM

School: _____ Year:_____

A. *Planning*

1. Key Result: Teach students to learn.

2. Specific Goal: Facilitate learning outside of the classroom.

3. Learner Impact Statement (must be stated in terms of *learner performance; what learners will achieve* or be able to do, *not what will be done to or for learners*):
   Eighty-five percent of all senior high students will be involved in at least one learning activity outside the classroom during the year, and 40 percent of the students will have at least three learning activities outside the classroom.

4. Need/Rationale for Change: Many students are not involved in outside activities and do not feel "connected" with the school. Often students who do not excel in the classroom become real leaders when involved in outside activities.

B. *Programming* (operational plan)

1. Target Learners: All students.

2. Resources Needed (personnel, materials, other): Cooperation between teachers, coaches, and advisors; clerical time for record keeping.

3. Methods/Strategies: Accurate records will be maintained of the involvement of all students in outside activities (field trips, off-campus learning experiences, extracurricular activities, etc.). Student populations not being reached by outside activities will be identified.

4. Impact of Change on/for Other Programs: Once it is determined which students do not participate in learning activities outside the classroom, it may be necessary to develop additional activities based on student interest. A long-term benefit may be that students will become more involved citizens who put learning to practical use.

C. *Budgeting*

1. Determination of How Budget Supports This Plan: Current extra-curricular and departmental field trip budgets are adequate to meet this goal.

D. *Evaluation*

1. Quantifiable Outcome Measures: A record of each student's involvement in outside learning activities will be maintained and reported at the end of the year.

2. Other Means of Evaluation: A student survey will be conducted to identify level of participation, attitudes toward outside activities, and reasons for participation or nonparticipant.

3. End-of-Year Results (to be completed in June of target year):
   a. Description of attainment level of learner impact statement.
   b. Results of tests and other assessment measures.
   c. Interpretation of results.
   d. Description of what you will do differently next year based on these results.

Principal's/Supervisor's Signature: _____

Date: _____

(Please attach any supporting materials—research, examples, data, etc.)

STRATEGIC PLAN: LEARNER IMPACT STATEMENT FORM

School: _____ Year: _____

A. *Planning*

    1. Key Result _____:

    2. Specific Goal:

    3. Learner Impact Statement (must be stated in terms of *learner performance: what learners will achieve* or be able to do; *not what will be done to or for learners*):

    4. Need/Rationale for Change:

B. *Programming* (operational plan)

    1. Target Learners:

    2. Resources Needed (personnel, materials, other):

    3. Methods/Strategies:

    4. Impact of Change on/for Other Programs:

C. *Budgeting*

    1. Determination of How Your Budget Supports This Plan?

D. *Evaluation*

    1. Quantifiable Outcome Measures:

    2. Other Means of Evaluation:

    3. End-of-Year Results (to be completed in June of target year):
        a. Description of attainment level of learner impact statement.
        b. Results of tests and other assessment measures.
        c. Interpretation of results.
        d. Description of what you will do differently next year based on these results.

Principal's/Supervisor's Signature: _____

Date: _____

(Please attach any supporting materials—research, examples, data, etc.)

Having described all the key phases and components of visioning and strategic planning, the next section shows how any principal can put it all together in a simple planning flow chart.

A FLOW CHART FOR EFFECTIVE PLANNING

Visioning and strategic planning are not episodes. Rather, they are cyclical and continuous efforts. The intensity and focus may be intermittent, but the process goes on. The kind of strategic planning described in this chapter works for schools because it doesn't stop. It relentlessly and incrementally moves the organization in the direction of its dream.

The following chart illustrates how all the steps in the process flow together in an uninterrupted pattern of choosing and rechoosing the future of the school.

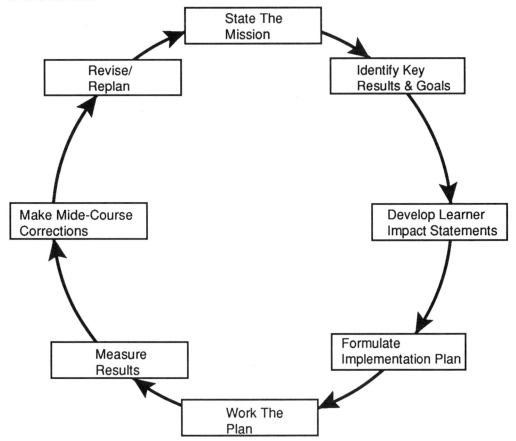

Successful leaders of championship organizations have discovered that envisioning and strategic planning give them the freedom to become what they want to be and the control to define their own destiny. The same thing can work for schools and school principals. The magic that energizes the planning process and provides ongoing momentum is *empowerment*!

WHAT SCHOOL LEADERS NEED TO KNOW ABOUT "EMPOWERMENT"

Empowerment is sharing decision making, authority, and responsibility. It is letting everyone in on the action. Good leaders know that if you expect people to share in a dream, you have to let them help make it happen. When power is shared, it grows and multiplies. This is one of the secrets of truly successful organizations.

In empowered schools, people share information, feelings, and goals and work together to solve problems. There is a sense of joint responsibility for quality control. Both credit and blame are shared. The entire staff is involved in the total operation of the school. Staff members are meaningfully engaged in making decisions concerning goals, curriculum, policies, hiring, evaluation, staff development, budgets, and so on. Principals who manage by empowerment don't abdicate leadership. They extend it by concentrating on the human talents of the staff and by giving permission for risk taking.

The benefits of plural leadership are many and varied. Empowerment:

- Enables all stakeholders to make a maximum contribution to the enterprise
- Frees staff members to function fully as true professionals
- Allows talented people to take on tough tasks
- Makes teachers better by forcing them to look at weaknesses and improvements
- Builds teamwork and a sense of community
- Provides energy
- Reduces isolation
- Creates an ethos of achievement
- Fosters an internal network and support system
- Promotes renewal
- Generates a "We Can Do It" attitude

Like its benefits, the obstacles to empowerment are also numerous and often built-in. One of the most common obstructions is resistance on the part of the staff to take on real responsibility for the school. Some teachers clamor for more freedom and authority and, then, back off when responsibility and accountability are added to the equation. Other common roadblocks include lack of trust, restrictive mandates and sacred cows, turf battles, skepticism, resistance to new ideas ("Ideacide"), and meeting overload.

All these obstacles can be overcome over time. Participatory management must be learned. It starts by keeping people informed and, then, increasingly involving them in decisions. It can happen without any formal new structure such as a site-management program. The prerequisites for effective empowerment are trust, training, openness, listening to each other, and a willingness to stumble occasionally.

The principal's main role in establishing and nurturing empowerment is fivefold:

1. Being an advocate for the system
2. Team building
3. Mentoring and modeling
4. Supporting decisions and those willing to make them
5. Tolerating ambiguity

Where those principles are practiced, empowerment flourishes and the organization grows stronger. Empowered staffs, in turn, empower students and parents. Thus, empowerment is the source and the force that can make the dream of the school come true.

This chapter has underscored the importance of the principal's role in managing and maintaining a vision that can pull the school into the future. Likewise, the strategic planning process necessary to translate the vision into reality has been outlined in detail.

Managing the dream of any organization is a function that can be performed only by the leader. The same is true for schools. Good principals don't let up on this endeavor. They not only orchestrate the visioning process, but they continually rekindle enthusiasm for the school's goals in much the same way that political party "whips" generate support for key legislative outcomes.

Some principals pooh-pooh visioning and strategic planning as being too time consuming and complicated for running a school. The truth is that some future planning is essential to a successful school. Otherwise, the staff is constantly reacting to circumstances created by others and the school is always running to catch up with the latest developments in the field. As many professional athletes can attest, "Good things don't happen when you're playing catch-up." Visioning and strategic planning are not too sophisticated for ordinary school personnel. They are simply a matter of knowing where you want to go and having a way to get there. No school should settle for less.

Chapter 3 moves from defining the goals of the school to guiding the people who must achieve those goals.

Managing the Total School Staff

All schools are people-oriented and people-driven institutions. The drama of the school comes alive and is shaped and played out through an ensemble of key actors which includes all members of the staff from principal to part-time custodian. It is this total staff that implements the mission and translates the school's vision into reality. More than any other single factor, the principal's ability to assemble and orchestrate an effective, efficient staff determines the success or failure of the organization. This portion of the guide spells out the essential elements in recruiting, selecting, motivating, and managing a staff that not only makes things happen, but makes the right things happen in the daily operation of the school.

HOW TO RECRUIT AND SELECT THE BEST POSSIBLE PERSONNEL

The single most significant decision school leaders make is selecting the right teacher to fill every classroom. Of almost equal importance is filling all the other assignments within the school from teacher's aide to food server. Most errors can be corrected, but choosing the wrong person to play a key role on the school staff can do irreparable harm to the lives and learning of countless young people and sabotage an otherwise successful program.

Staffing decisions are too important to be made alone and in isolation. The best rule for principals to follow is that *no one person should hire or fire any employee*. As in other fields, school leaders tend to surround themselves with like kind. Even when teachers assist in selecting other teachers, they often fall prey to the appeal of choosing colleagues who are like themselves, are known quantities (such as a familiar substitute), and will "fit in" with the existing staff. Since the best staff is a balanced staff comprised of diverse strengths and styles, more than one perspective should be represented in the selection process. The goal is to achieve a total staff that works like a kaleidoscope made up of varied elements that shift and adjust to changing situations, while always blending together to form an integrated, meaningful image.

Except in emergency situations, principals are well advised to employ a selection team to screen, interview, and select personnel for *all* positions in the school.

In most cases, a two- to five-member selection team provides a workable size group to expedite the selection process. Members of the team should be identified by the principal (or in some cases, a district personnel administrator) and may include the principal or designee, principals from other schools in the district, central office or supervisory representatives where appropriate, and at least one member of the employee group in which a vacancy is to be filled. The procedures that follow have proved to be effective guidelines for selection teams in the hiring process:

Selection Team Guidelines

- Within the limits of existing negotiated agreement, hiring procedures should be uniform for all categories of employees.

- All new employees will be selected by a selection team appropriate to the vacancy to be filled.

- Selection teams will screen applications, conduct interviews, and recommend a final candidate.

- The designated leader of the selection team will be responsible for scheduling interviews.

- All members of the selection team must participate in the interview process and are equals in the final decision making. (This is particularly important when there is some likelihood or possibility that the new employee may eventually serve in more than one role in the school or be assigned to another unit in the district.)

- In conducting interviews, all candidates will be asked the same set of predetermined questions by the selection team.

- The designated leader of the selection team will be responsible for checking references, as appropriate.

- In cases where candidates appear equal, where the team cannot reach agreement, where some intangible reservation persists regarding a strong candidate, or where a final decision seems unusually difficult, the selection team may call on outside parties (other administrators and professional consultants, etc.) to assist in finalizing the selection decision.

In using the selection team, it is critical that the principal and other team members bear in mind that every hiring decision is an opportunity to improve the school and its programs. Hiring can be a self-fulfilling prophecy. By holding high expectations and making known its intent to select only the most capable candidates, the school enhances the possibility of attracting the best and brightest applicants.

One decision that the principal must make early on is whether or not to involve the selection team in the recruitment phase of the selection process. Because of time constraints, it is often necessary or desirable for the principal to "go it alone" or to rely on the district personnel office to recruit potential applicants. In any case, the trick is to develop a sizable pool of candidates with quality training and experience relevant to the opening at hand, without being inundated by hordes of applicants holding minimal, marginal, or irrelevant credentials and qualifications. It is sometimes helpful and efficient to target the pool of potential candidates by developing a tailor-made posting (advertisement) and application form for the specific vacancy that exists. This can limit and eliminate extraneous applications from those who are underqualified, overqualified, or simply unqualified.

Throughout the recruitment and selection cycle, it is imperative that the principal and the selection team have some clear perception of the type of candidate desired for any specific position. The next section defines some critical criteria for sorting out candidates who have the "right stuff" for the particular job to be filled.

WHAT TO LOOK FOR IN THE STAFF OF THE FUTURE

Not all personnel decisions are permanent, but many are long lasting and difficult to rectify when the wrong choice has been made. In many situations, hiring for today is also hiring for many tomorrows to come. Knowing what to look for in filling each specific opening is the first step in effective staffing.

Obviously, the profile of the staff of tomorrow will differ in many respects from the historic/traditional view of what makes a successful teacher, school secretary, custodian, and so on. The convergence of a number of powerful forces such as those listed next will demand skills and expertise previously not requested of school personnel.

Forces Affecting Future School Staffs

- Changing societal expectations
- Heightened demands
- Continuing knowledge explosion
- New standards and tools of learning
- Runaway technology
- New audience of learners (see Chapter 4)

To make wise staffing decisions, the principal and selection teams must consider both current needs and future demands.

For the present, the selection team should weigh existing staff weaknesses and limitations, looking for gaps in talent and perspective. Filling these gaps can require selecting candidates who don't fit the existing mold and who will contrast or even conflict with present staff skills and expertise.

For the future, it can be both educational and worthwhile for the principal and team to solicit input from a variety of constituencies regarding what to look for in selecting tomorrow's teachers and other school personnel. These constituencies can include current staff members, students, parent groups, the school board, and community members. As an example, consider the following community committee's list of desirable traits/characteristics to search for in hiring future teachers:

Staff of the Future—Qualities to Look For

1. A well-developed sense of humor
2. Support for the concept of lifelong learning
3. Significant experience in the arts
4. Willingness to "give more" (101 percent) in time, caring, and so on
5. A solid liberal arts background
6. Ability to work with adults as well as with children and youth
7. Experience with cultural diversity
8. Broad experiences—including hobbies, reading, and travel
9. Strong commitment to the practice of democratic values
10. Ability to conduct effective parent meetings and conferences
11. Respect for childhood and adolescence
12. Understanding of cooperative learnings, teamwork, and team teaching
13. Awareness of recent findings on learning theory and the emotional/mental development of students
14. Ability to convey a sense of joy and delight in learning
15. Enthusiasm/commitment

Once criteria for shaping the staff of the future like these just outlined are defined, screening and selection become much easier. Another tool that can help the principal and team in filling vacancies and building a better staff is a well-crafted statement of philosophy on hiring and selecting personnel. The next section offers such a guide.

THE PRINCIPAL'S PHILOSOPHY OF TEACHER RECRUITMENT

A clear-cut statement of purpose and belief regarding teachers and other staff selection can serve as a needed frame of reference in filling all staff posts. The following philosophy provides one model.

A Philosophy of Teacher Recruitment and Selection

The goal of the teacher recruitment and selection program is to select the best possible candidate for every position within available resources. Selection procedures are designed to avoid discrimination and develop a total staff which reflects a healthy mix of age, sex, experience and educational/cultural background.

All hiring will be done on the basis of completed applications, reference checks, and the consensus agreement of an appropriate staff selection team. Other modern screening techniques, for example, writing samples, video clips, auditions, and teacher fairs will be utilized as appropriate. Consideration will be given to demonstrated knowledge of technological literacy, essential elements of instruction, teaching/learning styles, cooperative learning techniques, and other specialized competencies.

It is the school's intent to develop a staff of the future that is balanced and represents the state of the art in instructional and educational expertise.

Using established criteria and a definitive philosophy statement can guide and make the screening and selection process easier, but it is never easy. The successful principal is willing to exert every effort to seek out candidates of promise wherever they are and, then, to choose the very best. When building the staff for a newly conceived computer company, H. Ross Perot hired the best people he could find based on the motto, "Eagles don't flock. You have to find them one at a time." This motto can serve secondary school principals equally well. One innovative recruitment technique that has given some principals an edge in the eagle hunt is described next.

GETTING THE INSIDE TRACK ON TOMORROW'S "HIGH FLYERS"

When searching out and securing top-flight candidates from numerous applicants in a highly competitive market is crucial to maintaining and improving quality staffs, principals and other school leaders may take a cue from the private sector. Business recruiters have long wooed bright prospects with special attention and favored treatment. There's no reason that this same approach cannot be applied to attracting the best teaching talent coming out of training each year.

Using a "Star Search" theme, one school system has systematically identified top graduates from area teacher training institutions simply by contacting key professors and student teacher supervisors and asking, "Who are your top two or three seniors who have proven themselves in field and practicum experiences?" The school then issues a personal invitation for the best prospects to attend a special reception/dinner in their honor. Here is a sample invitation:

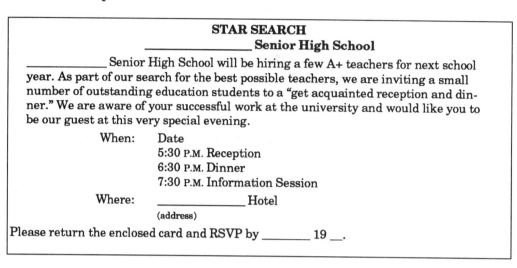

STAR SEARCH
_____ **Senior High School**

_____ Senior High School will be hiring a few A+ teachers for next school year. As part of our search for the best possible teachers, we are inviting a small number of outstanding education students to a "get acquainted reception and dinner." We are aware of your successful work at the university and would like you to be our guest at this very special evening.

When: Date
              5:30 P.M. Reception
              6:30 P.M. Dinner
              7:30 P.M. Information Session
Where: _____ Hotel
              (address)

Please return the enclosed card and RSVP by _____ 19 __.

Features of such a "Star Search" program may include informal mix and mingling time with school staff members (particularly first-year teachers familiar with the graduating seniors' dreams and fears), decorations associated with the school, entertainment by select school musical groups, information packets of school materials, and a welcome/briefing by the principal. Holding the event in an offschool site and presenting the college participants with souvenir mugs, pens, and so on can add a touch of class to a simple recruitment effort.

This unique "Star Search" affair can give the school the inside track on quality candidates, provide the school with some unusual positive public relations, and enhance the prospective newcomers' view of themselves, the school, and the profession as a whole.

With or without a special "Star Search" event, once the recruitment phase is over, the principal and selection team are faced with the formidable task of sifting and sorting through piles of paper applications in order to screen out the most viable candidates for interviewing. The next section offers tested techniques for getting a handle on the people behind the paper.

QUICK TIPS FOR SCREENING APPLICATIONS

Screening paper applications for teaching and other positions in the school is becoming increasingly complicated. It has become common practice for graduating teacher candidates and even experienced teachers, who are relocating or merely seeking a different position, to flood the market of potential employers with resumes and blanket applications. Many principals and other school officials now routinely receive literally hundreds of unsolicited applications each year. Sifting through the piles of files can be formidable and frustrating for busy administrators.

The screening process is further confounded by the frequent use of professionally prepared resumes that all look good and all tend to look alike. Even candidates who cannot afford to hire a professional to package their application materials often receive training in resume writing and enhance the appearance and appeal of their applications through the magic of computer desk-top printers. How can principals sort out what's real and relevant within the paper blizzard of application forms?

For some, the answer has been to employ consulting firms to conduct initial screening of applications and to rank the candidates, the premise being that if candidates can get professional help to prepare their applications, schools should hire professionals to evaluate the fact and fiction found in these application materials. Other schools hire retired administrators and/or teachers to sort through the annual avalanche of applications and identify the "keepers." In most cases, however, the screening burden falls directly on the principal and the selection team. Adhereing to two basic rules can expedite this process:

Rule 1—Look for reasons not to interview or hire: The first reading of applications should be done as quickly as possible and should focus on any cue or clue indicating that a given applicant is not right for the vacancy under consideration. Focus on the "soft spots" and the smoke screens in the applications—fuzzy answers, ambiguous recommendations, incorrect or incomplete responses, and so on. Don't get caught up in the rhetoric. Be relentless in looking for weaknesses. When the slightest doubt arises, eliminate the application from further consideration.

Rule #2—Whenever possible, have more than one person screen the applications: The greater the number of readers the greater the likelihood of spotting responses that are phony, misleading, or, at best, questionable. This rule argues for involving all members of the selection team in the reading, reviewing, and screening process.

Whoever screens paper applications for school positions, that person should have some yardstick against which to measure the myriad cover letters, resumes, forms, files and references confronting him or her. The following criteria have proved effective in screening applications for secondary teachers and other school employees:

Screening Criteria

- Academic achievement
- Teaching experience
- Teacher evaluations/recommendations
- Specialized training
- Postgraduate education

- Multiple licensure
- Potential for extra-curricular assignments
- Leadership experience
- Teaching style
- Summer employment
- Adult relationships
- Leisure/volunteer activities

All these tips can help school leaders get a handle on the tail of the paper tiger that wags much of the screening process. But paper sorting of written applications is only the first phase in selecting the best choices for a modern secondary school staff. Weeding out valid, viable candidates from a labyrinth of look-alike applications may be difficult, but conducting effective face-to-face interviews that really expose the best possible selections for school positions can be even more challenging and puzzling. The next segments pinpoint the fundamentals of successful interviewing.

ESSENTIALS OF AN EFFECTIVE STRUCTURED INTERVIEW

Careful and effective paper screening should eliminate about 75 percent of the applicants for any position by sorting out those candidates who truly have the technical skills for the job. It is the dynamics of interviewing, however, that can reveal the motivation, attitude, and savvy that mark the best prospective staff members.

Effective employment interviews have become increasingly important in an age where most resumes look alike. Most candidates for teaching and other positions in the secondary school now know all the power words and the "right buttons to push" on written application forms. It is only through the interaction of probing, face-to-face interviews that school administrators can spot the real person behind the paper resume.

The interview process represents the cutting edge of the organization's growth and improvement. Interviewing is an art that can be learned through practice. Principals lacking interview skills and experience should become students of the discipline and should seek help from others who possess interviewing know-how.

Since long-lasting staff decisions are often based on relatively brief verbal encounters, it is important to have a plan in order to maximize the information-gathering potential of each interview. This requires that interviews be carefully structured exercises, not random hit-or-miss situations. When more than one interviewer is involved, the chances of making sound staff selections are increased substantially. Most principals with successful hiring records use the same set of pre-determined questions for each candidate. This practice assures equal opportunity for all interviewees, reduces the risk of generating charges of discrimination, and provides a common base for comparing and evaluating candidates. Examples of frequently asked structured interview questions are the following:

Structured Interview Questions for Teachers

1. How do you get ready to teach a lesson?
2. How do you find out what students need to know?
3. What do you want your students to remember most? Why?
4. If a lesson fails, what do you do?
5. What gives you job satisfaction?
6. How do you handle angry parents?
7. Give examples of how you perform under pressure.
8. Describe the ideal teaching-learning situation.
9. Of all the supervisors you've had, which one(s) did you like the best? Why?
10. Who do you admire? Why?

More than the form (the questions asked), however, it is the substance (the process—what happens between the interviewer and the candidate) that is the key to successful interviewing. The basics for conducting an effective structured interview include the following:

- The interviewer must stay tuned in to the candidate's job ability rather than to interviewing skills. The interviewer's task is to use adult conversation to judge a candidate's ability to work with young people.

- Most of the interviewer's time should be spent in listening—listening for feelings as well as for facts.

- Timing and spacing of interviews should be planned carefully. Interviewing is intense and fatiguing. Research has revealed that the last person interviewed is three times as likely to get hired as the first candidate interviewed because of the fatigue factor. Usually, three to five interviews in one day provides for optimum comfort and sustained objectivity.

- The interviewer's total attention should be directed toward the candidate. The person being interviewed should be the most important person in the world during the time of the interview session.

- All interviews should include a variety of types of questions from these categories:

Closed questions	Reflective questions
Open-ended questions	Self-assessment questions
Probing questions	Situational questions

- Although every interview should be structured, there should also be enough freedom and flexibility to go with the flow.

Following these guidelines can enable any principal or administrator to use effective structured interviews to answer the ultimate question: Who can get the job done and make us a better school? Further tips for effective interviewing are laid out in the next section.

THE DO'S AND DON'T'S OF INTERVIEWING

Administrators skilled in the interviewing process follow a certain set of rules reflected in the following list of do's and don't's:

Successful Interviewers Do's:	*Successful Interviews Don'ts:*
• Put the candidate at ease	• Glamorize the position
• Treat all applicants equitably and as individuals	• Make decisions within the first few minutes
• Know what you're looking for	• Hurry
• Prepare for each interview (note areas on the application that need explanation)	• Put up barriers between the interviewer(s) and the candidate
• Use name tags to identify interviewers	• Spend time on irrelevant questions
• Avoid distractions	• Weigh nonrelated, negative information more than relevant positive information
• Listen	• Ask for information you don't need
• Be alert to body language	• Ask "taboo questions" (see examples)
• Ask only job-related questions	• Smoke
• Avoid yes/no questions	• Use a lecture approach
• Ask all mandatory questions (see examples)	• Ask leading or loaded questions
• Look for evidence of genuine love of youth and respect for the profession	• Abuse the power of the interviewer
• Value enthusiasm	• Interview too many candidates
• Try to get below the surface	
• Accommodate handicapped applicants in interviews	
• Ask questions that reveal values, surface experience and require life applications	
• Keep notes, using a rating scale where appropriate	
• Constantly review your part of questions and tailor-make questions for specific situations	
• Use callback interviews where necessary	
• Give candidates an opportunity to ask questions	
• Let candidates know what to expect	
• Use common sense	

Mandatory Interview Questions

(Due to legal requirements and to avoid possible future liability or litigation, the following questions should be included in all interviews.)

1. Have you ever been convicted of a felony?
2. Have you ever been disciplined by a professional organization?
3. Are you under court order to pay child support?

Taboo Interview Questions

(To avoid the risk of discrimination claims or charges, interviewers should never ask questions about the following areas.)

- Citizenship
- National origin
- Pregnancy/birth control
- Physical appearance
- Handicapped condition
- Economic status
- Home ownership
- Number of children
- Race, color
- Religion
- Parents place of birth
- Military service
- Arrest record
- Marital status (maiden name)
- Receipt of public assistance

Even when interviews follow all these rules and are conducted strictly according to the book, there are still times when the best choice for a new school staff member remains unclear. Fortunately, there are other tools available to the principal in making a final selection.

HOW TO GO BEYOND THE TRADITIONAL INTERVIEW

When all the questions have been asked and all the answers given, selection teams occasionally are still stumped as to who is the best prospect among final candidates. When this occurs, the use of multiple measures, beyond the traditional interviewing can provide the necessary additional information and insights to clarify the choices. Among the most effective additional selection measures are the following:

- Work samples (paper-marking, lesson designs, etc.)
- Videotape auditions
- Guest teaching
- Writing samples
- Callback interviews

- Visitations to observe the candidate in action
- Supplementary interviews by trained professional consultants
- Use of simulation exercises (Personnel Decisions, Inc., St. Paul, Minnesota, has developed an in-basket exercise that has been tested and adopted in a number of school systems.)

By combining one or more of these techniques with the traditional interview, the principal and his or her selection team can almost always agree on a final choice. But even when all parties reach consensus on the best candidate, there is one final crucial step in the selection process.

A FIVE-POINT APPROACH TO REAL-WORLD REFERENCE CHECKING

Exchanging information in an interview setting is, at best, an artificial situation. Sometimes the system fails, and even the most perceptive principal can be fooled, on occasion, by practiced answers, an articulate style, and a confident manner. The last step in selecting school staff members must always be a systematic process of reference checking. *Never* commit to hiring any candidate without talking to knowledgeable and reliable references who are familiar with the candidate as a person and as a professional. Reference checking is the final reality test necessary to successful staff selection. Reference checking is time consuming and, sometimes, difficult—but never hire without it! The five steps that follow are guides to getting the most valid results from contacting references:

1. Ask candidates for self-references ("What will your supervisor say about you and your work?") and compare answers with the actual report from selected references.

2. Speak directly in person or over the phone to all references. Many educators are more willing to give full information verbally than they are in writing. If possible, it is often helpful to have someone on your staff contact someone they *know* who has worked with the candidate to guarantee reliable reports.

3. Go beyond the original reference when possible. Ask the original reference for other sources to speak with. Sometimes, the farther you get from the original reference, the more candid the recommendations.

4. Use the reference check to obtain information not covered in the interview and to verify and confirm interview impressions.

5. Protect your sources to assure truthful references in the future.

Following the advice in the preceding sections of this chapter can go a long way in helping principals and other administrators to build a well-rounded staff that reflects the 3Cs of any successful organization: *competency, character,* and *chemistry.*

Selecting the proper mix of staff members, however, is only one piece of managing a total school staff. Baseball legend, Casey Stengal once observed, "Getting good players is the easy part. Getting them to work together is the hard part." The same is true in managing a winning team of professionals in the modern secondary school. The remaining segments of this chapter provide an unblinking look at what it takes to lead, supervise, and manage today's teachers and other staff members.

UNDERSTANDING THE NEW BREED IN THE WORKPLACE

Like most institutions, schools have undergone an array of both dramatic and subtle changes in recent years. These shifts have transferred the secondary school from a relatively simple social system to a highly complex community reflecting diverse needs, expectations, and interests. Almost every element that makes up today's school has undergone some cataclysmic alteration. The basic role is under redefinition. The curriculum has been turned inside out. The families served are taking on new forms. The student body poses new challenges requiring new techniques and delivery systems. Even the school staff represents a new breed of professional and support personnel.

In schools of all sizes, principals are facing a growing number of staff members whose views and values differ radically from those held by school employees in the past. Today's staff want more respect and autonomy than ever before. Teachers, in particular, are demanding a larger stake in decision making. (The proliferation of experiments with site-based management in all parts of the country gives testimony to this new paradigm in school structure and organization.) All employees, in schools and elsewhere, are relying less on their jobs as the primary source of the self esteem. Such employees tend to ignore traditional positional power or authority and to respond most readily to "earned leadership."

Some veteran administrators lament the passing of traditional docile teaching staffs and compliant support personnel. Nevertheless, the changing attitudes and actions among school staff members reflect the work ethic of the future. These changing values, beliefs, and behaviors are healthy signs that schools are still vital organizations capable of adapting to new societal demands and a new kind of student population.

The profile that follows illustrates some of the fundamental characteristics that differentiate present teachers and other school employees from traditional building staffs.

Profile of The Changing School Staff		
Values	Expectations	Behaviors
Privacy Recognition Sense of contribution	Opportunity to stretch Right to complain	Challenge goals Ask "why" questions

As staff members have changed, many historic approaches to administration have become dysfunctional. Increasingly, principals are called on to develop nontraditional strategies for shaping and leading the school staff. A new set of fundamental principles for managing and motivating school personnel is emerging:

1. The age of "administrative mystique" is over. Leaders must model their vision of teaching and learning.

2. Everyone on the staff must be committed to students as number one on the school's agenda.

3. High standards and expectations for staff members are fundamental in fostering commitment and positive attitudes toward the organization.

4. Principals must consistently focus on *all* the human resources in the school.

5. Downward loyalty is essential to the vitality of the organization.

6. Leaders must pay specific attention to the climate and culture of the school and nurture staff feelings of being valued and recognized.

7. All school leaders must develop eclectic/situational skills in team building, prioritizing, delegating, visioning, and goal setting.

8. Staff members at all levels should have a sense of making a valuable and valued contribution.

9. Effective principals encourage risk taking and accept mistakes.

10. Successful leaders manage themselves to manage others.

The nuts and bolts of applying these leadership principles are spelled out in the remainder of this chapter.

One of the most blatant examples of new phenomena in managing school staffs is the relatively recent challenge of dealing with employees involved with drugs.

HOW TO HANDLE AND HELP EMPLOYEES WITH DRUG AND ALCOHOL PROBLEMS

The scourge of drug abuse throughout American society poses one of the most monumental challenges of the times. This modern-day, man-made plague threatens to sap our national vitality by rotting our human resources from within. Unhappily, a focal point for the economics of the illegal drug industry is the youth of the nation and at the center of this devastating social problem is the school.

Principals are in the unique position of having to deal with the issues of drug and alcohol abuse at three levels: (1) providing preventative education programs to equip students to withstand the attraction and destruction of drug abuse, (2) reclaiming the educational lives of students already ensnared by drug abuse, and (3) handling school employees caught in the grip of substance abuse and/or addiction.

The incident of chemical use and abuse is no greater among educators than within any other social or professional group. Conversely, schools have no more immunity to the problem than other organizations. Unfortunately, when school staff members, particularly teachers, suffer with problems of chemical dependency, the entire school is at risk. Instructional effectiveness is jeopardized. The overall image and credibility of the organization is threatened, and vulnerable students may become endangered. When any member of the staff abuses drugs, the school immediately becomes part of the problem rather than part of the solution. Both the model and the message of the school are quickly tainted.

Principals have no choice but to deal forthrightly with drug problems among staff members. The more school leaders understand the "disease concept" of chemical dependency and the nature of state-of-the-art 12-step treatment programs (Alcoholics Anonymous, Narcotics Anonymous, etc.), the better position they are in to guide the actions and attitudes of the total staff in dealing with drug problems among students and employees. Many schools have found success by adopting a simple, proactive action plan for handling drug problems among school personnel such as outlined here:

Employee Drug Problem Action Plan

1. Develop a schoolwide philosophy that avoids being judgmental and that recognizes chemical dependency as a treatable disease that doesn't discriminate against any level or group.

2. Adopt and publicize a no-nonsense policy for dealing with employee drug problems (see personnel policy that follows).

3. Learn the physical and behavioral symptoms of drug abuse and dependency.

Personnel Policy on Chemical Dependency

The school recognizes chemical dependency as a treatable illness. Employees who are so diagnosed shall receive the same consideration and treatment opportunity as extended to employees with other types of illness.

The school's concern with chemical dependency is limited to its effects on job performance. No employee with chemical dependency will have his or her job security or promotional opportunity affected by diagnosis or treatment.

If job performance is affected by refusal to accept chemical dependency diagnosis or treatment or by failure to respond to treatment, the matter will be handled in the same way as similar refusal or treatment failure would be handled for other illnesses.

The purpose of this policy is to encourage recognition, early intervention, and subsequent support for the chemically dependent employee.

4. Provide appropriate inservice training on drug abuse for *all* employees.
5. Establish a chemical health counselor/specialist position within the school staff to spearhead efforts to prevent drug abuse problems and promote practical solutions (see job description provided).

Job Title: *Chemical Health Counselor*

   Responsibilities:

1. Act as a resource to all staff members.
2. Assist with making referrals and conducting interventions for staff and students.
3. Implement appropriate support and growth groups for staff and students.
4. Be responsible for awareness and education programs at all levels.
5. Provide continuing inservice training on chemical dependency issues.
6. Develop and implement preventative strategies.
7. Serve as liaison with community agencies.

6. Develop a trained cadre of staff members (counselors, social workers, health personnel, etc.) to assist the chemical health specialist in making help available to staff as well as students.
7. Never back away from necessary interventions.

8. When possible, establish an employee assistance program (EAP) that offers employees and their families confidential help at little or no cost.

9. Ensure that the five essential elements of a sound assistance program are available to all staff members: evaluation, referral, treatment/counseling, support groups, and follow-up.

10. Seek outside help (medical personnel, treatment facilities, law enforcement agencies, etc.) whenever necessary.

Following these steps provides principals with a workable strategy for dealing with employee drug problems in a professional, fair, effective, and humane manner.

Two final watch words for handling such problems should be kept in mind:

- The principal's *first priority is* to do everything necessary to maintain the integrity and effectiveness of the school and its programs and to safeguard students.

- The principal's *second priority* is to do everything possible to salvage and support all the valuable human resources of the school including staff members at risk.

Ranking alongside, and sometimes related to, drug abuse problems within schools are staff and student issues involving sexual abuse and harassment. The next section spotlights what the secondary principal needs to know about this growing area of concern.

DEALING WITH SEXUAL HARASSMENT AND ABUSE PROBLEMS

Like drug abuse, problems of sexual harassment and/or abuse may involve staff members at any level and are most often complicated, sensitive, and delicate to handle. Nothing promotes titillating media coverage and unbridled gossip within the school community more than allegations of sexual misconduct. All charges of sexual harassment or abuse must be dealt with by the principal or designee, but they must be handled with extreme care—reputations, careers, and, sometimes, lives are at stake.

The principal's first and foremost responsibility is to help all staff members fully understand today's new standards of behavior. Perceptions of appropriate and inappropriate conduct have changed dramatically in recent years. The "old boys club" mentality and mystique have no place in the school setting. Sensitivity and respect must be the overriding principles governing all relationships between and among staff members and students.

Without fail, incidents or allegations of sexual harassment involve heavy and emotionally charged issues. This is particularly true in situations regarding misconduct directed toward students. It is important that school leaders fully appreciate the enormous liability for administrators and the school district where sexual harassment or abuse exist. Heavy penalties have been extracted by courts from administrators whose only fault has been that they "should have known" that sexual misconduct was taking place.

By most legal definitions, sexual harassment may exist in two forms:

1. *Direct, overt sexual behavior* (unwelcome touching, unwanted advances, offensive comments, etc.). The most blatant examples involve the use of positional power by staff members (administrators and/or teachers) to gain sexual favors from students or other staff members.

2. *Presence of a "hostile environment"* (offensive displays of sexual materials, frequent repeating of sexually related stories or anecdotes, etc.).

Incidents of these forms of sexual harassment may occur between any combination of individuals in the school as depicted:

Employee ⟶ Employee	
M → F	F → M
M → M	F → F

Employee ⟶ Student	
M → F	F → M
M → M	F → F

Student ⟶ Student	
M → F	F → M
M → M	F → F

No matter at what level allegations arise, the principal must take direct action. The essentials of a sound plan for dealing with such situations include:

• A strong, proactive program of education and awareness for all staff (see the accompanying sample Sexual Harassment Fact Sheet)

• A definitive school policy statement prohibiting any form of sexual harassment or abuse

• Wide dissemination of the school's anti-sexual harassment policy

• Strict and consistent follow-through and implementation of the school's policy

More specific guidelines for dealing with allegations of sexual abuse situations are:

• Develop a simple, easy-to-use procedure for reporting or filing a complaint regarding alleged sexual misconduct. (The process should avoid intimidating students or staff members who want to report inappropriate behaviors and should include alternative methods of reporting.)

Sexual Harassment Fact Sheet
for
Staff and Students

Policy: The district has a strict policy prohibiting any form of sexual harassment of students or staff members.

Definition: Sexual harassment consists of unwelcomed sexual advances, requests for sexual favors, sexually motivated physical conduct or other verbal or physical conduct, or communication of a sexual nature. Sexual harassment may include but is not limited to

- Verbal harassment or abuse
- Subtle pressure for sexual activity
- Inappropriate or unwelcome touching, patting or pinching
- Intentional brushing against a student's or employee's body
- Demanding sexual favors accompanied by implied or overt threats concerning an individual's employment or educational status
- demanding sexual favors accompanied by implied or overt promises of preferential treatment.

Reporting: Anyone believing themselves to be the victim of sexual harassment by student or an employee of the district should report the alleged acts immediately. Students should report such complaints to a teacher, counselor, or other staff member. Employees should report complaints to their immediate supervisor or to the associate superintendent. A reporting form is available in all building offices, but reports may also be verbal or by informal written note. The district will act to investigate all complaints, as quickly as possible.

Consequences: Individuals who sexually harass either a student or staff member may be subject to civil or criminal litigation or both, as well as discipline by the school district, including possible suspension, expulsion, leave with or without pay, or termination.

Further Information: If you have further questions, contact the district personnel office.

- Don't trivialize or ignore any complaint or allegation.

- Always follow through and investigate every reported allegation or violation.

- Report all incidents of suspected or alleged incidents of sexual harassment or abuse to appropriate enforcement or protection agencies. (This is mandatory in many states.)

- Call on district office (e.g., personnel department) for help when needed.

- Don't hesitate to seek legal counsel in conducting investigations and acting on the findings.

- Have a predetermined plan for dealing with the media when sensitive issues are under investigation.

The action steps can go a long way in helping principals and other administrators in diffusing delicate situations and enforcing preventative and corrective measures regarding sexual harassment or abuse situations.

Although not as dramatic or spectacular as situations involving sexual misconduct, a more common and persistent problem in managing school staffs is the everyday concern about employee absenteeism. The next section details practical ways to bolster attendance and reduce unnecessary absences among staff members at all levels.

ACTION PLAN FOR REDUCING EMPLOYEE ABSENTEEISM

One of the fundamental rules for success in any organization is to "show up." In schools, this is as true for staff members as it is for students. Principals must always be concerned about excessive and chronic absenteeism whether it involves a single staff member or characterizes a sizable portion of the total staff.

In individual cases, irregular attendance may be caused by health issues, burnout, drug abuse, or a host of other personal circumstances or problems. When absenteeism spreads to a substantive segment of the staff, it is often symptomatic of some kind of "internal rot" within the organization. Problems lead to absenteeism and absenteeism leads to more problems. These problems often include diminished morale, reduced productivity, disrupted programs, and increased costs

Attendance problems can be contagious. Wherever a "culture of absenteeism" exists among the staff, it can rapidly infest the student body. Frequent absences by teachers and other staff members send the wrong message to students about the important relationship between consistent attendance and positive performance.

In schools, as well as in the private sector, the following measures have proved effective in avoiding or correcting problems of excessive staff absences:

- Careful record keeping to spot patterns before they escalate into major issues. Computerized attendance records can greatly assist administrators in monitoring staff attendance.

- The single, greatest deterrent to unnecessary absenteeism is to require employees to contact their immediate supervisor directly in *all* cases of absence. An answering machine or some unknown substitute caller may be easily conned, but most personnel are reluctant to feign illness or fabricate excuses when speaking directly to their boss.

- Some form of doctor's verification should be routinely required for all absences exceeding three days and should also be invoked in any situation where veracity is in question.

- Contract provisions and administrative regulations should be examined periodically to eliminate any undue incentives for absence (e.g., overly liberal personal leave clauses).

- It often pays big dividends to recognize and reward good attendance records (pay employees for unused sick leave upon severance, convert unused sick leave to vacation time where appropriate, etc.).

- Many schools have established staff wellness and fitness programs to promote healthier employees and reduce absences.

Following these guidelines can go a long way in assuring reasonable and responsible attendance by all staff members.

Although excessive absence is always a problem, some staff members pose an even greater problem when they are present. Employees at any level who habitually reflect a negative attitude can quickly poison the well of any school. Hints on handling the disciples of gloom and doom who seem to appear on every school's roster of employees are spotlighted in the next section.

WORKING WITH STAFF MEMBERS WHO HAVE AN ATTITUDE PROBLEM

Every school has one or more of them:

- It may be the custodian who files a grievance at every alleged slight.
- It may be the secretary who thrives on gossiping about vulnerable staff members.
- It may be the teacher who looks for fine points in the contract to sabotage new initiatives.

All schools have staff members who have an attitude problem. At any level, the principal may encounter antagonistic subordinates with deep-rooted anti-administration attitudes.

These negative staff members can be like cancers that sap the energy and undermine the health of the organization. A positive attitude among staff members doesn't guarantee success, but a pervasive negative attitude can predetermine failure. Effective leaders must develop a special antenna to spot nay-sayers and pick up signs of negativism:

Signs of Staff Negativism

Negative staff members tend to:

- Pocket veto management directives
- Bad mouth school leaders
- Feed the rumor mill
- Lack loyalty
- Bypass established channels of authority
- Form divisive cliques
- "Work to rule" at the slightest provocation
- Practice obstructionism
- Slack off on assignments
- Complain about working conditions

When negative attitudes become a problem within individuals or groups, school leaders have some leverage that may neutralize or turn around the attitudes that can polarize the staff and paralyze school programs. Choices available to the principal include:

1. Using the established performance appraisal system to influence change. It sometimes helps to step up the evaluation timetable for habitual complainers and other negative staff members.
2. Using peer pressure to redirect negative employees.
3. Reinforcing positive behavior ("catching them being good") to win over uncooperative subordinates.
4. Exercising the power of assignment (hall duty, lunchroom supervision, etc.) to get the attention of problem employees.
5. Taking disciplinary action (letter of reprimand, notices of deficiency, suspension, etc.) in cases of flagrant negative behavior.

The trick for the skilled administrator is to identify when action should be taken and what action to take. Administrators shouldn't expect or demand popularity; but they can and must expect effort, productivity, performance and a modicum of loyalty to the school.

Blatant negativism that is counterproductive to the success of the school must be dealt with head on. In some cases, however, a certain level of benign negativism can be tolerated in the name of respect for diversity.

When negativism arises, the principal or other school leader must weigh the pros and cons of confrontation. Winning some battles is not worth the internal political fallout that may result.

Nationally recognized consultant and "teacher of superintendents" Dick Foster admonishes administrators to avoid spending undue time and effort on the "bottom 15 percent (negative staff members) who cannot or will not change. When attitude problems are more of an annoyance than a fatal disease, the interests of the school may be best served when the principal refuses to dignify negative employees by directing attention to them, and, instead, concentrates efforts on the majority of staff members who will respond to challenge and adapt to change.

If action is necessary, the principal must take it. If action will merely do more for the ego of the administrator than for the good of the school, it should be avoided.

Previous sections of this chapter have dealt with generic principles and practices applicable to all categories of staff members. The next segment focuses on strategies for managing a specific group within the total staff.

SPECIAL TIPS FOR SUPERVISING SECRETARIAL/CLERICAL PERSONNEL

To manage the total staff successfully, the principal must be aware of and address the special characteristics and needs of each component within the overall team. Each subset within the staff differs in its makeup, its priorities, and its perceptions of how it fits into the grand scheme of the school. The clerical staff, which may include secretaries, aides, paraprofessionals, and other support personnel, is often underappreciated by administrators and teachers.

The best principals, however, fully recognize the value of the clerical staff as the school's first line of public contact and as the superstructure that supports the total school's activities and programs. Everyone can point to successful schools where key secretaries have made a parade of principals "look good" while drawing little attention to themselves. One of the secrets to effective management is to nurture, protect, and empower the clerical component of the overall school staff.

Numerous surveys in both the public and private sector reveal that the qualities clerical personnel most value in the working environment include respect, recognition, challenge, trust, and opportunities for growth. Sensitivity to these priorities should guide the principal's management and supervision of support personnel. Consider these specific strategies for providing maximum support to all members of the school's clerical staff:

- Integrate secretaries and aides into the decision-making processes of the school by including them in staff meetings, as part of interview teams, on committees, and so on.

- Be particularly sensitive to women's issues (sexual harassment, chauvinistic practices and "put downs," etc.).

- Encourage and facilitate networking with counterparts in other school and similar work environments.

- Promote personal and professional growth by supporting participation in workshops and seminars, arranging for "developmental assessments" for individual employees where appropriate, and encouraging membership in professional organizations such as Professional Secretaries International (PSI).

- Advocate pay equity plans that provide comparable compensation for comparable work.

- Include clerical personnel in school staff development activities.

- Provide opportunities for ongoing, meaningful input by the clerical staff.

- Use job titles that accurately reflect levels and areas of responsibility.

- Support fringe benefits of special interest to clerical employees (child care, cafeteria/flexible benefit programs, etc.).

- Respect the dignity and integrity of clerical personnel. Never ask or expect clerical staff members to lie, cover up, or provide false information.

- Pay attention to working conditions (private dining areas, adequate restroom facilities, proper lighting, ventilation, etc.).

In addition to these measures, one of the most effective tools for managing clerical employees is a clear-cut, easy-to-use performance appraisal process and instrument. Supervisors and secretaries alike favor an evaluation system that is based on identified standards of performance, promotes growth, fosters meaningful two-way communication, and is adaptable to changing conditions. The sample evaluation forms provided, developed by a cross section of clerical, aide, and administrative personnel, embody all the elements of a practical and workable performance appraisal program.

Just as clerical employees require special attention and consideration, the school's custodial/maintenance staff has unique features that call for some different management approaches.

Clerical/Aide Performance Appraisal

Directions and Definitions for Supervisors

1. The purpose of the performance appraisal program is to promote professional growth, help both supervisor and employee improve, and promote two-way communication.

2. An evaluation of every clerical/aide staff member *must be completed annually* prior to the end of the school year. (March–April is the suggested time frame.) The supervisor should initiate the evaluation process by distributing the Preparation Form, completing the Appraisal Form, and scheduling an evaluation conference.

3. An evaluation conference is required. The employee should complete the Performance Appraisal Preparation Form prior to each evaluation conference and bring to the conference for discussion.

4. The evaluator may use either the numerical rating, the comment portion of the form, or both. All comments should be as specific as possible.

5. In evaluating each performance standard, evaluators should consider the following definitions:

   - *Quality of work.* Accuracy, minimum errors, well organized.

   - *Quantity of work.* Volume of work, time management.

   - *Job knowledge.* Understands responsibilities, technical skill.

   - *Dependability.* Meets deadlines, achieves expectations, follows directions and established procedures.

   - *Working relations.* Demonstrates sensitivity, promotes teamwork, is responsive to others' needs.

   - *Attitude.* Is enthusiastic and positive. Has high self-expectations, sense of humor and sense of ethics; behaves professionally.

   - *Adaptability.* Anticipates problems, adjusts to circumstances, handles frustrations and pressure calmly and with renewed effort.

   - *Initiative.* Self-starting, performs tasks without prompting, exhibits problem-solving skills.

   - *Communication skills.* Communicates clearly in oral and written form.

   - *Accepts responsibility.* Readily accepts responsibility; seeks additional responsibility when appropriate.

Clerical/aide Performance Appraisal Preparation Form

Name _____ Position _____

Building _____ Date _____

In advance of each performance appraisal conference, the employee should complete this form and be prepared to review it with the evaluator.

1. *Areas/Accomplishments:* (May include work achievement, contributions to district or building goals, self growth activities, etc.)

2. *Areas of Growth/Improvement:* (Areas on which I would like to work)

3. *Ways My Supervisor Can Help Me Most*

Employee's Signature _____

Clerical/aide Performance Appraisal Form

Name_____ Position _____

Building_____ Date _____

Performance Appraisal Rating and/or Comments: (Supervisors should refer to the individual employee's official position description when completing this form.)

Performance Standards	Needs Improvement	Meets Expectations	Exceeds Expectations/ Exemplary	Comments (May substitute for and/or supplement numerical ratings)*
Quality of work	1	2	3	
Quantity of work	1	2	3	
Job knowledge	1	2	3	
Dependability	1	2	3	
Working relations	1	2	3	
Attitude toward work	1	2	3	
Adaptability	1	2	3	
Initiative	1	2	3	
Communication skills	1	2	3	
Accepts responsibility	1	2	3	

Employee's Comments:

_____

Evaluator's Signature

1 Copy—Employee
1 Copy—Employer

_____

Employee's Signature

Employee's signature indicates receipt of a copy and opportunity to discuss the evaluation and does not necessarily indicate agreement.

*Additional comments may be added on reverse side.

SPECIAL TIPS FOR MANAGING YOUR CUSTODIAL STAFF

Like the clerical staff, custodial and maintenance personnel represent a distinctive group within the school. Most often, this unit is largely a male-dominated group with strong ties to organized labor. The custodial force may be direct employees of the school or may be part of a contracted service. In either case, the members play an important role in creating first impressions of the school and frequently serve as ambassadors to the public. Managing this group warrants special attention by the chief administrator.

Because of the strong element of "union mentality" within this group, custodial personnel are often concerned with issues of seniority, wages, and benefit provisions. In recent times, this group of employees has also sometimes felt victimized by comparable-worth legislation and mandatory pay equity plans. Because of these forces, the principal's priorities must be to maintain high standards of work performance and to promote positive morale within the group.

Performance standards for custodians are often enhanced by holding weekly briefings (more often if needed) with the head custodian of the building, conducting periodic "walk-throughs" of the facility accompanied by key custodial/maintenance personnel, defining specific work areas and responsibilities for each custodian, and requiring that all work and special cleaning requests be submitted in writing. A carefully monitored probationary period for new hires and a systematic program of evaluation are also crucial to successful management of the custodial force.

Some schools have problems maintaining a full complement of custodians throughout the year because of frequent turnover and heavy vacation usage during peak periods (e.g., summer months when major projects can be completed). When the work force is depleted by vacancies or vacations, productivity, obviously, deteriorates. The most workable solutions to this problem include maintaining a list of substitute custodians, creating a "floating sub" position to fill in where needed, using commercial temporary help, and regulating vacation schedules (e.g., permitting no vacations during the month of August prior to the opening of school).

The keys to generating positive morale within the custodial ranks lie in recognition, involvement, praise, and encouragement. Providing and promoting training opportunities for custodians, coupled with an overt policy of promotion from within, can go a long way toward bolstering morale within this group. As with clerical employees, it is also important to involve and include the custodial staff in schoolwide decisions, committees, and staff activities. Among the many small touches that can make a big difference in managing custodial personnel are noting birthdays in the building's weekly bulletin, providing individual name tags for each custodian, and, occasionally, hosting special appreciation events (barbecues, picnics, etc.) just for the custodial staff.

Last, it behooves the principal to take extra measures to promote cooperating between teachers and custodians and to ensure that all custodial personnel are fully informed of school policies and regulations.

When the building looks good and systems work properly, everyone in the school feels better and the program flows more smoothly. Custodians make these things happen. It is up to the principal to do everything possible to see that the custodial staff succeeds. The management techniques just outlined contribute to this success.

Another segment of the staff that is often overloaded, but is critical to the day-to-day operation of the school, is the substitute teacher corps. Reserve teachers are another group that requires specialized management approaches as discussed next.

PUTTING OUT FIRES IN THE SUBSTITUTE TEACHER PROGRAM

Of all the unsung heroes in the school, substitute teachers may be the most overlooked and neglected. These replacement teachers are absolutely necessary to maintaining continuity, order, and quality instruction in the day-to-day program. Many times, they are also credible voices in the community that can provide accurate information to parents and patrons, dispel rumors, interpret programs, and enhance the school's team. For this reason, some schools have begun using the title "reserve teachers" to reflect more accurately their proper role.

The valued and valuable service performed by substitutes deserves the recognition and attention of school leaders. If the substitute system is operating well, the school program flows smoothly throughout the year. If it is in disarray, daily operations can unravel quickly.

Although most substitutes are positive contributors, there are certain common complaints that persist in many schools:

Eight Common Substitute Teacher Complaints

1. Low pay rates
2. Short notice of assignments
3. Delay and confusion in receiving payment
4. Lack of respect and recognition
5. Absence of daily classroom lesson plans
6. Lack of feedback
7. Partial day assignments
8. Inadequate communication and information

Where these concerns exist, principals should take proactive steps to resolve them and alleviate them for the future. Many of these issues can be handled by a substitute teacher handbook containing pertinent information on responsibilities, schedules, discipline policies, daily procedures, event calendars, parking rules, and so on. Some schools have also found it helpful to assign a regular staff member(s) to serve as substitute greeter and contact person each day.

The morale of substitute teachers can be heightened by including them in inservice activities, adding them to mailing lists for school publications, and encouraging teachers to have a special "sub folder" available in all classrooms.

Recognition for reserve teachers can be promoted by holding a back-to-school orientation program for substitutes, hosting a year-end reception for all subs who have served the building, and, where possible, providing bonuses for substitutes who have been unusually loyal to the school. Some districts have even initiated a Reserve Teacher of the Year Award program (see insert).

"Reserve Teacher of the Year" Program
(An Annual Award For An Outstanding, Representative Reserve Teacher)

Purpose:
The award is designed to honor an outstanding, representative reserve teacher each year in recognition of the valued and valuable service performed by reserve teachers as partners on the teaching team in the St. Louis Park Schools.

Selection Criteria:

1. Exhibited loyalty and dedication.
2. Performance reflecting the standards and quality indicators expected of teaching professionals.
3. Flexibility and adaptability in accepting a variety of assignments and challenges.
4. Commitment to continued growth within the profession.

Selection Procedures:

1. One elementary and one secondary reserve teacher will be honored each year.
2. Each May, classroom teachers will receive a ballot containing the names of all reserve teachers who have taught 60 or more days during the school year at the appropriate level. If no reserve teachers have taught the minimum 60 days at the appropriate level, no election will be held and no award will be given.
3. The elementary and secondary reserve teachers receiving the most votes will be honored as *Reserve Teacher of the Year.*

The Award:
An appropriate certificate will be presented by the school board to the selected *Reserve Teachers of the Year* at the district's annual spring presentation of "Class Act" awards.

As with all employee groups, some form of systematic evaluation should be conducted on a regular basis. In the case of substitutes, a simple form completed by the regular teachers should suffice. An example is provided:

Substitute Teacher Performance Appraisal

_____   _____

Substitute Teacher   Date of Substitute Teaching

Subject or Grade level(s) taught: _____

Building: _____

Rating: _____   Excellent (Comments optional)
         _____   Satisfactory (Comments optional)
         _____   Unsatisfactory (Explanation required)

Comments: _____

_____

_____

                           _____   _____

                           Regular Teacher's Signature   Date

                           _____   _____

                           Principal's Signature   Date

Please forward to Personnel Office. A copy will be provided for the substitute teacher. If there are any questions or concerns, the substitute teacher is encouraged to discuss this appraisal with the regular teacher or building principal.

By employing these suggested procedures, principals can successfully manage the substitute program and avoid breakdown when regular teacher absences occur.

In dealing with substitutes and all other groups within the school staff, it is important for administrators to understand the distinction between supervision and evaluation as discussed in the next section.

THE CRITICAL DIFFERENCE BETWEEN SUPERVISION AND EVALUATION

Although the terms "supervision" and "evaluation" are frequently used interchangeably, there is a fine difference between the two functions. To manage school personnel successfully, knowledgeable administrators should understand and act on this distinction.

Supervision, as used here, deals with the continuous personal and professional improvement of all segments of the staff. Evaluation, on the other hand, focuses on critical decisions regarding retention or dismissal of a small number of questionable employees. Everyone can benefit from effective supervision ("Even champions need coaching.") Only marginal and/or unsatisfactory staff members, however, require formal evaluation as outlined here:

What's The Difference?
(Supervision Versus Evaluation)

Supervision

- Provides feedback and opportunities for growth.

- Identifies areas for development and marshals resources to promote improvement.

- Is mutually accepted and carried out (collaborative).

- Is informal and unofficial (may be no permanent record).

- Is ongoing for everyone.

- Does not spell the difference between retention and termination.

Evaluation

- Follows strict requirements for due process.

- Focuses on unsatisfactory performance, requires measurable results, and may involve progressive discipline.

- Is usually imposed by administration (may be adversarial).

- Is formal, official, legalistic, and carefully documented.

- Involves a specific time frame for defined remediation or correction.

- Determines career futures job retention).

Supervision usually includes observation, scripttaping, follow-up conferences, job targets, and self-appraisal coupled with external feedback. By comparison, evaluation often involves identification of deficiencies and remedial measures, legal action, and penalties (suspension, dismissal, etc.).

By recognizing these distinctions and educating the total staff regarding the difference, principals can establish a practical framework for working to stretch all employees and for disciplining a few (bottom 15 percent) when necessary. The following section illustrates how changing situations bring into play the subtle nuances of both supervision and evaluation.

HOW TO HELP STAFF ADJUST TO CHANGING EXPECTATIONS

Even the most talented staff can fall prey to complacency and permit performance to lag behind elevating levels of expectation. Standards seldom stand still, but performance often levels off. In managing the school staff, particularly a mature, highly trained and highly experienced staff, principals must understand and deal with this phenomenon as outlined in the following principles:

Six Principles of Rising Expectations and Performance Levels

1. Both performance (output, productivity, and effectiveness) and expectations (societal standards and demands) usually increase over time.

2. Expectations tend to rise faster than levels of performance.

3. Performance tends to improve rapidly with added knowledge, experience, and training early in a professional career.

4. Performance often advances unevenly and may eventually plateau, while expectations continue to escalate without a lull or limit (see accompanying graph).

5. Performance may actually slacken or taper off; but expectations rarely diminish.

6. The gap between performance and expectations may widen without the professional staff realizing it.

Comparison: Improvement Patterns in Expectations and Performance

---

Performance:
Expectations:

When confronted with these principles, educators are often stunned by the prospect that, during a single career, a teacher's performance may be exemplary at one point and the same level of performance viewed as merely marginal at another point in time. It is extremely sobering for teachers to realize that today's superstar may have difficulty making the team tomorrow.

To assist teachers and other staff members to appreciate fully the need to adjust to changing expectations, it often helps to use a sports metaphor. Most of us readily understand that what once were world-class, record-breaking athletic feats might now be unheralded, lackluster performances.

It is only through effective supervision and realistic evaluation that principals can prevent the gap between expectations and performance from widening beyond reasonable limits of tolerance. School leaders must ensure that all staff members understand the necessity of continuing growth and improvement. This is a strong argument for an ongoing, dynamic program of staff development. All principals have a threefold obligation:

• To help staff members recognize the potential for disparities between rising expectations and static performance.

• To help teachers and other personnel identify the status of their individual performance in relation to existing standards.

• To help staff keep performance and expectations "in sync."

The next segment lays out suggestions for setting standards as the basis for supervision and evaluation and for matching performance to shifting expectations.

HOW TO SET STANDARDS FOR PROBATIONARY AND TENURED PROFESSIONALS

Without agreed-upon standards, a supervisor has no basis for meaningful supervision or evaluation, and staff members have no guidelines or benchmarks to help them judge if their performance remains in tune with professional and societal expectations. Without established standards, appraisal of professional performance is, at best, a hit or miss exercise.

A well-defined set of standards for teachers is a "must" management tool for principals. These standards should reflect *desired* levels of performance (not just minimal standards) and *all* areas of professional responsibility (not just the "teaching act"). The same standards should be set for both probationary and continuing contract teachers, although they may be applied differentially to account for varying stages of development.

Standards are the first step toward effective management, supervision, and evaluation. Standard setting should precede development of any evaluation instrument or process. Where standards do not exist, the principal should proact to have them developed.

In establishing such standards for teacher performance, principals should ensure that all the bases are covered:

- Standards should be mutually developed by a committee comprised of both teachers and administrators (equal representation is preferable).

- Input from students, parents, and other community members should be considered.

- All categories of teacher responsibility (instruction, discipline, parental releases, professional growth, etc.) should be identified and incorporated into the standards.

- The committee should be provided with whatever resources are necessary to produce a comprehensive set of standards. This may include use of an outside consultant or facilitator.

- Before finalizing the standards, a draft should be widely circulated for review and comment by all stakeholders.

A sample set of standards for probationary and tenured teachers developed according to these guidelines appears on the following pages.

In addition to adopted standards, supervision and evaluation of instructional personnel should be based on a generic job description for all classroom teachers.

Standards and Quality Indicators for Probationary and Tenured Teachers

A. *Instructional Skills*

1. Uses a variety of effective teaching techniques (role playing, discussion, etc.) and models (elements of instruction, cooperative learning, learning styles, etc.)
2. Uses a variety of evaluative techniques to drive instruction and diagnose and measure student learning needs effectively.
3. Sets high expectations for individual student growth.
4. Plans and organizes instruction to meet specific learning objectives.

B. *Student-Centered Focus*

1. Establishes a healthy, friendly, supportive classroom climate.
2. Generates interest and excitement in the classroom.
3. Knows each student and exhibits a genuine interest in students as individuals.
4. Shows sensitivity to the needs and feelings of students (e.g., family changes, chemical dependency, abuse).
5. Understands the basic principles underlying the education of young people, including those with special needs.

C. *Knowledge of Content and Use of Materials*

1. Demonstrates current knowledge of subject matter.
2. Demonstrates knowledge and use of district curriculum scope and sequence.
3. Designs and uses a variety of materials to supplement the textbook and achieve specific curriculum goals.
4. Uses multisensory approaches to accommodate a range of student learning needs.
5. Integrates appropriate real-life experiences and community resources into the classroom.

D. *Classroom Environment*

1. Organizes physical setting for effective and efficient learning.
2. Exercises classroom control in a positive, yet assertive manner, using a variety of effective behavior management techniques.
3. Provides a positive environment conducive to learning.
4. Follows current district and/or building discipline plans consistently.
5. Assists students to assume responsibility for appropriate behavior.
6. Establishes a climate in which students feel free to question and think creatively.

E. *Communication Skills*

1. Communicates clearly in oral and written form.
2. Communicates student strengths and weaknesses with honesty, tact, and understanding.
3. Encourages and initiates two-way communication.
4. Demonstrates responsibility in communicating student progress (progress reports, conferences, staffings, etc.).

F. *Interpersonal Relations*

1. Recognizes responsibility to foster positive staff morale.
2. Promotes a teamwork posture within the staff.
3. Displays fairness and consistency in dealing with students.
4. Displays compassion and sensitivity.
5. Recognizes the importance of parent and community involvement.
6. Shows responsiveness to community needs and concerns.

G. *Professionalism*

1. Sets high expectations for personal performance.
2. Practices ethical behavior, respects confidentiality, and follows proper channels of communication.
3. Demonstrates continuing professional growth and development.
4. Demonstrates an active interest and participates in professional activities (scope and sequence committees, etc.).
5. Holds teaching in high esteem and reflects a commitment to the profession.
6. Meets basic work expectations (promptness, attendance, recordkeeping, etc.).

H. *Attitude*

1. Approaches teaching with enthusiasm, energy, and optimism.
2. Demonstrates a positive problem-solving attitude in the workplace.
3. Demonstrates initiative to take risks and remains open to change.
4. Reflects self-confidence.
5. Exhibits a good sense of humor.

I. *Adaptability*

1. Monitors and adjusts teaching approaches as appropriate.
2. Recognizes own needs and is willing to ask for help.
3. Handles changes, interruptions, and last-minute requests effectively and calmly.
4. Responds to frustrations and adversity with patience and renewed effort.
5. Anticipates problems and devises ways to overcome them.

USING JOB DESCRIPTIONS AS THE BASIS FOR PERFORMANCE APPRAISAL

Personnel professionals are often aghast at the general absence of formal job descriptions for school employees. Many schools have no job descriptions at all or have very cursory listings of duties and responsibilities. Other schools may have position descriptions for various categories of classified personnel (bus drivers, cooks, custodians, aides, etc.), but none for teachers. This is a void that seriously hampers effective management of the school staff.

Although some purists might argue that teaching is an art and cannot be reduced to a written job description, the essence of accountability demands that functions and responsibilities be defined so that school leaders have a yardstick to measure if the job is getting done.

It is important to spell out what teachers (and other employees) are expected to do in order to hold them accountable and to point them in the right direction. It does little good to "empower" teachers if no one knows what it is they are empowered to accomplish.

It is possible to develop a position description for teachers. The description should be simple and direct and strike a balance between being too global and being overly prescriptive. Eight to 12 items are usually standard for any kind of job description. Many principals have found it preferable to adopt a single job description for all classroom teachers rather than attempt to delineate minute differences among the job responsibilities of teachers in different subject areas or grade levels.

If no teacher job description exists, the secondary principal is well served to see that one is developed. Once in place, the formal job description, coupled with established performance standards described earlier, gives the principal a workable framework in which to appraise performance, demand accountability, supervise for growth, and evaluate for corrective action where necessary. A sample job description for teachers follows.

JOB DESCRIPTION

Job Title: Teacher
Supervisor: Principal or designee
Responsibilities:

1. Plan, organize, and provide appropriate learning experience within assigned area(s) of responsibility.

2. Establish and maintain a classroom or instructional-area atmosphere conducive to learning.

3. Evaluate and interpret student learning in a professional manner.

4. Identify special needs of students and seek assistance of others as needed.

5. Make reasonable efforts to promote and maintain appropriate behavior of students.

6. Contribute to the continuous development of curriculum and the improvement of instruction.

7. Maintain records and submit reports necessary for the effective management of the school program.

8. Participate in faculty meetings, workshops, inservice training, and other appropriate activities.

9. Adhere to ethical standards adopted by professional teacher organizations.

10. Perform other special duties (supervision, attendance taking, conducting open houses, parent conferencing, etc.) as assigned by the principal or designee.

Job descriptions and performance standards give individual staff members something to shoot for. The next section describes how to help teachers set specific targets for improved performance.

A STANDARDS-BASED "JOB TARGET" APPROACH TO STAFF EVALUATION

As leader/manager of the school staff, the principal's responsibility is to translate performance standards and job descriptions into reality. A program of individual teacher job targets can provide the necessary bridge between rhetoric and real-world accomplishment.

Job targets are specific, measurable goals and strategies designed to help teachers, and others where appropriate, to grow and improve. The purpose of the job target is to lay out a precise personal plan for achieving a well-defined objective that contributes to the school's broader purpose. Most job targets include (1) a carefully crafted objective, (2) a step-by-step implementation strategy, and (3) an evaluation plan. Through the power of putting thoughts and action plans in writing, job targets help to :

• Define ends and means
• Facilitate teacher-administrator collaboration and discussion
• Focus teacher energy and effort
• Make it difficult to ignore or forget goals throughout the year
• Provide a basis for effective supervision and formal evaluation where necessary.

There are few rules governing development of job targets, but the following lists of "musts" and "mays" clarify their purpose and function:

Job Targets . . .

Must

- Be in written form
- Be clearly stated
- Include a specific time frame
- Be specific (sharply focused)
- Be personalized
- Include measurable or observable outcomes
- Be lofty enough to stretch the teacher but not unattainable
- Be mutually developed by the teacher and the supervisor

May

- Be formal or informal
- Be directed toward any facet of teacher performance
- Include personal, as well as professional goals
- Be goals that can be achieved alone or require support and assistance from others
- Originate with either the teacher or the supervisor

Where job targets are used most successfully, teachers are required to submit a limited number (often three to four) of individual goals annually. The goal statements don't have to be fancy or sophisticated (the less jargon the better), but should relate to the school's established performance standards, the teacher's job description, or other relevant school or district priorities. The targets do not necessarily have to focus of areas of weakness, but should occasionally include plans on how to build on areas of strength. A sample teacher job target follows.

Job Target

Objective:	To learn more about and introduce "cooperative learning" techniques into my classroom.
Method of Implementation:	1. Participate in district workshops on cooperative learning.
	2. Develop and implement a minimum of three cooperative learning lessons during the first semester.
	3. Use a teacher-made checklist to evaluate student success in cooperative learning activities.
Evaluation Plan:	Written lesson plans will be submitted to the principal. The principal will observe at least one cooperative learning lesson. Results of the teacher-made checklist will be reviewed and discussed with the principal.

To be effective, the job targets approach must be implemented in an atmosphere of trust where teachers know they have the "right to fail." Partially fulfilled job targets may, then, become the basis for redefined future objectives.

When used as outlined, a systematic program of job targets can serve as either guides for supervision or criteria for formal evaluation and remedial action.

While the job target process represents a fairly traditional approach to supervision and/or evaluation, the next section goes a step beyond by detailing alternative performance appraisal models.

ALTERNATIVES TO TRADITIONAL STAFF EVALUATION MODELS

Resourceful principals seek out a variety of means to help staff members grow, improve, adjust to evolving standards, or, when needed, scramble to get their act together to avoid possible discipline or dismissal. Traditional approaches to supervision and evaluation have too often been limited solely to interaction between the principal and the individual employee. To assist both in assessing personal performance and finding ways to work better and smarter, the following techniques provide viable and valuable alternatives:

1. *Self-appraisal.* Many teachers benefit dramatically from assessing their own effectiveness by viewing and analyzing videotapes of their performance in the classroom. Frequently, seasoned instructors are surprised, even shocked, to observe personal mannerisms and methods that impede optimal teaching and learning. By using the mirror of televised tapes to see themselves as others see them, teachers can often make minor self-corrections that result in major differences in student gains. Many experts advise that this approach is most successful when used exclusively as a self-help tool. There is often no need for tapes to be viewed by anyone other than the teacher involved. This makes performance appraisal up close, private, and personal.

2. *Peer review.* Some teachers learn best and most from other teachers. If the trust level and collaborative spirit of the school permit, principals should encourage peer reviews. This process enables staff members to observe each other in the classroom and to provide each other with the kind of credible feedback and advice that can come only from a fellow teacher. Such reviews should be voluntary, mutual, and strictly confidential.

3. *External Feedback.* A third source of help for teachers in examining their individual effectiveness and in identifying specific ways to improve instruction is external feedback from students and parents. Many teachers get such feedback through structured or open-ended surveys. A more sophisticated approach is to use an outside facilitator to conduct "focus group" meetings of randomly selected students or parents to elicit perceptions of teacher strengths and weaknesses.

In the crucial task of assessing performance and managing staff development, principals should be eclectic in using any and all of the approaches described in this chapter. "Whatever works" is the best advice for principals committed to maximizing staff growth through active supervision and evaluation. One further resource that should not be overlooked is the use of multievaluators.

HINTS ON USING MULTIEVALUATORS

Like physicians, principals sometimes need to get a "second opinion" in diagnosing teacher performance. In recent times, the use of multievaluators has gained in popularity in schools across the country—particularly in situations involving beginning or new teachers where long-lasting decisions regarding tenure must be made in a relatively short probationary period. The following guidelines can help the principal decide when and how to use a third-party evaluator.

1. Outside evaluators are most helpful in:
   - Validating perceptions of performance
   - Verifying observations
   - Providing different perspectives and fresh ideas for growth or remedial measures
   - Providing supporting documentation of deficiencies where due process discipline or dismissal are under consideration.
2. Second evaluators may include:
   - Other administrators in the school (assistant principal, dean, etc.)
   - District office administrators
   - Principals or administrators from other schools
   - Curriculum specialists, department heads, and so on (where permitted by the teachers' contract)
3. Except in cases where formal progressive discipline is pending, second evaluators should be used only with the knowledge, permission and consent of the teacher involved.
4. Second evaluators are most helpful when they bring some background or expertise that differs from the supervising principal's perspective.
5. Feedback from the third-party evaluator may be provided directly to the teacher involved or simply shared with the responsible principal for incorporation into his or her assessment. This feedback may be written or verbal depending on the situation.
6. Outside evaluators should limit their feedback strictly to teacher behavior that they have directly observed.
7. Except in extremely troublesome or complicated situations, no more than one outside evaluator should be used with a single teacher. Otherwise, confusion and concerns over intimidation or harassment may ensue.

Whatever approach is taken by the supervising principal or multi-evaluators, there is usually need to record or document the outcomes. Some school-tested formats for writing and the results of performance appraisal are presented in the next section.

SAMPLE FORMATS FOR DOCUMENTING PERFORMANCE APPRAISALS

Whether providing supervision to help good teachers get better or performing formal evaluations of marginal employees that may result in the nonrenewal of a teacher's contract, it is imperative that principals have some written record of the findings and outcomes. This record may serve merely as informal notes for future reference by the teacher and supervising administrator, may become part of a permanent personnel file, or may serve as evidence in a dismissal hearing. Whatever the purpose, the written record is an essential tool in managing the school staff.

Although harried administrators often deplore the time and work involved and view writing up performance appraisal results as an onerous task, the payoff is worth the effort. It always behooves the principal to prepare written documentation of appraisals with care, particularly if the record is to become part of an official file or serve as possible evidence or an exhibit in any hearing or litigation proceeding. As a time-saver, some principals use commercially published collections of evaluative statements/phrases that can be adapted or used verbatim to fit the situation at hand.

To assume completeness and consistency, the school should use a standardized form for documenting supervision and evaluation results. This should not be an exercise in writing "free verse" by the principal. The best evaluation instruments reflect teacher participation in their development, provide for teacher (evaluatee) input, include some form of specific action plan, require the teacher to sign off indicating knowledge of the content, and permit reaction or rebuttal.

In designing or selecting a performance appraisal format, the instrument should meet the following criteria:

- Objectivity
- Specificity
- Consistency
- Clarity
- Fairness
- Communication
- Improvement orientation

Historically, administrators have used a variety of performance appraisal formats ranging from highly structured, definitive checklists to some very global, open-ended instruments. Usually, more detailed documentation is required where decisions are being made regarding gaining tenure and in potential dismissal situations.

The forms that follow are samples of three different formats that have proved to be efficient and effective in successful secondary schools. Included are a job target approach, a standards-based appraisal document, and an open-ended instrument.

APPRAISAL OF PROFESSIONAL PERFORMANCE

Name:_____School:_____Position:_____

1. Commendable accomplishment (requires comments)
2. Completed job target
3. Partially completed job target (requires comments)
4. Failed to meet job target (requires comments)

Job Target No. ____ (This is related to Building Goal #____ and District Priority #____) *The Objective:* (What will I do?) *Method of Implementation:* (How will I do it?) *Plan of Evaluation:* (How will I demonstrate that I have accomplished the objective?) *Results:* (How well did I do at meeting the objective? Please refer to above Plan of Evaluation.)		

Comments by Appraiser:

Comments by Appraisee:

Probationary Teachers Performance Appraisal Form

Teacher Name:_____School: _____

Grade or Subject: _____Date: _____

KEY:
n/a indicates that the evaluator has no basis for rating the teacher on a given proficiency, practice, or characteristic.

Numerical ratings have the meanings indicated below:

Number	Meaning	Explanation
5	Clearly Outstanding	Performance is *exemplary*.
4	Exceeds Expectations	Performance is at a high level of accomplishment.
3	Satisfactory Performance	Performance meets expectations.
2	Below Expectations	Performance needs improvement and does not meet expectations.
1	Unsatisfactory Performance	Performance is clearly not acceptable; no significant improvement has occurred.

The numerical ratings are designed to facilitate communication evaluation and professional growth. They are not to be tallied, averaged, or used in isolation.

In addition to the numerical ratings, written comments are required for each standard on the appraisal form.

Together, the numerical ratings and written comments constitute the primary tool for evaluation of probationary teachers in the St. Louis Park Schools.

A. *Instructional Skills*

1. Uses a variety of effective teaching techniques (role playing, discussion, etc.) and models (elements of instruction, cooperative learning, learning styles, etc.)   n/a 1 2 3 4 5

2. Uses a variety of evaluative techniques to drive instruction and measure student learning needs effectively.   n/a 1 2 3 4 5

3. Sets high expectations for students growth.   n/a 1 2 3 4 5

4. Plans and organizes instruction to meet specific learning objectives.   n/a 1 2 3 4 5

Comments: _____

_____

_____

_____

_____

B. *Student-Centered Focus*

1. Establishes a healthy, friendly, supportive classroom environment.   n/a 1 2 3 4 5

2. Generates interest and excitement in the classroom.   n/a 1 2 3 4 5

3. Knows each student and exhibits a genuine interest in students as individuals.   n/a 1 2 3 4 5

4. Shows sensitivity to the needs and feelings of students (e.g., family changes, chemical dependency/abuse).   n/a 1 2 3 4 5

5. Understands the basic principles underlying the education of young people, including those with special needs.   n/a 1 2 3 4 5

Comments: _____

_____

_____

_____

_____

C. *Knowledge of Content and Use of Materials*

1. Demonstrates current knowledge of subject matter   n/a 1 2 3 4 5

2. Demonstrates knowledge and use of district curriculum scope and sequence.   n/a 1 2 3 4 5

3. Designs and uses a variety of materials to supplement the textbook and achieve specific curriculum goals.   n/a 1 2 3 4 5

4. Uses multisensory approaches to accommodate a range of student learning needs.   n/a 1 2 3 4 5

5. Integrates appropriate real-life experiences and community resources into the classroom.   n/a 1 2 3 4 5

Comments: _____

_____

_____

_____

D. *Classroom Environment*

1. Organizes physical setting for effective and efficient learning.   n/a 1 2 3 4 5

2. Exercises classroom control in a positive, yet assertive, manner, using a variety of effective behavior management techniques.   n/a 1 2 3 4 5

3. Provides a positive environment conducive to learning.   n/a 1 2 3 4 5

4. Follows current district and/or building discipline plans consistently.   n/a 1 2 3

5. Assists students to assume responsibility for appropriate behavior.   n/a 1 2 3

6. Establishes a climate in which students feel free to question and think creatively.   n/a 1 2 3 4 5

Comments: _____

_____

_____

_____

_____

E. *Communication Skills*

1. Communicates clearly in oral and written form. n/a 1 2
2. Communicates student strengths and weaknesses with honesty, tact, and understanding. n/a 1 2
3. Encourages and initiates two-way communication. n/a 1 2
4. Demonstrates responsibility in communicating student progress. (progress reports, conferences, staffings, etc.) n/a 1 2

Comments: _____

_____

_____

_____

_____

_____

F. *Interpersonal Relations*

1. Recognizes responsibility to foster positive staff morale. n/a 1 2 3 4 5
2. Promotes a teamwork posture within the staff. n/a 1 2 3 4 5
3. Displays fairness and consistency in dealing with students. n/a 1 2 3 4 5
4. Displays compassion and sensitivity. n/a 1 2 3 4 5
5. Recognizes the importance of parent and community involvement. n/a 1 2 3 4 5
6. Shows responsiveness to community needs and concerns. n/a 1 2 3 4 5

Comments: _____

_____

_____

_____

_____

_____

G. *Professionalism*

1. Sets high expectations for personal performance.   n/a   1   2   3

2. Practices ethical behavior, respects confidentiality, and follows proper channels of communication.   n/a   1   2   3

3. Demonstrates continuing professional growth and development.   n/a   1   2   3

4. Holds teaching in high esteem and reflects a commitment to the profession.   n/a   1   2   3

5. Meets basic work expectations (promptness, attendance, record-keeping, etc.).   n/a   1   2   3

Comments: _____

_____

_____

_____

_____

H. *Attitude*

1. Approaches teaching with enthusiasm, energy, and optimism.   n/a   1   2   3   4   5

2. Demonstrates a positive problem-solving attitude in the workplace.   n/a   1   2   3   4   5

3. Demonstrates initiative to take risks and remains open to change.   n/a   1   2   3   4   5

4. Reflects self-confidence.   n/a   1   2   3   4   5

5. Exhibits a good sense of humor.   n/a   1   2   3   4   5

Comments: _____

_____

_____

_____

_____

I. *Adaptability*

1. Monitors and adjusts teaching approaches as appropriate.   n/a   1   2   3   4   5

2. Recognizes own needs and is willing to ask for help.

n/a 1 2 3 4 5

3. Handles changes, interpretations, and last-minute requests effectively and calmly.

n/a 1 2 3 4 5

4. Responds to frustrations and adversity with patience and renewed effort.

n/a 1 2 3 4 5

5. Anticipates problems and devises ways to overcome them.

n/a 1 2 3 4 5

Comments: _____

_____

_____

_____

_____

Goals/plan For Improvement/comments (Add additional sheets if necessary)

_____

_____

_____

_____

_____

_____

_____

_____

_____

_____

_____

_____

_____

_____

_____

_____

_____ _____
Teacher's Signature   Date

Teacher Comments: _____

_____

_____

_____

_____

_____

_____

_____

_____   _____
Evaluator's Signature/Title   Date

Note to building principal: After the final evaluation each year, check one of the following:

☐ Recommend termination of contract

☐ Recommend continuance of probationary status

☐ Recommend tenure

_____   _____
Principal's Signature   Date

Note: The teacher's signature indicates that he/she has received a copy of this evaluation and has had the opportunity to discuss it. The signature does not necessarily indicate agreement with individual ratings.

PERFORMANCE APPRAISAL FOR TEACHERS

Name: _____   School: _____

Grade(s) or Subject(s) Taught: _____   No. of Students: _____

Performance Description	Recommendations
1. Acquires information from a variety of sources in order to appraise student learning levels, interests, and needs.	
2. Establishes learning objectives consistent with appraisal of student needs, requirements of curriculum framework, and knowledge of human growth and development.	
3. Plans and provides for involvement of all students in the learning process.	
4. Plans for and uses those instructional methods that motivate and enable each student to achieve learning objectives.	
5. Plans for and utilizes those resources that motivate each student to achieve learning objectives.	
6. Plans for and utilizes techniques that motivate and enable each student to achieve learning objectives.	
7. Establishes and maintains the environment required to motivate each student to achieve learning objectives.	

	Performance Description	Recommendations
8. Manages student behavior in a constructive manner by applying discipline policies consistently and fairly.		
9. Promotes positive self-concept in students by reinforcing accomplishment, accepting individual differences and needs, and promoting self-discipline and responsibility.		
10. Appraises the effectiveness of his or her teaching practices and instructional program not only in terms of achieving his or her own objectives but also in terms of the total school's instructional program.		
11. Participates in school management, shares responsibility for the total school program, and supports school regulations and policies.		
12. Established relationships with administrators, colleagues, students, parents, and community that reflect respect for every individual.		
13. Identifies areas for self growth necessary to maintain or improve effectiveness, acquires appropriate training and/or information, and demonstrates successful application.		

Overall evaluation:
Needs improvement _____
Meets expectations _____
Exceeds expectations _____

Recommendation:
Recommend for reappointment _____
Recommend for tenure _____

I have read and discussed this report with the evaluator.

_____   _____
Teacher's Signature   Date

_____   _____
Evaluator's Signature and Title   Date

Whatever instrument is used, it may prove inadequate when appraising teachers operating at the extremes of the performance continuum. A later section identifies the kind of documentation necessary when dealing with unsatisfactory employees. While these marginal staff members pose special problems, evaluating the truly "high flyers" on the staff may be equally difficult.

HOW TO EVALUATE SUPERSTARS

Far too many principals fall prey to the easy attitude that providing performance appraisal for outstanding teachers is either unnecessary or requires only a modicum of attention. "An occasional pat on the back should suffice." Nothing could be further from the truth. Even expert teachers need supervision and feedback. The best can get better. Most successful principals come to realize that investing time and effort in evaluating, encouraging, empowering, and enabling the top 5 percent of the teaching staff pays bigger dividends for students and learning than does expending considerable energy on the marginal and the mediocre members.

Unfortunately, most performance appraisal systems and instruments have severe structural limitations when it comes to supervising superstars. When dealing with the top 5 percent, the principal's supervisory role becomes primarily a matter of systematic coaching and cheerleading. For the very best, performance appraisal needs to be as personalized and individualized as possible. Self-appraisal should be encouraged. Documentation should be primarily narrative rather than numerical ratings or checklists.

The top teachers should play a greater role in their own appraisal by developing personal professional development plans and identifying ways to share their expertise. For the "high flyers," extra attention needs to be directed toward "How my supervisor can help me most."

Another handful of success secrets for supervising superstars includes the following:

1. The evaluation of excellence requires experts. As a generalist, the principal should incorporate reviews by other master teachers and subject area specialists in the appraisal process.

2. A clinical supervision model involving elements of instruction, scripttaping observed lessons and frequent reinforcement conferences often works best with the best teachers.

3. Outstanding teachers are not afraid to be assessed on the basis of product (student gains in learning). "How much is taught?" "How many students benefited?" and "How quickly is material mastered?" are the kinds of questions that should be answered in the appraisal of top performers.

4. Superior teachers can benefit greatly from feedback based on multi-data sources, including student descriptions of teaching behavior and performance.

5. To nurture talent, principals should do whatever they can to tie excellence to rewards. Where performance pays off, more staff members work to get into the winners circle, and those already succeeding strive harder to stay there.

One more gift that principals can give to their best teachers is to model the importance of performance appraisal by being willing to be assessed themselves. This sends a strong message that no one is above benefiting from effective supervision.

When all data have been collected, all lessons observed, and all written documentation completed, the culminating follow-up conference provides both the closure to the supervisory process and the beginning of an action plan for improved instruction.

PROFILE OF A PRODUCTIVE EVALUATION CONFERENCE

In dealing with the entire spectrum of the school staff, the performance appraisal conference constitutes one of the principal's most precious opportunities to manage behavior and influence change. In a busy and bustling secondary school, it is often possible to go for long periods of time without any focused, direct personal contact with many individual employees. The supervisory or evaluation conference, then, provides a unique setting in which to reinforce positive efforts, set goals, make midcourse corrections, and/or plan remedial measures. Such conferences should not be taken lightly.

The performance appraisal conference enables the principal to "bring it all together" as depicted in the accompanying figure.

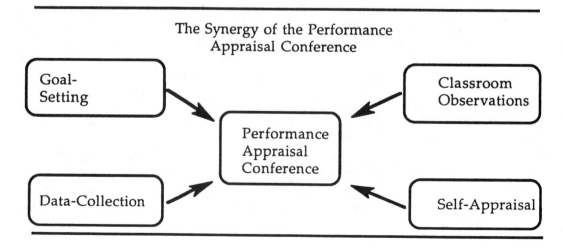

The Synergy of the Performance
Appraisal Conference

Goal-Setting → Performance Appraisal Conference ← Classroom Observations

Data-Collection → Performance Appraisal Conference ← Self-Appraisal

As indicated, the supervisory/evaluation conference provides a vital, one-on-one interpersonal link between the principal and each employee on a regularly scheduled basis. The essential elements for conducting a productive conference are as follows:

1. *Conference plan.* The performance appraisal conference is too good an opportunity to squander through inadequate or fuzzy planning. In advance, the principal should carefully define and design the objectives of the conference, the information to be shared, and the strategies that will be followed.

2. *Purpose.* The purpose of the conference will vary depending upon the experience and performance level of the employee involved. The focus should always be on action, not on personalities. Legitimate purposes include information sharing, two-way communication, feedback, counseling, reinforcement, reprimand, remediation, and/or goal setting.

3. *Content.* Some principals like to use a scattergun approach to the conference, while others prefer to focus on a narrow band of concerns and/or issues. Whatever the approach, the conference content should be well-planned and as specific as possible. The principal must determine what information should be shared and how much. It does little good to overwhelm the evaluatee with a flood of data and feedback that cannot possibly be analyzed or assimilated in a short conference period.

4. *Conference climate.* The atmosphere surrounding the conference should be businesslike, but as relaxed as possible. As school leader, the principal must exercise sensitivity and exhibit effective listening skills. The key is to treat each staff member with honesty and as an adult.

5. *Timing.* Conferences are usually most effective when scheduled in close proximity to a classroom observation. Proper advance notification is essential. Too many principals fall into the trap of procrastination and end up the school year trying to cram too many conferences into too little time. The basic guideline should be to hold conferences when both parties have adequate time to achieve the intended purpose.

6. *Location.* Effective conferences require a setting that is private, comfortable, and uninterrupted. Many principals have found it helpful to hold conferences in a neutral setting within the school or, occasionally, off the school premises (over coffee at a local cafe).

7. *Outcomes.* A successful conference requires closure. Every conference should result in a specific action/improvement plan. It is also advisable to follow up every conference with a written summary/record with copies to all parties involved.

In many instances, the performance appraisal conference is the punctuation point marking the end of the assessment cycle. In other situations, it marks the beginning of an ongoing process. This is the case where serious deficiencies have been identified and some further direct action is required.

HOW TO WRITE A LETTER OF DEFICIENCY OR REPRIMAND

All roads of supervision and evaluation may ultimately lead to an apparent dead end of deficiency. When supervisory skills and powers of persuasion fail and serious violations, infractions, inadequacies, or deficiencies persist, principals must consider employing some form of "progressive discipline." The degree of deficiency should determine the severity of the discipline. The usual progression of disciplinary or corrective measures follows this sequential pattern:

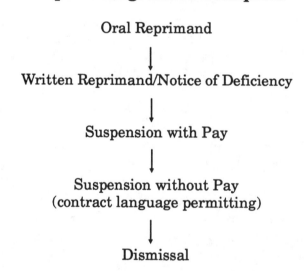

Steps in Progressive Discipline

Oral Reprimand

↓

Written Reprimand/Notice of Deficiency

↓

Suspension with Pay

↓

Suspension without Pay
(contract language permitting)

↓

Dismissal

Most administrators can handle delivering an oral reprimand, but too many shy away from taking the next step: putting it in writing. Letters (notices) of reprimand or deficiency are powerful tools. They should be used sparingly—but used, nevertheless, when necessary.

Sometimes such letters get results. They finally capture the attention of an unmotivated or misdirected employee and improvement occurs—things turn around. In other situations, these letters merely lay the critical foundation for more drastic or dramatic remedial action.

Letters of reprimand and deficiency can have far-reaching effects and may entail legal consequences. They must be carefully drafted, with legal counsel where possible. A model letter of reprimand is included in this section.

Following are exact specifications for formulating effective reprimand/deficiency documents that will stand the test of union challenge, arbitration, or possibly litigation:

(Use School District Letterhead)

SAMPLE

(Date)

(Name)
(Inside Address)

Dear Mr. _____ :

This letter constitutes a formal letter of reprimand based on your inappropriate behavior involving the physical touching of a 9th grade female student.

As a result of a parent and student complaint, I conferred with you on (date)___ concerning an incident in which you turned a female student over your knee and "softly spanked" her in front of the entire class. At that time, you were directed to refrain from such inappropriate touching of students. The female student involved subsequently withdrew from your class.

On __(date)__ , I received a second complaint from the same student indicating that you had "patted" her while passing her in the (hall, stairway—?). This incident was witnessed by at least one other student. On this date, I conferred with you a second time emphasizing the inappropriateness of such touching and instructed you to cease all such touching of students.

The intent of this letter is to direct you formally to refrain from any inappropriate touching, spanking, or patting of students from this time on.

It should be clear to you that this kind of behavior negatively impacts your reputation as a teacher and upon the reputation of the school district. Should any further incident of inappropriate touching of students occur, you will be subject to further disciplinary action.

Sincerely,

Principal

pc: Personnel File

This is to verify that I have received a copy of this letter.

_____   _____
Teacher's Signature   Date

Essential Features of the Written Reprimand

- Use a formal letter of reprimand in cases of severe or repeated infractions/deficiencies.
- Write the letter on school letterhead spelling out all relevant details (dates, times, locations, witnesses, etc.).
- Quote or cite any law, rule, or procedure that has been violated or established standard that has been unmet.
- Clearly state that the letter constitutes a formal written reprimand.
- Include an outline of what opportunities and resources for improvement will be available and what help the principal and/or other administrators will provide.
- Identify a specific and *reasonable* time-line for improvement (some problems, such as tardiness can be remedied immediately; others require sufficient time for planning, retraining, etc.).
- Emphasize that failure to correct unsatisfactory behavior or performance may result in further disciplinary action; but avoid specifying what the next disciplinary measure will be.
- Be sure that the employee receives a copy of the letter and a copy is placed in the employee's personnel file.

The rules for writing a letter of reprimand generally apply also to notices of deficiency, but these notices represent progressive discipline "cranked up a notch." The basic guidelines for writing formal notices of deficiency are outlined as follows:

Basics of Notices of Deficiency

- Use a formal notice of deficiency for only very serious infractions and deficiency. *It is the first step toward termination.*
- Cite any/all relevant statutes.
- Identify the document as a *formal* notice of deficiency.
- *Be specific.*
- Include *all* areas of deficiency.
- Spell out exactly what remedial action or correction is expected.
- Spell out an exact time-line for improvement.
- Spell out what the supervisor's role will be in the improvement process.
- Retain all notices of deficiency in the personnel file for at least five years.

As indicated earlier, a formal notice of deficiency positions the principal and the failing employee on the track toward termination. If positive results are not forthcoming, the principal must be prepared to take the next step.

HOW TO FIRE PERSONNEL WHO FAIL

After all reasonable management efforts have been exhausted and employee performance remains unsatisfactory, the principal must move boldly forward with the orderly dismissal of the individual from the school staff and, perhaps from the profession. Terminating a staff member is probably the most difficult and distasteful challenge of any school leader's career. The perceived power of unions and the tangle of teacher tenure laws throughout the country often makes termination seem to be unachievable. It can be done, however, with proper preparation and professional fortitude.

When confronted with the unpleasant prospect of firing an employee, many administrators will waver, waffle, and eventually "weasel out." If the situation warrants dismissal, the effective principal cannot cave in to this kind of leadership lapse. Sometimes the courage to tackle termination is found in answering these three simple questions:

1. Do I want this employee on my staff for the next five years?
2. Can I conscientiously continue to have this person influence the students under my responsibility?
3. Would I want this individual teaching *my* children?

When contemplating termination, the responsible administrator must be assured that there is "just cause." The possible causes for termination are varied and are often spelled out (although rarely defined) in state law. The most common causes for teacher dismissal cited in statutes from states across the country include

Incompetence

Immorality

Negligence of duty

Criminal activity

Noncompliance with legal requirements

Conduct unbecoming a teacher

When sufficient cause exists, the principal must proceed with dismissal action despite the legal, contractual, and practical barriers that must be overcome. A prime consideration in any termination process must be strict adherence to "due process," which is simply defined as fair play and the protection of the individual's rights. Following is a six-step test for assuring proper due process procedures:

1. Expectations and standards must be reasonable and must be clearly communicated to all staff members.
2. The individual involved must be given notice of the existing problem(s)

and of the possibility/probability of disciplinary consequences (including dismissal) if remediation does not occur.

3. Dismissal action must be preceded by a complete and objective fact-finding investigation.

4. Documentation must be thorough.

5. Disciplinary action (in this case, dismissal) must be reasonable. The consequence must be consistent with the seriousness of the offense.

6. Treatment for any offense must be consistent with that shown to others in similar situations.

In addition to satisfying these due process concerns, the principal should faithfully follow the accompanying directives that have been drawn from successful termination proceedings in a number of states and a variety of situations.

Termination Tips

- Obtain and follow legal advice.
- Effect immediate termination if the conduct is not remedial.
- Document everything (observation notes, conference summaries, appointment calendars, etc.).
- Use multievaluators and lean toward overvisitation and observation despite the risk of generating charges of harassment.
- Avoid using suspension with pay if termination is imminent.
- Remember that arbitrators and judges like to see a track record of progressive discipline.
- Provide the teacher (or other employee) with proper notice of pending termination action.
- Inform the employee involved of his or her right to a hearing where appropriate.
- Offer (but never demand) the opportunity to resign.

These measures can guide the principal through the agonizing termination process. Once it is completed, the school staff will be strengthened, the principal's professional integrity and credibility will be reinforced, and a clear message will be sent to all staff members that performance is the test of continued employment.

This chapter has covered from A to Z the rudiments for successful management of the total school staff. This is a key element in providing leadership for today's seconday schools. Of equal importance to the survival and success of the secondary school principal is the management of today's volatile audience of adolescent learners. The next chapter shows how to deal with the changed and changing teenage student.

Chapter 4

Managing Today's Adolescent Learner

There is a reason for schools. It's called students. Everything the principal and the staff do should somehow be connected with making things better for kids and helping students become what they need to be and even more. Just as successful businesses are increasingly customer conscious and service oriented, the best schools understand that they must be student centered.

Effective schools listen well, involve people in meaningful ways, care about learners as individuals and as a total community, and respond quickly and constructively when problems arise. Where such schools exist, the principal, more than anyone else, makes them that way.

Managing the student body of a modern secondary school is different and difficult. (See the discussion "Today's Changed and Changing Learner" in Chapter 1.) Today's students are more assertive, more worldly, more questioning, and more at risk than previous generations of learners. They are also more vulnerable and more in need of coping and problem-solving skills than ever before. Building a school that meets the needs of today's diverse student body is challenging—but it is also manageable, rewarding, and what the school is supposed to be all about.

This chapter shows how you can manage today's students in ways that:

- Impose order and organization on the chaos of adolescence
- Remove barriers to learner growth
- Establish a safe, sane, and healthy environment for students to learn what they need to know
- Maximize opportunities for students to be the best they can be (to release the hidden hero in every adolescent learner)

THE PRINCIPAL'S CREED: ALL STUDENTS CAN LEARN

Effective management of modern junior and senior high school students starts with an attitude of optimism, hope, and confidence in today's learners. This view of what is possible is most simply stated as, "All students can learn!" This is an attitude that starts with the school's leader and must permeate the entire organization.

Based on a growing body of research, this belief is expressed in a variety of ways:

- All students can learn and learning should be lifelong.
- The school expects all students to learn.
- Every learner can be successful—the only variable is time.
- The school has an obligation to teach every learner.

The optimistic concept that all students can learn challenges time-honored beliefs about the capacity of teachers to teach and shatters the previous presumed pattern of failure for many students. Too often, teachers have been led to believe that they can teach only so much, that some students are unsalvageable, and that much of what is taught in the school can be learned by only a limited proportion of the student body. This belief system has tended to make schools a proving ground for failure and make teaching a self-defeating profession. When teachers are convinced that they and many of their students can't succeed, it's no wonder that academic atrophy, discipline problems, and low morale flourish. It's hard to manage large numbers of predetermined losers.

The current attitude about students, however, is like a fresh breeze blowing new life into the organization. It changes the mind-set and the entire environment of the school. It creates a new set of possibilities. If you believe that you can teach every single student and that they, in turn, can learn and be successful, teaching becomes fun again.

The first step in managing today's adolescent learners is for the principal to champion the cause that every learner's success is the central focus of the school and its resources. If you believe that all students can learn and the staff believes it and the students believe it, managing a few hundred or thousand secondary pupils becomes a whole lot easier.

Believing that all students can learn implies a willingness to take on all comers—to accept and accommodate whatever mix of ethnic, economic, and cultural diversity the student population presents.

VIEWING THE STUDENT BODY AS A HUMAN MOSAIC

In many secondary schools, the diversity of culture making up the student body has increased dramatically in recent years. For some schools, this poses a problem of prejudice and racial tensions. It also offers an opportunity for differing groups to learn from each other and to expand multicultural awareness and understanding for all. The latter is one of the overriding values of *public* secondary education.

The demographics of American secondary schools have changed and will change even more. Many schools have experienced a large increase in the number and variety of minorities represented in the student body—often including a significant influx of immigrant students who do not speak the English language. Managing today's secondary student population means dealing with diversity in ways that avoid clashes between cultures and that build an equitable and inclusive school culture.

In handling a diverse student population, the worst things that school leaders can do is to ignore the existence of cultural differences or to try to impose the values, standards, norms, and expectations of one culture on others. The most reasoned approach is to strive to build bridges between cultures and to share the strengths of all cultural groups within the school. This helps make the school part of the real world.

The goal of the school should be to provide an educational environment that exposes students, staff, and the community to an inclusive program respecting all races, ethnic backgrounds, and cultural heritages. Previous integration efforts and civil rights movements have helped to make schools officially blind to differences. The next phase is to view the school as a human mosaic of many colors and to find ways to achieve common goals through diversity.

The first step in managing diverse student populations is for the principal and staff to have a clear picture of what's really going on in the school and to acknowledge their own blind spots, prejudices, and preconceptions. Beyond self knowledge, the strategies and opportunities for building a cohesive, multicultural school are as rich and varied as the number of diverse groups that make up the school community. Some of the best means of achieving an equitable/inclusive school culture are:

- Implement a multicultural curriculum integrated across all subject areas. Emphasize global awareness and avoid a quick-fix, tourist/tokenism curriculum. This means going beyond teaching about scenic attractions, colorful festivals, and national costumes and focusing on important cultural differences, practices, and priorities.

- Work with the student council to develop and adapt a schoolwide mission statement and related goals dealing with cross-cultural understanding (see the mission statement provided).

**Mission and Goal Statements
on Diversity**

Mission: _____School staff and students are committed continually to develop and maintain an atmosphere of respect for all individuals regardless of race, social class, sex, age, religion, or physical/psychological conditions.

Goals: To understand and respect the human diversity in our school and our community.

To promote individual participation in all facets of our school community.

To confront prejudice in our schools.

- Adopt a policy banning all forms of bias and prejudice, including biased instructional materials (print and media).

- Review all school policies and procedures to assure fairness and lack of discriminating practices.

- Review school testing programs to assure that assessment instruments reflect inclusive language.

- Heighten awareness toward any use of racial slurs by students or staff.

- Consider diverse cultures when planning school events.

- Be sensitive to the use of school mascots, emblems, and so on that may be offensive to minority groups. (Some schools have abandoned nicknames, such as "warriors" and "redskins," that have been determined degrading to Native Americans.)

- Stress special events that cut across all cultures such as Earth Week, United Nations Day, and so on.

- Provide appropriate staff development programs on the nature of prejudice and how to combat it.

- Recruit minority staff members and volunteers.

- Encourage contacts and interaction with students in other nations (cultural exchanges, "sister" schools, videotape exchanges, direct satellite communications, etc.).

- Celebrate cultural diversity through multicultural expos, around-the-world programs, and so on, keeping in mind that genuine understanding must go beyond food fairs and festivals.

- Hold leadership conferences for minority students.

- Pay special attention to the unique problem of new students from other cultures (loss, anger, fear, identity crises, confusion, guilt, etc.).

- Stress "cooperative learning" approaches throughout the curriculum.
- Make extra outreach efforts to parents from other cultures. Provide interpreters when necessary.
- Ensure that counselors and other school personnel respect student requests regarding what they want to be called.
- Initiate a human mosaic project within the school as depicted in the accompanying graphic.

Wheel of Activities Celebrating Diversity to Create Community in St. Louis Park High School

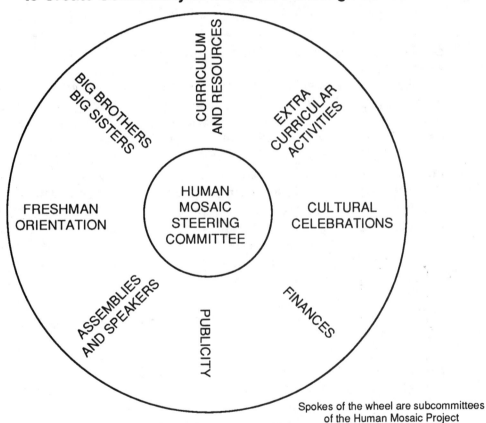

Spokes of the wheel are subcommittees
of the Human Mosaic Project

The Human Mosaic Project is part of the school's community building efforts to enhance and encourage an environment which promotes the celebration of diversity. Its goals are to expand equality, enjoyment and enrichment of diverse students and staff in the learning and living community of St. Louis Park High School and eventually the entire community of St. Louis Park.

- Use panels of ESL (English-as-a-second-language) students to help staff members understand the problems of students caught between cultures.

- Showcase role models representing all cultures.
- Work with minority leaders throughout the community to promote understanding and solve problems.
- Include articles on diversity in school publications.

The future of our society depends on cross-cultural cooperation. It should start in the school. If school leaders can handle diversity by turning differences into assets, they've gone a long way toward successful management of today's adolescent learners.

HOW TO HAVE A DRUG- AND ALCOHOL-FREE SCHOOL

Drugs and serious education don't mix. Some observers view chemical dependency as a deadly dry-rot eating away at the underpinnings of our society. This has to be a paramount concern for everyone who works with and for young people. Fortunately, there are some hopeful signs that certain kinds of alcohol and other drug use among secondary students may be plateauing or even declining. Nevertheless, there is no question that drug use and abuse lie at the heart of many current behavior problems in and out of school. No principal can successfully manage today's student populations without meeting school drug problems head on.

Educators are deluged with prepackaged drug education, prevention, and intervention programs. Some work, some don't. The most successful build on knowledge, communication, positive peer pressure, and healthy role models. Smart principals select the best and realize that no piecemeal program is enough. Following is a commonsense ten-point program to managing students and drugs that can work in any school.

A TEN-POINT APPROACH TO ALCOHOL AND OTHER DRUG PROBLEMS IN THE SCHOOL

Point One: *FACE REALITY—KNOW WHAT'S GOING ON*
Schools can be enablers if they ignore or downplay the impact of student drug use. It's imperative that principals and staffs remain in touch with what is happening with students and drugs. Many schools have benefitted from conducting anonymous student surveys of existing drug use and experimentation. Students are often surprisingly candid in responding to such needs assessments. Often, adult perceptions of student life and the real world of what's happening in the lives of students are miles apart.

All school personnel should learn to be effective observers of students and should know what to look for (see "Signals for Concern," which follows). Staff antennas should be especially attuned to marked changes in behavior and performance on the part of individuals or groups of students.

Signals for Concern

Apathy	Frequent vomiting
Absenteeism	Chronic fatigue
Tardiness	Vandalism
Noninvolvement	Cheating
Grade plunges	Irresponsibility
Sudden outbursts	Negativism
Diminished sense of time	Erratic behavior
Dropping old friends	Withdrawal
Overuse of eye drops	Slurred speech
Hyperactivity	Paranoia over privacy
Excessive thirst	

Since most of what goes on with students and drugs is illegal, patterns of use, drugs of choice, the language of drugs (see "Drug Culture Terms"), and strategies for concealment are constantly changing. It is important that the adults in the school keep current as the drug culture evolves through various transformations.

Common Drug Culture Terms*

Bag	Packet of drugs
Cap	Capsule containing drugs
Chipping	Irregular drug use
Cooker	Cup, spoon, and so on, for dissolving drugs
Cut	Adulterating drugs
Flea Powder	Poor quality drugs
Fruit Salad	Mixture of drugs
Hot Shot	Fatal dose of heroin
J	Marijuana cigarette
Mule	Drug courier
Roll Over	Turning Evidence
Spike	Hyperdermic needle
Step On	Dilute drugs
Toke	Drag on a marijuana cigarette
Yard	$100
Zig-Zag	Cigarette rolling papers

*The language of drugs changes frequently as new terms are coined and old terms disappear or change meaning.

Point Two: TAKE A STAND

School officials should send a clear and consistent message declaring the school off limits for drugs. Every school should have a hard-hitting, no-nonsense policy prohibiting any form of drug or alcohol possession or use. Consequences should be certain and enforcement consistent. The purpose of a firm schoolwide policy banning drugs is twofold:

1. To provide clear and immediate consequences
2. To offer aid and counseling for students who need help, are ready, and/or reach out for it

Point Three: ORGANIZE THE STAFF FOR ACTION

Every secondary school must have someone on staff specially trained to deal with drug problems and with students and families victimized by drugs. This may mean providing staff development programs for counselors, social workers, the school nurse, health instructors, or other specialized school personnel. In the best situations, however, the school will have a full-time certified chemical health professional or substance abuse prevention coordinator on staff.

A cadre of trained personnel should be designated as the school's chemical assessment team. The team should be responsible for developing prevention programs, crisis intervention plans, student assistance programs, and follow-up support services. All staff should know "the plan" and how to activate it.

Point Four: TEACH HEALTH AND PREVENTION

Drug education programs at the secondary level may be too little, too late, but the school cannot afford to stop trying. The principal should take the lead in establishing a sound, sequential instructional program dealing with healthy, life-style concepts, coping skills, and self-esteem building, including attention to the "gateway drugs" (tobacco and alcohol). It makes little difference if the curriculum is commercially developed or locally designed as long as the goals are clear and the facts are straight.

In addition to offering the best possible program in their own school, secondary leaders should be champions of early education programs at the elementary level.

Point Five: SHOWCASE SPECIAL PROJECTS

The school has a responsibility to keep the message of drugs and drug dangers before students, staff, and the community-at-large. Special projects and events can be an effective medium for this message. In many schools, student organizations such as SADD (Students Against Drunk Driving) serve as the catalyst and focal point for these activities. Some of the most popular special anti-drug projects include:

Red ribbon campaign (for car antennas)

Drug awareness weeks

Peer counseling projects

Drug-free clubs

Student-parent contracts

No-drug-use pledge campaign

Postprom free rides for intoxicated students

Vigils for victims of drunk drivers

"Say No" buttons, banners, bumper stickers, and so on

Point Six: *PROVIDE A SAFETY NET OF SUPPORT*

Schools must be "second chance" institutions for students with drug problems who are trying to reclaim their lives. When students get into serious trouble with drugs, it is the school's responsibility to facilitate treatment and recovery and stand ready to accept and support them on their way back. Every junior and senior high school should have a reentry program for students coming out of treatment, including a system of support groups (e.g., small peer groups focusing on individual experiences and feelings).

In some cases, school officials should assist students to get a "fresh start" by changing schools. The increasing popularity of choice and open enrollment make starting over a viable option for any student at risk. Where appropriate, the schools should link up with other community organizations and agencies to provide necessary support for recovering students.

Good schools don't write off any student. Helping young people kick addictions and rebuild lives is one way to prove it.

Point Seven: *NURTURE THE PARENT CONNECTION*

Of all the areas that require close-knit parent-school cooperation, dealing with student drug problems takes a top spot. Where drug use is pervasive, the school and the home both need help and need each other. Educational leaders should elicit total parental support in preventing and combatting drugs in the school. Alert schools are proactive in providing needed drug-related parenting education programs.

Many schools have also had success in developing a parent communication network (PCN) whereby families sign pledges to supervise their teenagers and to provide drug-free activities for their children and others. A directory of PCN members can be a valuable resource for both parents and school personnel when specific help and support are needed.

Point Eight: *DEAL WITH STAFF DRUG PROBLEMS*

Dependency on alcohol and other drugs is not a teenage disease. It cuts across all age groups. It starts with "crack babies" and extends to an increasing number of senior citizens. School personnel are not immune. In a comprehensive drug-control program, the principal must be prepared to deal with drug use and abuse by staff members, as well as by students (see the discussion in Chapter 3, "How to Handle and Help Employees with Drug and Alcohol Problems"). There is no room for a double standard when it comes to drugs.

Point Nine: *KEEP AT IT*

An effective school campaign against drugs cannot be episodic. It cannot succeed by fits and starts. It must be relentless and on-going. Drug dealers and users show up every day, and so must the forces out to stop them. More than anyone else, the principal must keep antidrug efforts on the school calendar every day of the year. Weekly messages in the school bulletin, frequent public address announcements, and regular features in the school newspaper are common means of maintaining and continuing focus on drug problems and solutions.

Point Ten: PROVIDE OUTLETS AND ALTERNATIVES

Like adults, students take drugs because substance use serves some personal purpose or satisfies a need. Part of the school's role is to open up options and alternatives to drug use and to help students with problems of depression and dysfunctional family situations. An exciting and varied student activity program can assist in establishing the school as a "drug-free zone" and help in the successful overall management of today's adolescent learners.

HOW TO ESTABLISH A TOBACCO-FREE ENVIRONMENT IN THE SCHOOL

Positive peer pressure can be one of administration's most effective tools in managing the student population. In a growing number of schools, the force of peer power has been successfully channeled to help snuff out tobacco use—making the school a cleaner, healthier, better place for everyone.

One means of harnessing peer pressure to alter behavior is to conduct a comprehensive opinion survey and use the results as leverage for change as illustrated by the questionnaire that follows.

Where survey results show a preponderance of opinion favoring a tobacco free environment, school officials are perfectly positioned to establish an across-the-board ban on all tobacco use.

The next step is to adopt a full-blown policy declaring the total school tobacco free (see the accompanying policy).

Student Tobacco Policy Survey

1. Indicate how often you are bothered by smokers at school:
   ___ a. Frequently
   ___ b. Occasionally
   ___ c. Seldom
   ___ d. Never

2. Indicate how often you are bothered by someone using smokeless tobacco (chewing/dipping) at school:
   ___ a. Frequently
   ___ b. Occasionally
   ___ c. Seldom
   ___ d. Never

3. If you are bothered by tobacco use in school, in what ways are you bothered (check all that apply)?
   ___ a. Clothes and hair smell
   ___ b. Eye irritation
   ___ c. Coughing
   ___ d. Headaches
   ___ e. Allergies
   ___ f. Concern about future health
   ___ g. Interference with work/study
   ___ h. School building smells
   ___ i. Tobacco juice on floors, in fountains, and so on
   ___ j. Butts at entrance ways
   ___ k. Others _____

4. Do you think the school system should offer programs for students who want to quit tobacco use?
   ____ Yes   ____ No

5. What is your opinion of a total ban on tobacco use in the school and on school grounds for students, staff, and community members?
   ___ a. Strongly agree
   ___ b. Agree
   ___ c. Don't care
   ___ d. Disagree
   ___ e. Strongly disagree

6. Would students be more likely to follow a tobacco policy if it was the same policy for adults who use the school?
   ___ Yes   ____ No
   ___ Maybe
   ___ Don't know

Tobacco-Free Policy

Background

_____ High School is dedicated to providing a healthy and productive environment. The school is concerned about the health of employees and students and recognizes the importance of adult role models for students. Therefore, the school promotes nonuse of tobacco among students and adults and commits itself to:

- Total elimination of tobacco use on school property and at school activities
- Educational programs to help students resist tobacco use and cessation programs and support services for both employees and students

Policy

Smoking and the use of tobacco products shall be prohibited on all school property, in school vehicles, and at school-sponsored events.

Enforcement

The success of the policy will depend upon the thoughtfulness, consideration, and cooperation of smokers and nonsmokers. All persons on school premises share responsibility for adhering to and enforcing this policy.

Violation

Employees and students violating this policy shall be subject to progressive discipline in accordance with applicable contract provisions, state law, and district discipline policies.

Once the schoolwide policy is in place, the following measures can help assure smooth implementation with a minimum of controversy:

1. There should be considerable lead time before the policy becomes effective. Some schools have allowed up to a full year for students and staff to assimilate and adjust to the policy and plan for implementation.

2. The policy should be widely disseminated and publicized community-wide.

3. A vigorous ad campaign (monthly posters, skits, displays, etc.) should be conducted to explain and support a tobacco-free environment and to alert all parties to the pending policy.

4. As the effective date draws near, highly noticeable signs declaring the school tobacco free should be posted in prominent locations in and around the school (see the sample provided by the American Lung Association).

5. Plans should be made to offer assistance to all students and staff members who want to quit using tobacco, including cessation clinics and classes and support groups.

When the pendulum of student opinion swings in the direction the school wants to go, the staff should move quickly to seize the opportunity

for change. The same principle can apply to solving problems of school absenteeism.

BUILDING A STRONG STUDENT ACTIVITY PROGRAM

Managing an active teenage student body is easier when every student can find a positive "niche" in the school—a situation in which they can succeed, grow, and be recognized. Many find their "comfort zone" within the student activity program.

Cocurricular/extracurricular activities constitute what some educators call the "second half of the curriculum" and are an essential part of the texture of the school. The extent of student involvement in activities is often a measure of school climate. Many problems can be averted by energizing the activity program and broadening participation.

Good student activity programs do not happen by accident. They grow out of staff creativity, commitment, and sensitivity to student and community needs. As chief architect of the school's activity program, you should keep certain essential design features in mind:

Features of an Effective Student Activity Program

- Is inclusive
- Has flexibility
- Is congruent with overall school philosophy
- Develops skills/talents
- Stresses learning
- Teaches goal-setting
- Enhances self image
- Reinforces ethical behavior
- Provides carry-over activities
- Develops leadership
- Is student centered (not adult driven)
- Does not exploit students
- Teaches life skills
- Develops interpersonal skills
- Promotes health
- Promotes a safe environment
- Builds pride
- Promotes positive attitudes
- Is handicapped accessible

To succeed in reaching the greatest number of students, the activity program must strike a balance:

- Between athletic, artistic, career related and service organizations
- Between small group and large group activities
- Between competitive and cooperative activities
- Between activities for males and females

Such balance can occur only if students join in. To boost participation, many schools have found the following measures helpful.

- Provide transportation (activity bus)
- Increase team size
- Vary schedules (not all activities have to occur between 3 and 6 P.M.)
- Hold parent meetings to promote participation
- Make it easy for students to start participating and worthwhile for them to continue
- Try nontraditional activities to reach students not normally involved (a "Battle of the Bands, bicycle derby, skateboard competitions, etc.)

A modern-day impediment to school activity programs is the increasing number of students holding outside jobs and working long hours each week. Most students work at a "part-time" job sometime during their secondary school career. Some jobs offer many of the same opportunities for growth and self-actualization as the student activity program. Many, however, offer little but minimum wages and hard work. In some districts where the part-time job work load has begun to make both the school and the students "losers," schools have issued suggestions for working teens and their parents.

Guidelines for Working Teens

1. Limit part-time jobs to 15 to 20 hours per week.
2. Balance work with study, entertainment, and rest.
3. Don't let the job interfere with school attendance.
4. Set aside time for homework.
5. Maintain involvement in some school activity.

Just as the curriculum requires regular review and revision, the activity program needs periodic assessment to keep it current, relevant and in tune with changing student interests. Every activity should be evaluated on a systematic basis (see the "Student Activity Evaluation Survey.")

Student Activity Evaluation Survey

	Agree	Disagree	Don't Care (n/a)
1. The activity was well organized.			
2. Facilities/equipment were adequate.			
3. I learned something worthwhile and valuable.			
4. The activity was fun.			
5. Adult leaders understood student needs.			
6. Everyone was treated fairly.			
7. The group worked well together.			

8. I particularly liked:

9. I suggest improving:

*To be completed following each activity or sports season.

Guided by feedback from students, coaches, advisors, and parents, the school's activity program should be dynamic and responsive. One of the key roles of the principal should be to assure that new programs and activities can be initiated easily and quickly.

Your greatest responsibility to the activity program, however, is to provide qualified and energetic adult leaders. Whenever possible, coaches and advisors should come from the ranks of the regular teaching staff. When student activities function best, there is an expectation that every staff member will provide leadership for one or more extra-curricular activities.

A well-rounded student activity program takes times and effort on the part of the entire staff. The pay-off is better behavior and better feelings in the school.

In addition to sports and other extracurricular activities, the next section includes other ways to provide leadership opportunities and help students experience success.

PROVIDING OPPORTUNITIES FOR STUDENT SUCCESS AND LEADERSHIP

It is hard to cause trouble or show disrespect for an organization that finds out what you're good at, appreciates your contributions, respects your individuality, and gives you chances to succeed and lead. This is one of the secrets of successfully managing a school full of active adolescents. Everyone (young and old) deserves some glory in their daily lives. Schools work better when students know they count and are counted upon.

It is not easy to catch every student being successful or to let certain students lead anything, but there are ways to do it. The following ideas have worked and are working in many secondary schools.

- Use students as consultants to administration. Include a cross section of student representatives on panels, committees, site councils, and so on. Form a "principal's cafeteria cabinet" of inside student advisors.

- Provide special leadership training sessions for *all* kinds of students.

- Put different students in charge of important school events and activities.

- Rotate leadership positions frequently.

- Expand the size of student leadership groups.

- Publish lists of student achievers (nominated by any staff member for any legitimate accomplishment).

- Facilitate teens helping teens. Form peer counseling groups.

- Make students spokespersons for the school (e.g., ambassadors to civic clubs).

- Appoint students as liaisons to each subject area department.

- Recognize students of the month, athletes of the week, artists of the month, and so on.

- Showcase all kinds of student work via exhibits, public displays, art shows, literary publications, and so on.

- Use students as tutors for peers and younger pupils.

- Let students serve as teacher aides for pay or credit where appropriate.

- Recognize students for service to others and community work.

- Have students help make and enforce the rules (e.g., student discipline boards).

- Expect teachers to write encouraging notes to students throughout the year (not just at report card time).

- Honor minor sports competitors along with major sports athletes at pep fests, assemblies, and so on.

- Stage a number of one-act plays rather than one or two major productions a year.

- Hold academic awards and fitness awards nights.

- Award school letters for music, drama, speech activities, and so on.

- Assign and train students as tour guides for visitors.

- Sponsor talent shows for students who have not appeared in regular performances.

- Form student welcome committees to assist newcomers.
- Let a variety of students become "media personalities" over school operated radio and/or TV stations.
- Link students with adult mentors for career exploration.
- Spotlight student achievers at public school board meetings.

It is up to each principal to find the most practical ways for his or her school to provide opportunities for student success and leadership. The goal is to help all students experience a cycle of success:

Cycle of Success

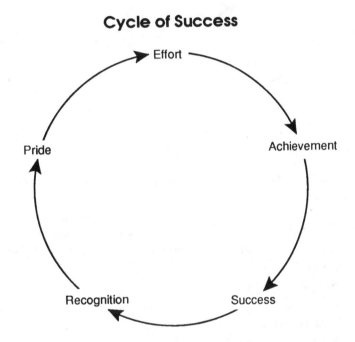

Guaranteeing respect and recognition for every student takes a lot of the mystery out of managing today's secondary school population.

NEW WAYS TO HANDLE THE OLD PROBLEMS OF ATTENDANCE AND TRUANCY

The first rule of success for students, as well as adults, is to "show up." Attendance has to be one of the principal's top priorities in managing the school's student population. Students can't learn in absentia, and teachers can't teach empty seats. The school simply won't work if marred by lack of regular attendance.

An initial sign that a school is struggling is often a high rate of absenteeism and truancy. Some schools suffer from an overall low attendance rate. Others are victims of a form of hidden truancy when students disappear for a few periods each day. Any significant incidence of absentee-ism is a symptom of problems at hand and trouble yet to come. Attendance problems frequently precipitate a downward spiral of both performance and behavior:

Downward Spiral of Deteriorating Attendance

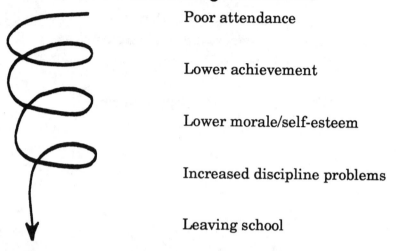

Poor attendance

Lower achievement

Lower morale/self-esteem

Increased discipline problems

Leaving school

As leader of the school, the principal must understand and convince others that good attendance is rooted in good instruction. Where teaching is relevant and students experience success, regular attendance becomes fashionable, and peer pressure works against absenteeism. The best solu-tion for chronic attendance problems is the power of attraction generated by a vital curriculum and dynamic teaching.

In addition to sound instruction, the school needs a hard-hitting truancy policy (see the policy statement provided) and an attainable master plan for maintaining daily attendance.

The best attendance plans keep the process simple and streamlined. Attendance procedures shouldn't be so complicated that they become all consuming and actually detract from instruction. The trick is to organize the staff for effective attendance monitoring. Principals don't have to take atten-dance, but they are responsible for seeing that the job gets done. It is essential that the school *follow up on every absence.* With proper training, however, aides and clerical personnel can handle the entire tracking, recordkeeping, and reporting process. Where necessary, volunteers can also help implement attendance procedures (e.g., calling homes during evening hours to reach parents after working hours). To keep attendance procedures working smoothly and efficiently, some schools form an attendance council made up of the principal, assistant principal, nurse, counselors, and teacher representa-tives to study attendance patterns and make necessary adjustments.

The most critical element of a successful attendance plan is the swift, certain, and consistent application of consequences for all violations. The most common consequences include:

Student Attendance Policy

School policy requires attendance everyday that school is in session. Illness, family activities, court appearances, religious holidays, and school-sponsored projects are the only excusable reasons for nonattendance. The determination of an excusable absence is made by the principal or his or her designee.

Procedure:

1. When an absence occurs for a nonschool-related reason, the parent/guardian involved should phone the school and clearly state the reason and probably length of the absence.

2. If the parent/guardian does not phone, the student must report to the principal's office upon returning to school with an explanation for the absence signed by the student's parent/guardian. The absence will be considered unexcused until the foregoing information has been presented from the parent/guardian. *Students and parents have two weeks to correct an unexcused absence situation.*

3. *Every student must check the attendance sheets posted throughout the building each morning.*
   - If student was incorrectly marked absent, student must get a verification form from the office and have it signed by the teacher involved.
   - If student was excused, student must get the absence cleared with the office.
   - If student was unexcused, student must report to the office.

   This procedure must be followed the day of or the day after the absence. After this time period, the absence will be considered unexcused and detention will be assigned.

4. Students who become ill during the day must be excused through the health office or principal's office so that parents/guardians can be notified.

Verified unexcused absences will result in detention, parent notification and possible loss of credit.

- Individual conferences
- Parent notification
- Detention
- Mandatory makeup
- Saturday makeup classes
- "Quiet lunch" periods
- In-house suspension
- Suspension from school
- Withdrawal from class/loss of credit

In addition to penalties, a well-engineered attendance plan should contain a variety of proactive measures such as:

- Stressing the importance of student attendance records to college admissions officials and future employers
- Publishing attendance figures by class and teachers
- Providing incentives for perfect attendance (prizes, exemption from final exams, etc.)

The ultimate purpose of all these attendance strategies is simply to make it easy for students to come to and remain in school and both difficult and uncomfortable for students to skip or leave school without legitimate cause.

Well-defined attendance regulations serve as the cornerstone for the school's overall structure of discipline policies and rules as described in the next section.

STEPS TO ESTABLISHING EFFECTIVE DISCIPLINE POLICIES AND PROCEDURES

Discipline is where the school makes it or doesn't as an effective place for young people to learn and grow. Teaching and learning can occur only in an orderly environment. The purpose of the school's discipline program should be to provide direction, set limits (structure), and promote self-discipline. The trick is to create an educational setting that is neither overly permissive nor overly oppressive. The desired state for any secondary school is orderliness and organization without bureaucratic booby traps or a "police state" mentality. Once the principal and staff have a clear sense of what reasonable discipline is and is not, how to achieve it becomes much easier.

Discipline is a full-time job for some principals. Where this happens, both the principal and the school are in deep trouble. The school leader is important to the conduct code of the school, but he or she is only one resource for defining and achieving behavioral expectations and standards.

Good discipline begins and ends in the classroom. Teachers can't hide from their responsibility for helping make the entire school happy enough, safe enough, and sane enough for real learning to occur. The discipline tone of the school is the creation of the total staff (not just one or two administrators). It is a product of the overall culture (attitudinal atmosphere) of the organization (see Chapter 2) and is driven by whatever self-fulfilling prophecy the staff chooses to believe and act on. The only way to change behavior is through feelings and teachers have the greatest impact on the way students feel in and about the school. Positive discipline must be an agenda item for everyone.

Good discipline doesn't develop from the helter-skelter stamping out of brush fires. It is more than rules and regulations. The school with the healthiest culture, not the heaviest rule book, enjoys the best discipline. The answer to managing today's secondary school students is a holistic approach that addresses curriculum, instruction, student activities, and overall school climate. Rules and regulations are only one piece of this approach.

A well-defined discipline code shows what is important to the school and serves as everyone's guide to getting things done without chaos or confusion. A good discipline code should be:

- *Clear*—no legal language allowed
- *Honest*—no phony rules that no one intends to enforce
- *Fair*—no favoritism
- *Simple*—see sample school rules provided
- *Flexible*—some groups, for example, students from other cultures and special education students—may require unique accommodations
- *Based on legitimate student needs*
- *Consistent*—same rules apply to all
- *Reasonable*—no rule without a good reason
- *Responsive to due process for all*

School Rules

An effective student discipline code can be as simple as this:

1. Show up.
2. Obey all laws.
3. Respect others.

Good discipline doesn't happen overnight. It develops over time and is tended to on a regular basis. The following steps show how it works:

Steps in Establishing Good Discipline

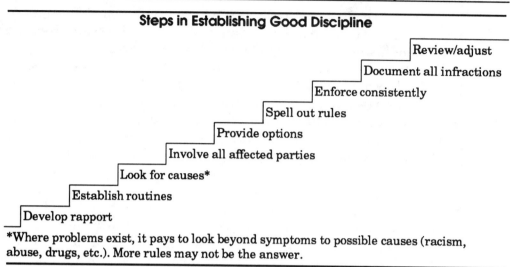

*Where problems exist, it pays to look beyond symptoms to possible causes (racism, abuse, drugs, etc.). More rules may not be the answer.

Although there is no perfect formula, following these steps provides the greatest assurance of achieving desired discipline goals.

To avoid or resolve discipline problems, school officials must also look at such alternatives merely to adding rules such as:

- IEPs (individual educations plans)
- Student contracts
- Early identification/intervention
- Group counseling
- Active learning
- Support groups
- Time-on-task strategies
- Behavior modification techniques

In many schools, the following measures have also helped in establishing productive and harmonious discipline standards:

- Be visible and show a genuine interest in students.
- Avoid scapegoating.
- Provide ways for students to responsibly challenge the system (grievance procedures, school cabinet, etc.).
- Insist on a goverance system that accentuates accessibility.
- Hold town meetings on discipline.
- Organize the staff so that no one person has to serve as the full-time "hatchet man" for the school.
- Help teachers to understand that they don't have to be angry at students and to learn that there are at least two views of every discipline incident.

- Guarantee that someone on staff knows every kid (certain daily contact with every student).

Some schools create their own losers and generate their own discipline problems. By following the principles and practices just outlined, schools can make better choices for establishing effective discipline. It is the principal, however, who is ultimately the "responsible chooser."

The final concern for school staffers is to keep control once they have it. In managing large numbers of teenage learners, the staff can never afford to relax completely. When it comes to discipline, staff members have to "earn their wings every day."

The next section applies the basic principles just outlined to an emerging menace within the school—the threat of gang rivalry and violence.

WHAT TO DO ABOUT GANGS

Street gangs are not new, but gang activity has taken on a menancingly new face of violence. Likewise, gangs are not everywhere, but their presence is increasingly being felt in communities of all sizes throughout the nation. The upsurge of street gangs has to be a cause of reasoned alarm for all school personnel. What happens on the streets spills over into the school. Even where gang activity is excluded from the school grounds, its presence inevitably damages the school by generating fear and insecurity. Every secondary principal today owes it to both students and the community to understand gang culture, gang appeal, and what to do about gangs.

Most modern youth gangs are drug driven and crime oriented. The proliferation of today's street gangs roughly parallels the evolution of adult gang organizations during America's prohibition period.

At worst, gangs can place schools under siege and turn entire communities into war zones. To manage the school and its students effectively, principals must have a strategy to deal with gang activity and gang influence. This strategy starts with a real-world knowledge of what today's gangs are all about.

Gangs are usually loosely structured with no two exactly alike. Nevertheless, certain features characterize the commonality of culture shared by most contemporary youth gangs. The typical street gang today looks something like this:

- The bulk of gang membership is made up of 14 to 24-year-olds, although some members are recruited as young as third grade and a growing number of gang leaders are well into their adult years (some mature leaders are rumored to continue heading up gang activity while in prison).
- Most gangs adopt distinctive, and often ominous names (Vice Lords, The Bloods, etc.).

- Each gang stakes out a specified territory and members often view themselves as "soldiers of the neighborhood." Turf battles are frequent and violent.

- The gang has an intense sense of loyalty and allegiance. Members often take an oath for life like, "I will not—and could not—withdraw from this nation [gang] and will be a part of it even in death. Death is the only means in which I can be considered inactive."

- Gangs value violence. Beatings and murders are common. Weapons are sophisticated and high tech. Walk-by and drive-by shootings are a way of life. Most gang violence is not random, but consciously targeted toward rival groups. Remorse is rare.

- Gang aims are antisocial. Profits from drug trafficking and other illegal activities are the lifeblood of most gangs. Frequently, members have criminal specialties (auto theft, shoplifting, con games, murder, etc.).

- Gangs practice a code of silence. Members are usually referred to only by first initials or nicknames. They are also bound not to provide information about other members nor to cooperate with police investigations. The police are often viewed as just another rival gang.

- Gang membership is usually drawn along ethnic or racial lines— blacks, Hispanics, Jamaicans, whites (skin heads), and so on.

- Gang leaders are most often the oldest, strongest, or gutsiest members. It is not uncommon for these leaders to gain obedience through force and to use their power to extort money and sex from the membership.

- Gang life begins and ends with crime. New members usually undergo an initiation requiring them to commit some illegal act. Gang members who try to resign or leave the gang are sometimes assassinated.

- Most gangs are male dominated. Female members are generally viewed as "property" and serve primarily to provide support, cheerleading, and sex for the males in the organization.

- Each gang develops its own distinctive symbols, slogans, chants, signs, and so on (see "Gang Signs" in subsequent section).

Besides knowing the basics of street life culture, it pays for school personnel to appreciate why teenagers join gangs.

Gangs exist and flourish for reasons that make sense to many young people and that school staffs need to understand. For many members, who are often victims of neglect, abuse, or abandonment (kids raising themselves), the gang serves as an extended family and as the only available support system. Other common reasons driving young people into the arms of gang membership include the following:

- Identity
- Drugs
- Money
- Intimidation
- Protection
- Rebellion
- Hate
- Need for structure
- Gang "mystique"

- Excitement
- Brotherhood
- Acceptance
- Recognition
- Approval
- Frustration
- Hopelessness
- Sense of power

The first step to separating gang life from school life successfully is for all staff members to know and watch for the signals of gang activity (see the following "Gang Signs").

Gang Signs

- Gang graffiti (on walls, cars, notebooks, etc.)
- Gang colors (on jewelry, clothes, tennis shoes, etc.)
- Tattoos
- Gang dress (bandanas, scarves, caps, rolled-up pants legs, gloves worn only on one hand, etc.)
- Weapons
- Heavy jewelry (some jewelry items double as weapons.)
- Beepers and portable phones
- Buttons and insignias
- Hand signs/gestures (similar to sign language for the deaf)
- Off-beat haircuts
- Satanic paraphernalia

The appearance of any of these signs does not necessarily indicate the infiltration of gangs into the school Often nonmembers copy gang apparel or symbols. School officials should look for more than one sign to avoid premature action or overreaction.

The worst thing you can do is to deny the possibility of a gang problem. On the other hand, the presence of gang members does not destine the school to uncontrolled turmoil. Crime goes where it is allowed to exist. Gangs only become as strong as the school or community-at-large allow. It is possible for a committed staff to establish the school as a "neutral zone"—off limits to gang rivalry or violence. The following measures have worked for many administrators in curtailing or eliminating gang activity within the school:

- Enforce a reasonable dress code prohibiting known gang colors and costumes.
- Remove all graffiti as soon as possible.

- Keep out outsiders.
- Maintain high staff visibility throughout the building at all times.
- Administer a fair and consistent discipline code, including a tough weapons policy.
- Identify known gang members within the student body and closely monitor their behavior.
- Provide staff development programs to promote understanding of gang culture.
- Conduct campus pride and self-esteem programs.
- Elicit community support in antigang efforts (parent networks, neighborhood responsibility for teenagers, etc.).
- Encourage antigang programs for young children who are often used by gangs as couriers for delivering drugs.
- Lobby the media to refrain from publishing (advertising) names of gangs involved in crime incidents.
- Support antigang legislation (see the following box, "Gang Law Examples").

Gang Law Examples

- Extra penalties for bearing arms in the vicinity of the school.
- Added penalty for crimes committed by gang members.
- Make it unlawful for gang members to carry guns.
- Make it against the law to be a gang member.

(All these legal measures have been adopted in one or more communities. Some have worked. Some haven't. In most cases, more laws are not the final answer.)

Where gangs exist, principals and staff members must make every effort to establish the school as an "oasis" from gang activity—a safe zone where students are secure and free to learn without fear, intimidation, or violence.

In maintaining the school's neutrality from gang activity, there may be circumstances when it is necessary to exercise the principal's prerogative of involving suspension or expulsions discussed in the next section.

WHEN AND HOW TO IMPOSE SUSPENSION AND EXPULSION

In managing students and student behavior, suspension and expulsion have traditionally been trump cards of last resort for school authorities. This is still the case. However, in any situation involving violence, lethal weapons, or other life-threatening conditions, principals should not hesitate to dismiss students from school. Swift, decisive dismissal action sends a powerful and unmistakable message to the entire community.

School authorities may suspend a student temporarily from school quickly and with a minimum of due process when circumstances warrant. Permanent expulsion of a student, however, is a much more cumbersome process requiring compliance with a labyrinth of legal requirements. (Precise statutory regulations vary from state to state.) Expulsion should be invoked only when the student involved poses a direct, immediate, and serious threat to persons or property. In applying either suspension or expulsion, administrators must consider: (1) proper provocation, (2) protection of student rights, and (3) appropriateness of the action commensurate with the seriousness of the offense:

Pupil Dismissal Flow Chart

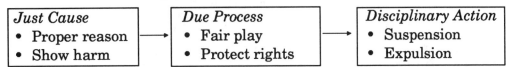

Just Cause	*Due Process*	*Disciplinary Action*
• Proper reason	• Fair play	• Suspension
• Show harm	• Protect rights	• Expulsion

In any dismissal situation, the principal's action must meet the standards of legality, liability, and perceived fairness. Special care must be taken to avoid allegations of discrimination against minorities or violations of federal and state mandates requiring educational access in the "least restrictive environment" for handicapped students. Legal counsel should be enlisted whenever needed.

The principal's greatest protection lies in a squeaky-clean process of documentation and a predetermined (legally tested) dismissal procedure. The framework for an effective suspension/expulsion process is outlined here:

Framework for Pupil Dismissal Action

(The school's procedure for students dismissal should incorporate all of these elements.)

1. Definitions of terms (suspension, expulsion, hearing, etc.)
2. Documented grounds for dismissal
3. Due process guidelines
4. Provision for notification of rights
5. Dismissal hearing procedures
6. System for documentation
7. Time line for dismissal action
8. Statement of duration and/or limitations
9. Identification of responsible parties
10. Appeal process
11. Readmission timetable and process

In addition to the procedural outline provided, another important safeguard against errors or omissions that may invalidate a principal's dismissal action is a carefully crafted district or building policy (see accompanying policy).

Policy on Student Suspension and Expulsion

Suspension:

A principal may suspend a student from school for a period of five consecutive school days for just cause.

A suspension may be extended beyond five days when the pupil is a substantial danger to other persons or pending school board decision in an expulsion hearing.

Any suspension shall be preceded by an informal conference between principal or designee and the affected student. In the case of a suspension of more than one day, the following process shall be used. A written notice containing

- Grounds for suspension
- Statement of facts
- Description of testimony
- Readmission plan
- Copy of pertinent statutes

shall be served by the principal or designee upon the pupil at or before the time of suspension takes effect. Every effort shall be make by the principal to notify the parent or guardian as soon as possible. In any instance, a written notice shall be sent by registered mail within 48 hours of the conference.

Expulsion:

The school board is the final authority for expelling a student. The process to be followed by the school board shall be prescribed by pertinent statute. A handicapped pupil may be placed, through a team meeting and the IEP, in a more restrictive environment, but shall not be expelled when the misconduct is related to the pupil's handicapping condition.

In any expulsion situation, parents or guardians may and often do waive the right to a hearing. If the hearing is held, however, special precautions must be taken to assure the absolute integrity of all student and parent rights as follows:

- The student must be entitled to legal representation.

- An unbiased, experienced third-party hearing examiner should preside.

- School authorities must ensure that the student and parents or guardians fully understand what is going on and appreciate the gravity of the situation. (Interpreters should be used when needed.)

- The school board retains final authority and may not follow the recommendations of the hearing officer.

Expulsion is an extremely serious action resulting in the student's long-term or permanent dismissal from the school. It does not, however, end the school's professional obligation to the learner. Caring schools continue to search for means to help expelled students gain readmission to an appropriate educational program, pursue alternative learning opportunities, or secure whatever help is needed to get their lives on track. Good schools (and good principals) never give up on any student.

The next section shows how you can use special allies on the staff to help manage student behavior.

EFFECTIVE USE OF COUNSELORS AND OTHER SPECIAL STAFF

Managing a secondary school student body is the business of every staff member. Every person on staff should try to live out the creed, "Let's go out and get better today." Participatory decision making and plural leadership should extend to all aspects of student management. Everyone on staff has an interest in all the learners, the general school climate, and the total health of the organization.

No principal can achieve an orderly, safe, and productive school environment alone—but a focused and committed staff can make it happen. All staff members have an obligation to be visible in the building, attentive to what's going on, knowledgeable and supportive of school rules, and willing to help stop bad things from happening in the school.

All teachers, counselors, administrators, and so on, who have direct, significant contact with students and parents should be involved in the disciplinary process and overall student management. All have specific knowledge of certain pupils and a personal investment in the success of all students. When all staff members are actively engaged in the control and management of student behavior:

- Early intervention is facilitated.
- Congruence of discipline philosophy is easier to achieve
- Sanctions and consequences are more consistently applied
- All parties are more likely to understand the rules and the reasons for the rules.
- Problems are resolved more quickly.

While all staff members should be involved in student management, counselors, and other specialized personnel may be particularly helpful in influencing and controlling pupil behavior. Traditionally, purists have maintained that counselors cannot be involved in discipline without jeopardizing their effectiveness. Actually, the opposite is true. Where counselors do play an active role in the discipline process, they take on a "real-world" image among other staff members, their credibility is enhanced and their direct impact on students is greater.

Counselors can play a unique role in student management through the following specialized functions:

- Providing insight into the needs and motivation of individual students
- Consulting with teachers on what specific behavior means and what a student in trouble may be trying to communicate
- Helping students cope with the realities of the school
- Serving as an advocate for the adolescent in relationships with peers, school authorities, and so on
- Assisting others to understand "where students are coming from" and why
- Serving as liaison between students, parents, and outside agencies in solving problems

Just as counselors can serve as unique allies to school leaders in student discipline, other specialized staff members have particular expertise and special roles related to the management of student behavior.

Roles of Special Staff in Student Management

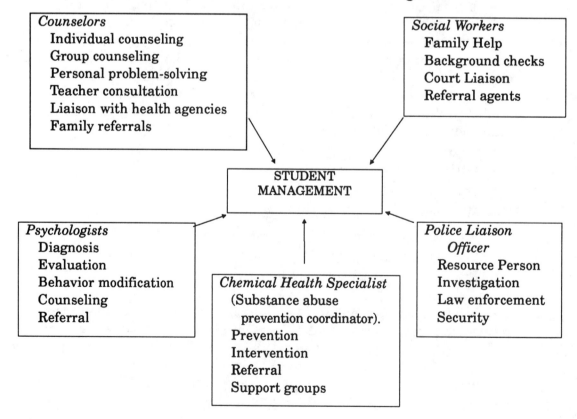

As principal, your responsibility is to capitalize on the unique contributions of all specialized personnel in managing student behavior and achieving a proper balance between freedom and structure within the school.

THE PRINCIPAL'S ROLE IN BALANCING FREEDOM AND STRUCTURE

Active teenagers need both freedom and structure. The principal must be the "equalizer" who insists that the school achieves some reasonable equilibrium between students running rampant and out of control, on one hand, and the staff imposing overly harsh, restrictive, or punitive controls, on the other.

The day-to-day operation of the school involves a dynamic tension between the forces favoring structure and those advocating freedom. Good principals find a middle ground. More than anyone else, the chief administrator must see that the school strikes a balance between the structure necessary for orderly learning to occur and the freedom young people need in order to test themselves and their environment.

Effective schools are orderly, businesslike, and productive. They are also interesting, exciting, and fun. It is up to you to balance freedom and structure and to guarantee that students are treated as individuals, not inmates.

An essential element in balancing license and limits within the school is an unflinching commitment to due process for all students.

WHAT TO DO ABOUT DUE PROCESS: GRIEVANCE PROCEDURES FOR STUDENTS

In a democratic society, all parties are guaranteed freedom and opportunity to call attention to unfair treatment, to right wrongs, and to overturn injustices. Democracy should not stop at the school entrance.

All students must have a way to stand up for their rights, to challenge the system, and to keep it honest. This is what due process is all about.

The purpose and intent of modern due process requirements is simply to ensure fairness for all. If the school does not stand for this principle, it does not qualify as a viable educational institution by American standards.

The essential elements of due process are:

- Fair and equitable rules/regulations
- Proper notification of the rules of the game
- Opportunity for hearing (a day in court) and appeal

In schools, due process involves (1) procedural safeguards, (2) equal protection, and (3) unequivocal applications of fair standards and consistent consequences.

Although some few educators still view adherence to students rights requirements as an unnecessary added burden on school personnel, *the leaders of the school must be champions of due process for all students.*

Every secondary school should have a straightforward grievance procedure for students that is readily understood and easy to use (see sample policy and sample grievance form).

Student Grievance Procedure

When misunderstandings arise between students and teachers or coaches, the following grievance process is available to all students to resolve the problem:

1. When feasible, the student should meet with the teacher or coach to discuss the issue.

2. If the initial meeting does not resolve the situation, the parent or guardian may confer with the teacher or coach involved.

3. If still unresolved, the matter should be referred to the principal.

4. In extreme situations, unresolved issues may be referred to the superintendent of schools, and, ultimately, the school board.

5. Students may file a grievance or submit a request for remedy by completing a formal grievance form available from the school office, by informal written statement or by verbal statement to any licensed staff member. A parent or guardian may also file a grievance in behalf of the student.

Student Grievance Form

Student name: _____ Grade: _____

Date of grievance/incident: _____

Description of facts:

Remedy of relief requested:

Other comments:

Date: _____ Student signature: _____

Parent/guardian signature: _____

WHERE TO GO FOR HELP WITH DIFFICULT PROBLEMS

No matter how important you are or how good you are, some problems of student management cannot be solved by even the most creative and resourceful principal or school staff working alone. Some professional educators are hesitant and embarrassed to admit that any problem exceeds their personal powers of resolution. Such denial is the first sign of faltering leadership. The most effective leaders eagerly seek out help whenever it is needed and from wherever it is available.

Student management and school discipline are concerns for the entire community and for society at large. Within every community, there are many groups, organizations, and agencies ready and willing to help the school that are often overlooked.

In addition, every school has a wealth of resources and assistance from individual and groups at the local, state and national level. Usually, the best help is closest to home. Some outside resources administrators can draw on to help solve student management problems are provided in "Sources of Help for School Administrators."

In addition to the more formal resources listed, many principals find that their best resource of help, advice, and assistance comes through *networking* with other practitioners in the field. Every administrator should establish contacts and linkages with a variety of professional colleagues. Peer support and assistance can be an invaluable force in fostering effective leadership for improved student behavior and enhanced school climate.

This chapter has laid out the philosophical precepts and the nuts and bolts of successfully managing today's adolescent learners in the school setting. Chapter 5 provides concrete directions for how principals can effectively manage the school's curriculum and ensure that teachers are teaching and students are learning the "right stuff" for life in the changing modern world.

Sources of Help for School Administrators

Local Resources

- School district specialists
- District legal counsel
- Local teachers association
- PTSA and PTSO organizations
- Ministerial associations
- United Way agencies
- Civic clubs (many are willing to contribute funds to support special youth projects)
- Youth service agencies (YMCA, Boys and Girls Clubs, etc.)
- Chamber of commerce
- Big Brother/Big Sister organizations
- Family counseling and mental health clinic
- 12-Step programs (Alcoholics Anonymous, Al-A-Teen, Narcotics Anonymous, Cocaine Anonymous, etc.)
- Commercial consultants
- Police
- "Help" Hotlines

State/County Resources

- Child protection unit
- State department of education
- Health department
- Vocational rehabilitation services
- Highway patrol
- Sheriff's office
- Colleges/ universities
- Mothers Against Drunk Driving (MADD)
- State attorney
- State teacher's association

Federal Resources

- U.S. Department of Education
- National Institute on Alcohol Abuse and Alcoholism
- National Institute on Drug Use
- Educational Research Service (ERS)
- National teacher organization (NEA, AFT)
- Phi Delta Kappa professional fraternity
- National Association of Secondary School Principals
- American Association of School Administrators
- National School Board's Association
- Centers for Disease Control

Chapter 5

Managing the Curriculum and Instructional Program

The curriculum defines the program and provides the substance of learning. Without a vital curriculum, even the best staffed and run school is academically bankrupt.

A well-designed secondary curriculum is more than a set of disjointed topics and activities. It is the total planned program of experiences available to individual learners. It includes educational goals, learner outcomes, subject offerings, course outlines, and even the student activity program. In many ways, the curriculum is the script that guides and fuses the interaction of all the key actors in the drama of learning.

As instructional leader, the principal sets the tone for program development and curriculum review. The best principals don't delegate direction and coordination of the instructional program. This chapter establishes the basis of curriculum leadership for secondary school principals.

THE PRINCIPAL'S ROLE AS INSTRUCTIONAL LEADER

The principal doesn't have to be a master teacher in all subjects or know everything about curriculum. But every effective principal needs to know and understand what good teaching is and what a good curriculum looks like.

The principal doesn't dictate curriculum, but is accountable for ensuring a sound instructional program that works today and meets the needs of tomorrow. Just as a corporate chief executive officer (CEO) insists on and stands behind a quality product, the principal should be the driving force, chief advocate, and champion of the school's curriculum. Without leadership from the top, curriculum revision, instructional review, and staff development will be sputtering and sporadic at best.

Following are straightforward strategies and basic leadership techniques that many principals have found effective in managing the school's curriculum and instructional program:

The Role of the Principal in Curriculum Leadership

- Know what the current curriculum is. More than anyone else in the school, the chief administrator should have firsthand knowledge of what is being offered and taught in all courses and at all levels. Many principals insist that an up-to-date file of course outlines and syllabi be maintained in the school office at all times.

- Admit ignorance in some areas while modeling behavior of analyzing data, planning, developing, implementing, and evaluating instructional initiatives.

- Insist that what is being taught is important and relevant and makes sense to learners.

- Emphasize that good curriculum is designed. Don't let it just happen.

- Block out quality time for curriculum and instructional leadership—for both yourself and others on the staff.

- Put in place a systematic process of curriculum review (see "Who Plans Curriculum and How" later in this chapter).

- Get the right people involved. Put the best minds on the staff to work on critical issues.

- Provide leadership in defining what a good curriculum is (see "What the Principal Needs to Know About Curriculum" later in this chapter).

- Define the roles of all those involved in curriculum design and find new ways for them to work together.

- Encourage experimentation. Some of the best teaching and learning takes place in *terra incognita* (uncharted territory).

- Tolerate mistakes. Don't penalize good faith flops.

- Bend the rules to free up promising innovations.

- Build in a nuts and bolts staff development program to help teachers understand the curriculum and gain the skills to implement it.

- Identify and provide the resources needed for encumbered curriculum research, design, and evaluation.

- Demonstrate energy, excitement, and enthusiasm for curriculum reform.

- Challenge status quo thinking. Ask the tough questions.

- Market the curriculum. The principal should be the number one sales representative for the school's instructional program.

One other key role of the school leader in curriculum development is to serve as a liaison with district personnel in meshing system-wide goals with building initiative.

WAYS TO BLEND DISTRICT CURRICULUM WITH SCHOOL GOALS

Despite increasing cries for decentralized decision making, there remains the need for a coordinated district curriculum planning process and model. Individual schools cannot go it entirely alone.

Accelerated social mobility and the growing role of "choice" in school selection and attendance argue against a separate building-level curriculum. In its most extreme form, a decentralized curriculum may result in a highly prescriptive and provincial program of studies that limits learning and does a disservice to students and society at large.

Unquestionably, schools have unique needs—but curriculum must be multidimensional and must be developed on many levels. Effective learning requires instructional content that spans all levels and schools and a step-by-step, grade-by-grade plan designed to help all students learn.

Principals who know curriculum and instruction best want to work in a system with a common set of desired outcomes and an integrated planning process that accommodates individual school needs and cultures. In this kind of learning context, the principal's role is to contribute to and influence district curriculum decisions while defining and defending programs that make sense at the building level. It is up to the principal to make room on the district agenda for building priorities as depicted:

District Curriculum Areas

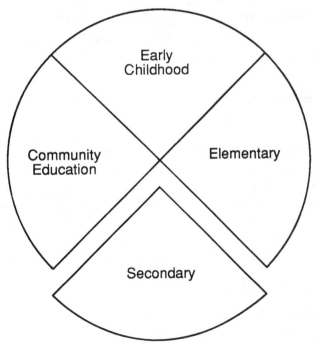

To ensure that each area receives a fair share of the pie, principals need to take specific steps to blend district curriculum with their respective building goals. The practical tactics that follow can help school leaders achieve what the district has in mind, while advancing their own building interests at the same time.

1. Insist that your school be adequately represented on all district curriculum committees (text selection groups, scope and sequence committees, staff development committees, curriculum advisory councils, etc.). Don't let staff representatives take their assignments lightly.

2. Encourage key staff members to become active in curriculum matters on a district-wide basis.

3. Initiate joint middle, junior, and senior high subject area department meetings.

4. Replicate district curriculum committees at the building level as a ready means of feeding in ideas from the bottom up.

5. Keep district curriculum personnel informed of building needs and concerns on a regular basis. Many principals make it a point to meet one-on-one regularly with the superintendent or district curriculum administrator to share school-level plans and provide curriculum updates.

6. Track developments in elementary programs and anticipate their impact on secondary curriculum.

7. Be creative in linking building goals to district priorities. Suggest broadened meanings for district strategic plan language and new twists to old ideas that support school aims.

8. Lobby the district office for special curriculum projects.

9. Network with other principals at all levels to keep abreast of embryonic curriculum developments.

10. Analyze where the school board wants to put its money and capitalize on all opportunities to promote important building initiatives.

Although some maverick principals seem to enjoy bucking the system, it is always prudent to balance district and building needs by whatever means possible. When the two are in conflict, the school usually loses. By meshing building improvements plans with district-wide curriculum goals, the school does its part to support the organization and increases the likelihood of success for its own priorities and programs.

At both the school and district levels, the best curriculum is shaped by

• What students already know
• What students don't know
• What students need to know

This requires rigorous and ongoing assessment as the basis for curriculum and instructional decision making.

A RECIPE FOR RESULTS: USING ASSESSMENT TO DRIVE INSTRUCTION

The first thing that principals need to know about curriculum making is that assessment should drive instruction. All decisions about what is to be taught should be based as much on knowledge of where students are as on identification of where the school wants them to be. This requires a cycle of assessment that includes:

- Assessment before instruction to determine if learners have the skills needed to prepare them for instruction
- Assessment throughout the teaching/learning process to pinpoint progress—what's working and what's not
- Assessment after instruction to verify basic learning or mastery

To most people, the purpose of tests and measurements is to rank and rate students. From the principal's perspective, however, the real reason for using assessment is to shape, pace, and personalize instruction, not to label individuals. Evaluation is at the heart of curriculum and instructional decision making because it tells the decision makers (teachers, administrators, curriculum personnel, etc.) the degree to which students have attained predetermined outcomes. The regular assessment of student program and achievement is essential to guide the teacher's instruction. In its simplest form, an assessment-driven model of instruction looks like this:

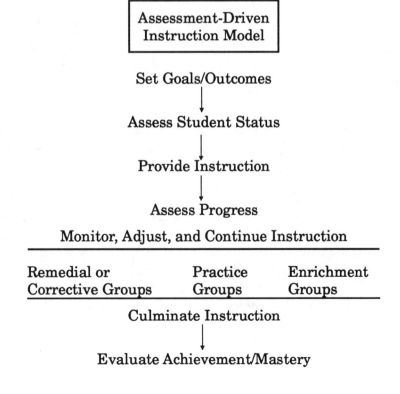

```
          ┌─────────────────────┐
          │  Assessment-Driven  │
          │  Instruction Model  │
          └─────────────────────┘

              Set Goals/Outcomes
                      │
              Assess Student Status
                      │
               Provide Instruction
                      │
                Assess Progress

      Monitor, Adjust, and Continue Instruction

  Remedial or        Practice      Enrichment
  Corrective Groups  Groups        Groups

              Culminate Instruction
                      │
            Evaluate Achievement/Mastery
```

Assessment-driven instruction is a practical way of holding the staff's "feet to the fire" in curriculum development, testing, and implementation. One of the most practical applications of this approach is the outcome-based education movement that has been adopted by many schools and is outlined later in this chapter.

The assessment-driven instructional model is a tool that principals can use with all individuals and groups responsible for curriculum and instructional planning as described in the next section.

WHO PLANS CURRICULUM AND HOW?

Principals don't make curriculum. Even teachers don't always have the last say in what is taught. The curriculum is forged by many forces. What teachers teach and what students learn is shaped by a variety of influences at the building, district, community, state and national levels (see "Curriculum Influencers" following):

Curriculum Influencers

- Tradition
- Social issues
- Legal requirements
- Economics
- Student interests
- School reform movements
- Collective bargaining
- Accrediting agencies
- Textbook publishers

- Research
- Political agendas
- Accountability demands
- Public pressure
- Court decisions
- Foreign competition
- Teacher specialties
- Special interest groups
- Test makers

To be a successful instructional leader, savvy principals need to understand these forces, to learn how the system works, and to know what "hot buttons" to push to orchestrate outcomes.

While many curriculum choices are ultimately made by individual teachers behind closed classroom doors, most sweeping decisions and goal setting are accomplished through groups and committees. No single leader can serve on all the numerous groups affecting curriculum, but it pays for the principal to have emissaries on as many as possible.

While curriculum committee structure may vary from school to school and district to district, most of the nuts and bolts of curriculum and instruction are hammered out by one or more of the following kinds of groups:

- Scope and sequence committees

- Summer curriculum writing teams
- Textbook selection committees
- Ad hoc task forces
- Advisory committees
- School effectiveness teams
- Curriculum chairs/department heads
- Building leadership teams
- "Think tanks" (educational focus groups)
- Curriculum advisory councils (see "School Curriculum Advisory Council Guidelines" following)
- Staff collaboration teams
- Teacher assistance teams, TATs (discussed later in this chapter)

The purpose of such teams and task forces is to serve as a sounding board, a catalyst for planning, and a cadre of practitioners to help introduce new programs. Where such committees exist at the district level, each secondary school needs to be represented and may want to establish similar groups at the building level. If no such committees function on a district basis, the principal should set in place a working curriculum committee arrangement at the school level to ensure systematic curriculum review and revision. The trick is to not have too many committees, to avoid committees that are too large, to stay away from using the same people over and over on committees, and to never have more than one committee working on the same thing.

School Curriculum Advisory Council (CAC) Guidelines

Role
- The role of the CAC is to (1) provide for discussion of curriculum issues and (2) provide feedback/ideas about the overall program of instruction. The CAC is strictly advisory in nature and is not a rule-making body.

Membership
- Ten parents/community representatives (two of which are recent graduates).
- Six student representatives (two from each grade level).
- Eight staff members, representing all major departments.
- Membership terms to run for two to three years, at discretion/interest of the individual.

Qualifications
- Special interest/experience in curriculum issues.
- Skill in establishing positive working relationships in groups.
- Availability for meetings
- Competence in analyzing data, examining options, and reaching consensus.

The modern secondary curriculum is both complex and comprehensive. Thus, it is no mean task to keep track of what's being taught, where and by whom. Part of the principal's responsibility is to manage the curriculum so that no area goes unattended and nothing "falls through the cracks." To accomplish this, most curriculum experts suggest a systematic cycle for curriculum review such as the five-year plan spelled out here:

Curriculum Program Review Cycle

This plan provides for continuous curriculum review, evaluation, and validation/revision by all subject areas over a self-repeating five-year cycle. The five separate phases are intended to last approximately one year as follows:

Phase I Program Mission   Phase III Program Development
Phase II Program Evaluation   Phase IV Program Implementation
              Phase V Program Refinement

Year	Phase I (Mission)	Phase II (Evaluation)	Phase III (Development)	Phase IV (Implementation)	Phase V (Refinement)
1	Language Arts	Math, Foreign Language	Science, Music	Social Studies, Physical Ed., Vocational Ed.	Health, Art
2	Health, Art	Language Arts	Math, Foreign Language	Science, Music	Social Studies, Physical Ed., Vocational Ed.
3	Social Studies, Physical Ed., Vocational Ed.	Health, Art	Language Arts	Math, Foreign Language	Science, Music
4	Science, Music	Social Studies, Physical Ed., Vocational Ed.	Health, Art	Language Arts	Math, Foreign Language
5	Math, Foreign Language	Science, Music	Social Studies, Physical Ed., Vocational Ed.	Health, Art	Language Arts

(Repeat Cycle)

Once a planning cycle has been established, a standardized review process should be set in place to be followed by all groups responsible for curriculum improvement. It is the principal's job to see that the integrity of the process is maintained and that no committee or task force is permitted to cut corners or skip steps. A typical curriculum development process is illustrated here:

Curriculum Development Process

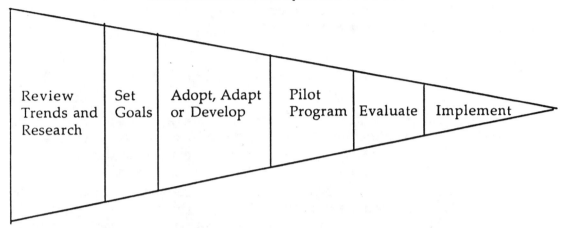

In many situations, curriculum study groups have the options of "buying" a commercially prepared curriculum package or of developing their own program. There are advantaged and disadvantages to both approaches as follows:

> **Program Options: Pluses and Minuses**

Commercial Programs

PLUSES:
- Save time
- Built-in lesson plans and materials
- May be less expensive
- Developed by experts

MINUSES:
- May not meet local needs
- Can jeopardize articulation and transfer
- May avoid controversial topics

Local Programs

PLUSES:
- Build on existing curriculum
- Foster ownership and commitment
- May address local issues

MINUSES:
- Cost more
- Lack teacher expertise
- Involve considerable time

Many principals encourage curriculum committees to enjoy the best of both worlds by combining commercially prepared programs with locally developed units and materials. This approach maximizes opportunities for integration and articulation and can result in an instructional program that is both globally aware and locally sensitive.

As program decisions become more decentralized, the principal's role in managing the curriculum is intensified and magnified. This section has explained the *process* of curriculum development. The next section details what any school leader needs to know about the *product*.

WHAT DOES THE PRINCIPAL NEED TO KNOW ABOUT THE CURRICULUM?

Some principals feel ill equipped for curriculum leadership. A few wouldn't know a good curriculum if they saw one. In most cases, however, any principal can become a competent curriculum leader once they know where they want to go and what it will look like when they get there.

Principals who are front-runners in instructional leadership understand that they cannot and need not know all the minutia of every subject area—but they do have to know what's happening, what's important, what's needed, and what's possible (and maybe a little beyond possible).

The curriculum of the school is not ethereal or mysterious. It is made up of down-to-earth stuff that students need to learn, know, and do to succeed on a daily basis in the modern world. It is about what everyone needs to live life, enjoy life, and make life better.

School leaders don't have to be scholars or research giants to manage the instructional program successfully. Here's all the principal *really* needs to know about curriculum:

- The best curriculum is a *balanced* curriculum.
- The curriculum is for all learners. You don't need a totally different curriculum for different ability levels.
- The curriculum must be learnable and doable.
- Subject matter should be logically ordered and sequenced.
- There is probably no single fact or knowledge bit that everyone absolutely has to know, but there should be an academic core of content to provide focus and coherence to the curriculum.
- Most students learn best from a hands-on, real-world curriculum.
- The curriculum should be rooted in learner outcomes, or exit expectations (what students will know, do, and be like when they complete the program).
- The curriculum must always be focused on the learner.
- Parents and students should have a say in curriculum planning.
- All aspects of the curriculum should be tied directly to the school's vision, mission, and goals.
- The curriculum should be flexible and dynamic enough to allow for "bird walks" and unique "teachable moments."

- A good curriculum is about the future. It should not be limited just to what teachers already know.
- The curriculum should be inclusive, unbiased, and globally oriented.
- Do not go overboard on requirements.
- The curriculum should consistently emphasize higher-level thinking skills for all students.
- An information society requires a curriculum that is resource based, not textbook driven (see "Resource-Based Instruction" later in this chapter).
- The best curriculum grows out of *dialogue*.
- Every curriculum is partially political.
- Teaching process is usually more important than teaching product.
- Most students learn best from an action-oriented instructional program.
- Where possible, the curriculum should be interdisciplinary.
- The curriculum should reach beyond the classroom.
- Somewhere in the school program every student should have an opportunity to dig a "post hole" for depth.
- Where the instructional program is largely locally developed, the principal must guard against mutations in the curriculum.
- Technology is not a separate course. In many ways, technology *is* the curriculum of tomorrow.
- No school can allow its curriculum to stand still. It needs continuous evaluation and ongoing attention.
- The curriculum is only as good as the staff development program that supports it.
- The curriculum does not have to be bland, antiseptic, or value free.
- The curriculum should not get in the way of real learning. Nobody needs a curriculum that is bureaucratic, obscure, or full of tricks and traps.
- The curriculum can be *fun*. There is joy in learning and it ought to show.

These guiding principles constitute the basics for managing the school's curriculum and instructional program. One effective means for incorporating these tenets, making them tangible, and making them work is to adopt a program of outcome-based education as described in the next section.

PRINCIPLES OF OUTCOME-BASED EDUCATION

Today's secondary schools are operating in a time and place that demands results. Society's growing emphasis on proof and productivity has led a number of schools, districts, and even entire states to initiate programs of outcome-based education (OBE). The OBE model is an assessment-driven vehicle for translating sound curriculum theory into classroom reality. This is one tool that instruction-oriented administrators will want to use.

Outcome-based education is a formal, structured process for:

- Applying "assessment to drive instruction" (see earlier discussion in this chapter)
- Screening and shaping curriculum decisions in the classroom
- Raising "red flags" concerning curriculum and/or learner problems
- Implementing curriculum in a way that assures alignment of learner outcomes, assessment, and instruction

The whole process is illustrated here:

OBE Made Easy

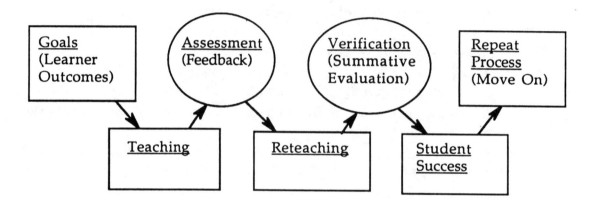

Throughout the OBE model, assessment is used to gather data on student progress toward curriculum outcomes to make better decisions for improving instruction. To keep the curriculum on track, assessment techniques are employed to measure progress at all critical instructional levels, that is, program outcomes, grade/course outcomes, unit outcomes, and even lesson outcomes.

The philosophical underpinnings of an outcome-based education program are simple and straightforward:

- All students can be successful learning.
- Success spawns more success.
- Schools can make success happen.
- Learning standards should be held constant for all learners.
- Time is the variable that determines when (not if) students will succeed.

This is a philosophy that appeals to more and more school leaders. Outcome-based education is not a curriculum—it is a means of imposing quality control checks on all aspects of the instructional program.

Outcome-based education is an instructional model that administrators need to understand to stay current in the field of curriculum leadership. Another development that is transforming curriculum thinking is the movement toward resource-based instruction.

RESOURCE-BASED INSTRUCTION IN TODAY'S SECONDARY SCHOOL

When adopting a new curriculum, the easiest (and probably the worst) thing the school can do is merely buy a new textbook. In a world awash with information sources, no single text (not even any single medium) should define the curriculum. In an age of "information power" and untethered technology, the entire universe can be the classroom. If the school is doing its job, today's students can access information from literally everywhere on and off this planet. This is why an increasing number of secondary schools are using resource-based instruction (RBI).

Resource-based instruction/teaching is simply the use of multiple resources in a variety of formats and technologies to achieve curriculum goals. The focus is on information, not on the package it comes in. This is the antithesis of a traditional textbook-driven curriculum. The underlying premise is that by using all available materials and technologies, more can be learned in less time. RBI can teach much of the content of the curriculum quicker and better and, at the same time, empower students with critical information-access skills. Thus, the *curriculum* (whatever it is) *becomes* the *medium* for ensuring that students are effective users of information and ideas from all sources.

The goals of RBI are as tightly targeted as the technologies that make them possible:

- To teach students how to locate information, think about it, compare it, analyze it, and synthesize it
- To help students take facts and discover meaning from multiple information sources
- To enable students to question, combine, communicate, and create information
- To teach students to develop their own data bases and to use technology to construct alternative scenarios
- To teach skills in evaluating and presenting information from traditional and new data sources.

Under RBI, students learn from all the same real-world resources that are increasingly found in their daily life such as:

- Printed material
- Computers/modems
- Cassette tapes
- Filmstrips
- Camcorders
- Interactive videodisc players
- Videotapes
- Telephones
- Teleconferencing
- Hypermedia
- Microfilm/microfiche
- TV/VCRs
- Graphics
- Hard disc players
- CD ROM systems
- Satellite transmissions
- Film slides
- Fax machines
- Artifacts
- Optical character recognition (OCR) devices

The basics for effective implementation of RBI are:

- Teachers who are comfortable with technology and are willing to take risks
- Competent media personnel who are technologically literate and capable of becoming coteachers and codesigners of instruction
- Information-rich media centers designed as the center of learning, not just an appendage to the curriculum

As in all innovative ventures, there are certain risks and potential pitfalls involved in moving toward resource-based instruction, including:

- Misuse of media (If used improperly, the media may detract from the subject matter.)
- Use of inappropriate media
- Temptation to spend too much time on topics because of the attraction of the media
- The expense of equiping the school's library-media center as an environment rich in materials and technologies
- Challenge of reteaching or replacing traditional library personnel

Despite the obstacles, the pay-off can be enormous. Like OBE, resource-based instruction is not a curriculum; it is, however, a vehicle that can breathe life into the instructional programs and prepare students better for living in an information age. As a by-product, it also provides a natural catalyst for interdisciplinary teaching.

One of the most powerful things a principal can do to energize the curriculum and position the school program for success in the twenty-first century is to influence the staff to take a hard look at resource-based instruction. Once they try it, the students may not let them back away and teaching and learning in the school may never be the same!

Any new curriculum or new delivery system such as RBI involves some staff retraining. The next section offers tips on establishing an effective in-house staff development program.

THE HIDDEN HALF OF THE CURRICULUM: STAFF DEVELOPMENT

The hidden half of the curriculum is staff development. Even the most well-designed curriculum or instructional innovation is "bookshelf bait" unless teachers know it and know how to use it. This requires ongoing inservice training.

In top-notch corporations, everyone from the CEO on down is committed continually to getting better and doing better. In schools, improvement of instruction and professional growth should be an expectation for every staff member every year. The best teachers are good learners.

Part of the principal's role in managing the curriculum is to orchestrate opportunities for the entire staff to learn, grow, and improve. There are lots of staff development options open to educators from universities, state agencies, professional organizations, commercial consultants, and district programs. Good principals lobby to keep a piece of the action (and a piece of the budget to support it) at the school level to help achieve building goals.

The purpose of a dynamic staff development program is to enhance effective decision making for successful learning—to help teachers make good choices in the classroom. Building-level staff development activities should assist the staff to both design and deliver the school's program. The key to successful staff development is to involve teachers and others in identifying needs and planning appropriate inservice programs. The formula looks like this:

Leadership + Ownership = Enthusiasm and Commitment

A few simple strategies can guide the principal in conducting a solid professional growth program that supports the curriculum and promotes better teaching:

1. Learning opportunities for teachers should deal with both the science and the art of teaching.
2. The school needs programs that improve teachers on both the *professional* (theory, knowledge, skills) and the *personal* (health, wellness, morale) *levels.*
3. Good staff development programs stress philosophy and rationale, as well as practical applications. Teachers have to believe in the curriculum before they can and will teach it.

4. Teachers need to see the payoff for participating in the school's inservice programs. Don't forget the WIFM Factor (*What's In It For Me?*).

5. The best programs feature choices for professionals (see "Staff Development Offerings for Secondary Teachers").

6. More teachers get involved when staff development is offered through varied delivery systems (released days, weekend workshops, summer sessions, late afternoon/early evening program including dinner, etc.).

7. One-shot inservice infusions don't work. To be effective, professional growth programs must allow for *feedback, follow-up,* and *follow-through.* Teachers need time to assimilate and practice new skills.

Staff Development Offerings for Secondary Teachers

*   Thinking skills: ideas for classroom integration
*   Resource-based teaching
*   Thinking skills and data bases
*   Digiters and graphics
*   Developing multicultural lessons
*   Gender-fair issues
*   Strategies for low-achieving students
*   Advanced learning styles
*   Cooperative learning styles
*   Expanding parent involvement with students
*   How to implement OBE instruction

One management tool that can help principals design and monitor a comprehensive building inservice program is to require all staff members to complete an "Individual Professional Growth Plan" for the year (see the form provided.)

Just as assessment should drive instruction for students, evaluation should guide professional growth programs for staff. To fine-tune the school's inservice program, every workshop or activity should be evaluated and the results used to determine future directions. An evaluation form is provided.

In planning a staff development program that works, school leaders need to recognize that teachers learn best from other teachers. Whenever possible, inhouse experts and/or cadres of existing staff members should spearhead and carry out the school's inservice training program. The next section illustrates how this can work.

Individual Professional Growth Plan Form

Name: _____ Teaching Assignment: _____

My choice(s) for my personal professional growth plan are indicated below.

I. _____ I want to enroll in the following inservice programs to be offered by the school:

_____

_____

_____

_____

II. _____ My professional growth plan will include leadership/service on the following staff committee(s):

_____

_____

_____

_____

III. _____ I want to follow a customized professional growth plan this year. I will (describe your selected topic and your planned activities):

_____

_____

_____

_____

_____

_____

_____

_____

_____

_____

Date:_____ Teacher Signature: _____

Please return this form to the principal's office by November 1.

Staff Development Evaluation Form

The Staff Development Committee is interested in your opinions and suggestions regarding the inservice program. Please fill out this evaluation and return it to the principal's office by _____.

Title of Inserts Program:_____ Date: _____

	High		Low
1. Please rate the degree to which the program achieved its purpose.	3	2	1

Comment(s): _____

_____

2. Please rate the usefulness of the program for you personally.	3	2	1

Comment(s): _____

_____

3. Please rate the usefulness of the program for the staff as a whole.	3	2	1

Comment(s): _____

_____

4. What specifically was informative or of value to you about the program?

_____

_____

_____

5. In planning future programs, I would suggest:

_____

_____

_____

_____
Teacher's Name (optional)

HOW TO GET THE MOST OUT OF TEACHER ASSISTANCE TEAMS

Some of the best professional growth occurs when teachers learn by doing and working together to solve real school problems. One way that principals can facilitate this is to create a collegial consultation model by forming one or more teacher assistance teams (TAT) within the school.

The TAT concept was originally designed to assist teachers in "mainstreaming" special education students and/or to better handle individual learning or behavior problems in the classroom. The TAT approach, which has proved successful in a number of settings, usually works like this:

1. One or more (up to three) teacher teams are elected by the staff. The number of teams is determined by school size. Membership may be rotated among interested and willing staff members.

2. Classroom teachers identify and refer specific individual problems to the team for advice and assistance.

3. After reviewing background information, the teacher assistance team meets with the referring teaching and follows a structured problem-solving process as follows:
   - Define the problem and set desired outcomes.
   - Generate alternative solutions (usually 10 to 25 suggestions).
   - Refine strategies and negotiate objectives.
   - Establish possible timetable and evaluation procedures.

4. The referring teacher selects the most viable solutions and tests them in the classroom.

5. Follow-up meetings with the team are held as necessary to assess progress or brainstorm additional alternatives.

The TAT system that has worked well for integrating and handling problem students in regular classrooms can also be applied to solving curricular and instructional problems—and provide some practical staff development at the same time.

By creating one or more instructional teacher assistance teams, the principal can build a support system for classroom teachers to promote building-level problem solving. The TAT approach focuses on constructive answers to curriculum and instructional problems, shares teacher competence, and deals with individual immediate classroom concerns. It provides prompt, accessible help and gives teachers more ideas for dealing with specific problem situations.

The underlying premise for TAT is simply that teachers can solve more problems working together than they can alone and can learn from each other in the process. The TAT model features maximum flexibility and school-level applicability with a minimum of cost, time, or paperwork. The forms provided next illustrate the ease of implementing the TAT process.

TAT Assistance Request Form

I. Teacher's name: _____ Course title:_____

II. Describe curriculum/instruction problem:

III. State desired outcome:

IV. What has been tried so far?

V. Other background information:

Date: _____ Teacher's Signature _____

TAT Recommendation Form

Teacher's Name:_____ Course Title:_____Date: _____

Desired outcome:

TAT suggestions	Alternative(s) selected for classroom use	Evaluation procedure	Timetable

The principal's role in the TAT program is simple and straightforward as follows:

1. Establish one or more teacher assistance teams.
2. Conduct the first meeting to clarify the process.
3. Provide support for TAT (meeting time, resources, etc.).
4. Monitor process.
5. Recognize TAT participants.

In many ways, the TAT model is a classic example of exercising leadership by pointing people in the right direction and getting out of their way. When school leaders must deal with limited staff development resources, TAT offers a cost-effective means of using peer problem-solving groups to provide greater service to both staff and students, to foster meaningful professional growth, and to improve instruction.

Managing the school's staff development program is a big job that is getting bigger as demands on school programs increase. The next section shows how principals can avoid the futility of tilting at too many windmills by pulling it all together in an integrated staff development program.

SOLVING THE STAFF DEVELOPMENT EQUATION: AN INTEGRATED APPROACH

One of the biggest complaints teachers and principals have about staff development programs is that they cram in too much too quickly. Each year brings forth a proliferation of innovative programs and new delivery systems that teachers are supposed to learn and assimilate. The plate gets too full for teachers to handle. Just as students lament the fact that teachers never run out of things to teach, the professionals, themselves, complain that there is too much to learn and not enough time to learn it. At any given time, a school may have several staff development balls in the air that teachers are expected to catch and hold on to as illustrated on page 170.

In the role of instructional leader, the principal is in a unique position to make staff development manageable for everyone. As in all facets of leadership, timing is critical. If too many ideas are introduced in rapid succession, none can be mastered or internalized. Teachers need time for follow-up with practice and feedback. Most experts agree that the standard for "institutionalizing" a new school practice or program is three to five years.

Part of the principal's job is to help solve the "time" issue and the problem of inadequate opportunity for classroom practice and integration of new ideas. This means that every staff development program must take

The Juggling Act of Inservice Education

(example)

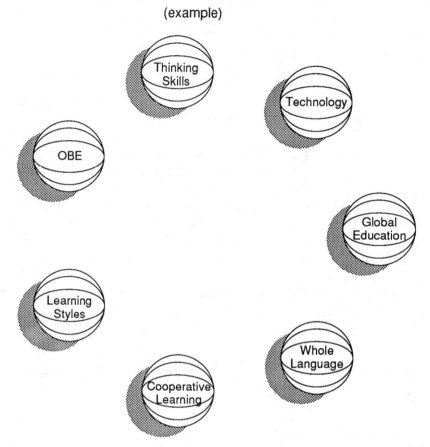

into account "readiness," which is as important for adult learners as for children and youth. New ideas often need to be phased in over a reasonable period of time—starting with those teachers who are most ready, willing, and interested. If teachers aren't ready, *wait*. Don't force it.

Staff development programs are effective only when teachers see a need and purpose for dropping old practices and learning new ways. The most important thing the principal can do in guiding professional growth in the school is to make learning for teachers meaningful by tying what they are expected to learn directly to agreed-upon goals. Every growth activity for the staff should relate clearly to the school's vision and mission.

Both old and new programs need to be integrated under the umbrella of existing building goals. The principal is the one who must show teachers how each new piece fits in and helps take them where they want to go.

The best staff development plan is one that weaves together initiatives and goals, combines strategies, and integrates key components into a program of professional growth that hangs together and makes sense to teachers.

Evaluation of existing programs and practices is the screening mechanism that administrators have to use to determine "what to include in" and "what to include out" of the school's staff development program as explained next.

BASIC TOOLS FOR EFFECTIVE PROGRAM EVALUATION

Program evaluation gives school leaders a diagnosis of the curriculum that tells them where it hurts. It pinpoints which areas need review, which practices need fine-tuning, and which teacher skills need updating. All curriculum review and staff development should grow out of an assessment of what is working and what isn't in the school program.

In some schools, evaluation is just a ritual—an annual rite performed to satisfy the school board and make good copy for the local newspaper. In the best schools, however, program evaluation is systematically employed to provide answers that administrators need to keep the curriculum on track. An effective program evaluation process starts with identifying learner outcomes and ends with deciding what happens to specific programs and practices as outlined here:

A Typical Program Evaluation Process

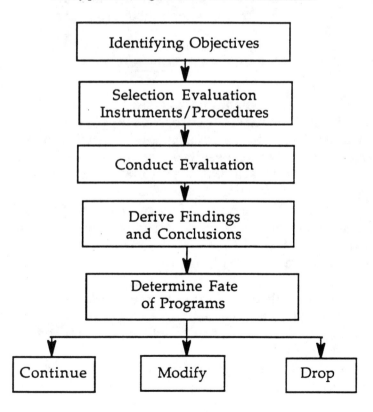

The only criterion a principal needs to manage a workable system of program evaluation is the following four-point test:

1. What information do you really need to make the right curriculum decisions? (Evaluate only what is important.)

2. How will you use the information? (Don't collect extraneous statistical data or "junk information" that will only confuse the main issues.)

3. How can you get the information you need? (Does the right instrument exist? If not, what other evaluation procedures/techniques might work?)

4. Is it worth the time and effort to get the information? (Consider costs versus payoffs.)

Most traditional program evaluation systems have been built around pencil and paper tests including (1) norm-referenced tests (standardized, commercial instruments), (2) criterion-referenced tests (teacher-made instruments), (3) state assessment devices, and (4) college entrance exams.

Every principal needs to understand tests, what they can and cannot do, and how to use the results. But test results aren't enough to provide all the answers needed to manage successfully today's complex secondary school curriculum. The final section of this chapter describes alternative nontest techniques for assessing school programs.

NONTEST TECHNIQUES FOR EVALUATING SCHOOL PROGRAMS

With today's expanding expectations, many of the learner outcomes that schools have for students can no longer be reduced to discrete bits of information or knowledge measurable by pencil and paper test items. Many curriculum goals are not easily quantifiable. Much of what the school wants learners to attain are skills, attitudes, and processes that do not lend themselves to traditional means of measurement.

To gauge the success or failure of the curriculum and instructional program, modern educators need a variety of assessment techniques. Tests simply do not tell all that school personnel need to know about how the school program is working.

To manage successfully the curriculum, principals need to be creative and willing to use (and convince others to use) a broad range of evaluation tools. Assessment can come under many guises. More and more secondary schools are adopting or inventing alternative means of program evaluation.

In addition to traditional means of measurement, many schools are now using the following nontest techniques for diagnosing and documenting program success or failure:

Nontest Techniques for Program Evaluation

- Consumer surveys (of students, parents, and community members)
- Classroom observations
- Analysis of materials and lesson plans
- Follow-up studies
- Monitoring subject area trends
- Curriculum mapping (tracking)
- Writing samples and portfolios
- Checklists
- Interviews
- Demonstrations, exhibits, performances, and so on
- Professional judgments
- Research
- Accrediting association evaluations
- Progress charts
- External evaluation by outside consultants
- Video portfolios

The principal's responsibilities are to assure that continuous program evaluation takes place, that every reliable means of measurement is used to evaluate the curriculum, and that the "right" tool is used for each area of assessment. Last, it is up to the principal and others who run the school to use evaluation results to make appropriate curriculum decisions.

This chapter has provided the essential groundwork that every principal needs to manage the curriculum and to function effectively as instructional leader of the school. Chapter 6 offers similar suggestions for handling internal and external school communications.

Managing Communications in and out of the School

Communication is what education is all about. It is the lifeblood of every school. As in most areas, the principal has the primary responsibility for assuring an effective communication flow throughout the school and between the school and its multiple audiences.

Unfortunately, some principals fail to realize that they are constantly communicating. Every action by the leader sends a message that has the potential for being misread, misconstrued, or misinterpreted. In many situations, secondary principals have a special communication obligation because everybody in town wants to know about the junior and senior high school. In these cases, every communication is partially a sales pitch.

This makes effective communication too important to be left to chance. You can't just let communication happen. It has to be carefully planned, systematically managed, and continuously monitored and refined. This chapter provides the basics for a sound system of internal and external communications for any school.

UNDERSTANDING THE ELEMENTS OF SCHOOL COMMUNICATIONS

Communication isn't just about sending messages. It's also about receiving information and giving feedback. Communication works only if it's a two-way street. As chief communicator for the school, the principal must consider not only the content to be conveyed, but also the capacity of the intended audience to receive it and the likelihood that it will be understood.

The goal of all communication efforts is to transfer ideas and/or information from the source to the intended audience essentially *unchanged* (what is heard is more important than what is said).

175

In every communication situation, the key questions to be asked and answered are:

1. What do you want to communicate?
2. Why do you want to communicate it?
3. Who needs to get the information?
4. How should the information be communicated?
5. When is the best time to communicate it?

A successful communications loop looks like this:

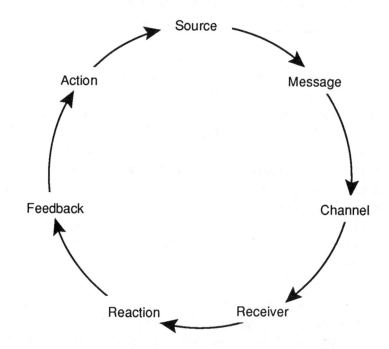

The tricky part of effective communication is that it can break down at any point in the cycle. All of the essential elements have to be in place and properly addressed.

One of the first rules of good communication is to secure the attention of the intended receiver. This requires knowing who your exact audience is and how best to reach them.

HOW TO IDENTIFY AND TARGET YOUR AUDIENCES

Not many executives are called on to play to as many audiences as a secondary school principal. At one time or another, the principal has to communicate specifically to each of the groups identified here and more:

Students	School board
Teachers	Supervisors
Secretaries	Legislators
Custodians	Civic organizations
Cooks	Business groups
Paraprofessionals	Professional organizations
Bus Drivers	Realtors
Aides	Feeder schools
Coaches	Colleagues
Volunteers	Union leaders
Substitutes	Senior citizens
Parents	Alumni
Nonparent taxpayers	Government agencies

Communication does not come in one size that fits all. Not all forms of communication work equally well for all groups. The licensed staff may readily understand the jargon of the profession, but senior citizens may not. Business leaders in the community may be able to grasp and interpret statistical financial information that is only "gobbledy gook" to most parents. Some audiences can and will read published materials prepared by the school, and some will not. Some groups are readily accessible, while others are hard to reach.

A good school communications plan takes into account all these audiences and factors. Each of the school's diverse publics has distinct interests, needs, and agendas. Each, at least sometimes, must be targeted separately.

To be effective in reaching various groups, it helps to keep the specific audience in mind each time you plan a communication strategy. One way to do this is to visualize the targeted individual or group as you draft a memo, prepare a speech, or edit a newsletter. It is also advisable to test communications on representatives of the targeted population before going "public."

When customizing communication for a specific audience, care should be taken to consider not just the content or message, but also the format, medium, delivery, timing, duration and location. Examples of targeted communication strategies include the following:

Targeted Audience	Communication Strategy
Working parents _____	Schedule evening meetings and provide child care
Immigrant families _____	Translate parent letters into appropriate language(s)
Single Parents _____	Avoid use of negative labels (broken homes, nontraditional families, etc.)
Hearing-impaired parents _____	Provide signing interpreters at school functions
Senior citizens _____	Hold meetings in nursing homes and provide large print handouts
Realtors_____	Develop packets containing school information, attendance boundaries, bus routes, and so on
Taxpaying groups _____	Provide truth-in-taxation information showing the impact of proposed bond issues on individual residences
Legislators _____	Provide information through lobbyists and hearing testimony

When trying to match the medium and the message to a particular public, some principals have found it beneficial to call on language arts, speech, and journalism teachers, as well as district public relations personnel, for advice. These specialists can help package generic information to best meet each group's specific areas of interest.

The place to start in designating an effective overall school communication plan is with traditional means of communication that have stood the test of time and still work.

GETTING THE MOST OUT OF OLD STAND-BYS

Recent technologies have given school personnel a new array of communication techniques. Nevertheless, there are certain "bread and butter" tools that continue as the pillars of every school's communication plan. These are information vehicles with which parents and others are familiar and comfortable and that they have grown to trust and count on. The five mainstays of school communication continue to be

1. School newsletters
2. Open houses
3. Progress reports (report cards)
4. Parent-teacher conferences
5. Parent committees

Just because these traditional techniques are as old as the principal and staff members themselves doesn't mean that they are outdated. They still work. You don't discard old stand-bys that continue to get the job done. What principals must do is to dust off these traditional modes of communication, polish them up, and recast them to fit today's needs. Some of the best ways to get the most out of these communication cornerstones are outlined in the paragraphs that follow.

School Newsletters

District publications often go unread by lots of people, but individual school newsletters have extremely high interest appeal and maximum readership. People want to read about their students, other people's kids, and what's happening in "their school." The school newsletter is the principal's most personal and powerful means of communicating with the parent population and others. (Where budgets permit, it's good public relations to mail the school newsletter to all residents.)

With modern desk-top publishing technologies, there is no excuse for any secondary school not having a classy, appealing, and professional-looking parent-community newsletter. One of the first things a school leader can do to upgrade the school's image and public information program is to dress up his or her parent newsletter.

The problem with too many school newsletters is that they are too vague, too long, too preachy, and too boastful (or, sometimes, too defensive). Other common pitfalls in school publications include overusing technical terms and acronyms, sending mixed messages, and talking down to readers. These are the initial things to look at when upgrading your school newsletter.

Other ways that professionals use to improve newsletters are:

- Develop an interesting, appealing and catchy name and logo for your publication—something that sets it apart and establishes your school's identity.
- Refuse to be boring. Don't print filler or stacks of statistics.
- Use bold, attention-grabbing headlines.
- Include lots of student quotes, student writing, and other examples of student work.
- Don't be afraid to use a "Principal's Corner" column to get across your personal priorities as school leader.
- Concentrate on a brisk to-the-point writing style.

- Insert calendars whenever appropriate. Parents love to clip calendars for refrigerator display.
- Insist on clear photographs and reproductions of student artwork. With today's technology, these reproductions don't have to look amateurish.
- Don't whitewash controversial issues. Face them squarely with all the facts you can marshal.
- Don't hesitate to intersperse white space with print. Crowded copy doesn't get read.
- Use tear-off sheets to generate feedback and encourage two-way communication.
- Have several people proofread all copy. Somehow, even minor errors appear glaring when they crop up in school publications and sometimes can be quite embarrassing (example: the misprinted masthead that read, "Pubic Schools").
- The school newsletter that goes into the home of every parent is the single most important public relations and communications document you prepare during the year (preferably on a quarterly basis.) Give it your best effort and get professional help when needed. Two partial examples are included to illustrate effective newsletter formats.

Open Houses

Just as school newsletters continue to be read faithfully by most parents, the traditional "open house" still draws a remarkably high percentage of attendance. This annual event provides a rare chance to bring large numbers of parents and other relatives into the school to meet face to face with the professional staff. It is too good an opportunity to let pass without making the most of it.

An open house should be much more than a time for parents to visit the school, see classrooms, and match up teachers' names and faces. It is the best opportunity of the year to give large numbers of people first hand information about school programs, goals, expectations, and procedures in one place at one time. Principals should insist that all teachers provide parents and others will all the following information, orally and in writing, as part of the open house program:

- Syllabus/course outline
- Homework expectations
- Grading requirements/standards
- Discipline policies
- Attendance and other pertinent procedures

Other ways to make your open house work better are to provide child care; offer refreshments, supply building maps and student guides, show videos of school activities, and solicit feedback through brief evaluation forms.

A Publication of St. Louis Park Senior High School — A National School of Excellence

NOVEMBER 1989

EMERGENCY INFORMATION

A reminder to parents and guardians who have not completed the school emergency procedure card and health form. It is very necessary to have this information in the event your child is injured and unable to provide us with emergency phone numbers.

If you need any additional forms, call or have your child pick them up in Health Services.

PARENT-TEACHER CONFERENCES

St. Louis High School will be hosting our annual Parent-Teacher Conferences November 15–17. Conference time is an excellent opportunity for parents to provide teachers with insights regarding their sons and daughters and for teachers to update parents on their son/daughter's progress. If parents are unable to attend the conferences at any of the times listed below, teachers would be happy to arrange an appointment for an individual conference.

Conference times for 1989–90 are:

Wednesday, November 15	6:00–9:00 P.M.
Thursday, November 16	11:30–3:15 P.M.
Friday, November 17	5:30–8:30 P.M.
	8:00–11:45 A.M.

ADVANCED PLACEMENT COURSES

Advanced Placement (AP) is a program sponsored by The College Board which offers high school students the opportunity to take courses within high school for college credit. At the end of each year The College Board administers examinations for students who have participated in Advanced Placement courses. The results of these examinations usually provide a student with college credit and advanced placement in college classes. Although each college determines its own policy on accepting AP exams, most colleges give advanced placement credit for scores of 3 to 5 on the College Board scale which ranges from 1 to 5.

In May of 1989, 53 St. Louis Park students tested in four different areas for Advanced Placement courses—in the English Literature, and Composition, European History, American History, and Calculus. Of those students, a total of 38 received scores of 3 or above in The College Board test. The following chart indicates student's scores for the Advanced Placement classes. It is an extraordinary accomplishment to have 70 percent of the students testing in the course to receive a grade of 3 or above. The students who participated in these classes, as well as the staff members—Marjorie Bingham, MaDonna Leenay, and Rollie Hanks, are to be congratulated for their accomplishments.

Score	1	2	3	4	5
U.S. History	3	6	4	6	5
European History	0	1	1	4	3
English Lit/Comp.	2	2	1	7	3
Calculus	0	1	1	2	1
Total	5	10	7	19	12

Building Bridges

Between School And Home

St. Louis Park Junior High School

October, 1990

STUDENTS WIN DESIGN CONTEST

by Paul Preus

Last spring three Park Junior High Technology students were awarded prizes for designing posters on recycling for a state competition in MR PREUS' seventh-grade Industrial Technology classes. JODY PAULSEN received first place honors, JENNY TRAN captured second place, and JENNY MADSEN took third place.

In April twelve posters were selected by art teacher MR. GULSTRAND and sent to state. In June Park Junior High was notified of the winners. Accordingly the Minnesota Technology Education Association awarded $250 to Park Junior High.

Receiving honorable mention were AMY DONAHUE, ROBERT GANGL, CLAIRE GOLDSTEIN, SARA GRIMALDI, SARA KLATT, SHANNON KLINEPIER, CHELSEA KNUDSEN, and ANGIE STORLIE.

First place, Jody Paulsen

Progress Reports (Report Cards)

Students and parents expect report cards and pay attention to them. The pupil progress report is the one piece of communication from the school that is read by virtually all members of the intended audience. Rightly or wrongly, most people believe that report cards tell them something relevant and important. It is up to the school and its leader to make sure that this expectation is fulfilled.

The traditional A,B,C progress report no longer fills the bill. The school owes students and parents more complete and definitive information about individual progress and mastery of specific learner outcomes. A few schools have begun to use pupil mastery profiles to replace the traditional report card. Even where parents demand the time-honored A,B,C format, efforts should be made to supplement letter grades with more precise progress charts and checklists.

Whatever form the report card takes, it should meet the following criteria for effective progress reporting:

1. It should mark and report what the school purports to teach.

2. It should communicate clearly.

3. It should contain as much information as possible (including data on attendance, effort, and behavior).

The report card is the most personal information that the school provides to students and parents. For this reason, teacher comments can provide a significant added dimension to progress reporting. It is unrealistic, however, to expect all teachers to write personal comments for 150 or more students each marking period. One solution is to initiate an automatic system whereby teachers can choose comments from a preselected list of frequently used statements that can, then, be printed out on individual report cards. A list of comments for report cards follows.

Comments for Report Cards

Comments Indicating Positive Behavior

Actively participates	Positive attitude
Applies skills	Respects others
Conscientious	Responsible
Displays self control	Uses study time well
Excellent work	Shows initiative
Follows directions	Well organized
Good listener	Well prepared
Good study habits	Helpful to others
Shows improvement	Works independently
Seeks help if needed	Takes pride in work

Comments Indicating Need for Improvement

Assignments late	Poor use of time
Creates disturbances	Unacceptable language
Disorganized	Work incomplete
Insufficient effort	Lacks interest
Needs more practice	More effort needed

Probably the best way to beef up the communication aspects of progress reports is to issue them more frequently. Many school are now encouraging teachers to issue interim (midterm) reports for all students, not just those who are failing or falling behind.

Anything that improves progress reporting makes a significant improvement in communication between the teacher, the student, and the parent. The report card is the student's individual ledger sheet of learning. It should accurately reflect the pupil's academic debits and credits and should add up to a complete picture of how well the student is doing in junior or senior high school.

Parent-Teacher Conferences

With some reluctance, most secondary schools now have a system of annual parent-teacher conferences. In the best schools, such conferences are conducted at least twice a year.

Some schools follow a format in which parents move from room to room individually with teachers. Others set up the school gymnasium and/or cafeteria with teachers stationed around the area to be accessible to parents. The latter approach saves time, but doesn't permit parents to get a feel for individual classrooms. Under both systems, it's usually difficult for parents to visit with all of the teachers who work with their student. This is the biggest complaint parents have about conferences at the secondary level.

Secondary teachers can thank their elementary colleagues for the advent of parent-teacher conferences in junior and senior high schools. Parents have demanded that conferences be extended to secondary schools because they worked so well in the lower grades.

Parent-teacher conferences are often the only opportunity during the year for the teachers to meet privately, one-to-one with the parents of most of their students. (Attendance at secondary conferences often runs as high as 70 percent and up.)

Individual conferences are usually too brief and, often, incomplete—but they *are* up close and personal. Done right, they are the most effective communication tool available to the school and make the most lasting impression on parents.

Conferences should do more than deal with numbers and grades. Report cards can do that. Teachers should use conference time to talk about feelings, impressions, attitudes, and values. They should also use this opportunity to show parents examples of what the student has accomplished and how the pupil's work stacks up against his or her potential and the work of others. More and more schools are developing individual student portfolios (collections of student work, projects, tests, reports, etc.) to use as the basis for evaluating students and conducting parent conferences.

One way to wring the greatest value out of a brief conference session is to have both parents and teachers prepare for the conference in advance.

Some schools have had success in issuing guidelines for parents to follow in preparing for conference time (see the following "tips").

Tips for Parents in Preparing for Conferences

- Decide in advance which teachers absolutely have to be seen at conference time and which should be seen only if time permits.
- Discuss with your student any items that should be brought up at the conference.
- Plan to share any special conditions or concerns that will help teachers better understand your student.
- List in advance the questions you want to ask and things you want to find out from each teacher.
- Ask how you can help at home with any problem area.
- Take notes during the conference if necessary.
- Review the conference with your student.
  - Praise/reinforce strengths and positive accomplishments.
  - Don't shy away from discussing problems and areas for improvement.
- If needed, develop an action plan with your student and follow through.
- Feel free to check on your student's progress between conferences.

The principal sets the tone and attitude of the staff regarding parent conferences. The message should be clear that parent conferences are an opportunity, not just an obligation.

Parent Committees

Many administrators abhor committees. We've all had nightmarish experiences with committees that did more bickering than business, didn't know what they were supposed to do or how to do it, wasted time, and ended up accomplishing nothing. It doesn't have to be that way.

Committees can be extremely useful to:

- Gather information
- Learn different views
- Sample opinions and perceptions
- Discuss problems and alternatives
- Brainstorm solutions
- Reach consensus on issues
- Help reach decisions
- Feed communication back into the broader community

As a principal, you might as well get used to working with committees. They are an inevitable and integral part of the school's communication and decision-making system.

Committees can work. It is up to the school leader to see that they do. The following measures will help get the most out of any parent committee:

1. Define the committee's purpose or the problem to be solved up front. Spell out the parameters clearly and honestly. If the committee is advisory only, make that fact clear and indicate for whom the advice is intended.

2. Determine membership carefully. Broad-based representation is usually best, but size must be a consideration. Any committee larger than ten is likely to run into problems of logistics and scheduling and consensus will be harder to reach.

3. Establish early on the time frame in which the committee will function. Most committees should eventually work themselves out of business.

4. Explain clearly what product is expected from the committee (summary of finds, recommendations, etc.)

5. Identify what reserves (funds, clerical support, etc.) are available to the committee.

6. Provide a suitable environment for committee work.

7. Start with a process for enabling members to get to know each other.

8. Provide all members with sufficient (and the same) background information.

9. Distribute agendas prior to all committee meetings.

10. Insist on setting, starting, and ending times for all meetings and enforce them.

11. Develop a process for keeping some record of committee progress and accomplishment.

12. Evaluate each committee separately and provide the members with some follow-up concerning the outcomes of their work.

All parent committees serve as important communication links with the community. In many schools today, however, a new breed of committee has assumed special significance—the parent advisory council (PAC).

GUIDELINES FOR SUCCESSFUL PARENT ADVISORY COUNCILS

Although somewhat recent in origin, parent advisory councils have become common in elementary and secondary schools across the country. Some districts (mostly major cities) have even taken the concept one step farther by the escalating the PAC to the level of a quasi-governing body for the school (see site management discussed in Chapter 1).

With or without any governance authority, parent advisory councils are a powerful conduit for communication throughout the community. As such, they need to be properly conceived, clearly defined, well organized, and carefully guided in their year-to-year operation.

Many principals get extremely nervous and uptight when they hear about parent advisory committees. They fear loss of control, threats to authority, and, perhaps, ultimate insurrection. If you're one of these, you might as well prepare yourself for a major attitude change. Increased parental input and involvement in school operations is a reality. PACs are here to stay.

The good news is that apprehension about working with PACs is usually a needless overreaction. Used properly, parent advisory councils can be a forceful ally for the principal in supporting decisions and carrying accurate information out into the community. PACs often serve as an effective communications network capable of spreading information rapidly to the school's parent population.

The secret to a successful parent advisory council lies in clearly delineating the purpose and role of the council from the beginning. The operable word in the name of the council is "advisory." Effective PACs give suggestions and advice. They don't set policy, make decisions, or take action. They deal with general issues and matters, not with specific practices or procedures. It must be understood from the outset that the principal remains the responsible and *accountable* leader of the school. The purpose and role of the PAC should be put in writing and normally includes the following functions:

- Acting as a sounding board
- Eliciting and identifying concerns
- Learning more about school programs
- Finding out what the community's questions are
- Brainstorming alternative solutions to problems
- Informing the public about school matters

Once the purpose is spelled out, the way is clear to use the council to help the principal make better decisions and to keep all interested parties better informed about school affairs. The guidelines provided can also assist in getting a PAC off to a good start and helping it to work more smoothly once it is established.

As indicated earlier, the place to start to improve school communications is to fine-tune the five basic information vehicles—newsletters, open houses, pupil progress reports, parent conferences, and parent committees (including PACs). Beyond these old stand-bys, however, there is a virtual cornucopia of communication tools now available to school personnel as described in the next section.

Guidelines for PACs

I. *Membership*

   A. The size of the council must be limited to be workable. (Anything over 15 is probably too cumbersome.)

   B. The membership should consist largely of parent representatives, but some staff members (besides the principal) should always be included.

   C. Only one parent representative should be included from a family.

   D. Potential members may be nominated, but the final election should remain with the principal.

   E. The membership should be representative of different grade levels.

   F. There should be a balance of male and female members and minority populations should be representative.

   G. Terms should be limited to one or two years. (Rotation of membership is healthy for the council and keeps it fresh and vital.)

II. *Officers*

   A. Officers should include, at a minimum, a chair, vice chair, and secretary. (Picking a vice chair to serve in the absence of the chair is critical since busy parents aren't always available for every meeting.)

   B. Officers should be elected by the membership, not hand-picked by the principal.

III. *Meetings*

   A. Regular meetings should be scheduled quarterly. Other meetings may be held as needed.

   B. Meeting times should be set at the convenience of the membership, not the school. Evening meetings are usually best.

IV. *Agendas*

   A. Meeting agendas should be developed mutually by the principal and the other chair.

   B. Any member should be allowed to suggest agenda items.

   C. Agendas should always be distributed prior to each meeting.

BETTER WAYS TO INFORM AND INVOLVE PARENTS AND THE COMMUNITY

Schools now have more means of informing and involving parents and community members than ever before. (Some even manage their own radio and cable television stations.) With today's technology and know-how, there is no excuse for communities being uninformed about school issues or for school leaders to be out of touch with constituent concerns.

Successful principals operate on the basis of full disclosure—no secrets and no surprises. This requires maximum use of all the communication tools at their disposal. Following is a sampling of information strategies and techniques that have worked for schools in all parts of the country.

- Start a parent resource center in the school.
- Include an "open mike" (public concerns) portion at all PTA meetings.
- Institute parent hot lines providing updated school information.
- Hold coffee klatches and brown bag seminar minisessions for parents.
- Arrange to have school messages included on billboards and marquees throughout the community.
- Conduct "whistle stop" tours at the beginning of the year. Have key staff members ride the school bus, stopping at regular stops to visit with residents and answer questions.
- Hold neighborhood meetings throughout the year.
- Make more creative use of the telephone:
  - Call parents who are normally uninvolved in the school.
  - Call parents of students who have extended illness.
  - Call to congratulate parents on school successes.
  - Have students call citizens with invitations to special events.
- Include noncustodial parents in all important school mailings.
- Avoid sending all communications on "official" (and sometimes intimidating) school stationery.
- Expand the number of advisory councils to include separate committees for such areas as:
  - Vocational education
  - Athletics
  - Special education
  - School safety
  - Drug prevention/intervention
  - Gifted education
- Provide incentives for teachers to make home visits prior to the opening of school.
- Encourage local churches to include school information in weekly bulletins and newsletters.

- Hold open office hours on selected evenings and Saturdays.
- Arrange for school displays and expos in local malls.
- Plan a computer fair for parents.
- Invite parents to follow their students' schedule for a day and to eat lunch at school.
- Conduct periodic opinion polls and focus group interviews.
- Develop special publications for parents such as a "Glad You Asked That" pamphlet, parent's manual, gifted program brochure, report card manual, school fact sheets, and so on.
- Develop spot announcements for use with telecasts of athletic contests.
- Convert an old school bus to use as a "school mobile" to carry school displays throughout the community.
- Make maximum use of local residents as volunteers and paid aides in the school.
- Seek legislation to require employers to let workers off with pay to be involved in school activities.
- Develop special "parent kits" such as homework hints or summer activity sheets.
- Use local public access TV to promote school activities.
- Develop an adult-in-the-classroom program so that parents and other citizens can audit high school courses.
- Arrange for students and staff members to appear on local radio and TV talk shows.
- Encourage booster clubs for school activities other than athletic teams (theater, debate, etc.)
- Issue press releases or hold press conferences when needed.
- Organize joint parent-student community service projects.
- Boost attendance at parent meetings by featuring local celebrities, legislators, famous alumni, and so on.
- Organize calling campaigns when communication is critical and time is short.
- Encourage businesses to include tributes to a student of the week in their weekly advertisements or commercials.
- Organize a speaker's bureau of key staff members or student leaders.
- Develop special publications for alumni.
- Display yearbooks in physicians and dentists waiting rooms. (The yearbook serves as an "annual report" of the school.)
- Use social occasions or write a letter to the editor to set the record when necessary.

The communication techniques described have taken on a new meaning as parent choice programs are now making marketing of the school a major responsibility for principals and other administrators.

HOW TO USE CHOICE TO MARKET YOUR SCHOOL

An effective public information program has always been one of the secrets of successful schools. Now it has become a survival technique for many.

Widespread parental "choice" and open enrollment systems are making marketing the school a necessary function of the principalship. It's not surprising, however, that some administrators are less than enthusiastic about this new role. Principal preparation programs seldom include training in sales or public relations. Nevertheless, all principals have to be ready to help their school compete in the educational marketplace.

Gimmicks won't get parents to choose your school. Neither will false modesty nor an inept communication program. The schools that end up winners in the "choice game" will be the ones that offer the best programs, excel at customer service, and know how to tell their story better than others. This is where managing the school's communication program comes in.

Your school's past track record of performance is your best marketing tool; but people have to know about it. Taking the steps that follow will better inform the public and help get parents to pick your school:

1. Make the school the best it can be by using the leadership and management techniques outlined throughout this guide.

2. Use the communication strategies spelled out in this chapter to tell your school's story *simply* and *honestly*. Point out the unique strengths of the school, but don't ignore or deny trouble spots. If the school has problems, talk about how the staff is working with parents to create the school's future. If the student body is racially mixed, talk about the value of diversity. Parents appreciate candor. They know no school is perfect, respect professionals who are unafraid to face, and solve problems and get excited about opportunities to roll up their sleeves to help make their school of choice a better place to learn.

3. Be open to inquiries. Encourage visitations to allow parents to get a feel for the climate and the way people are treated in the school.

4. Prepare a special parent choice packet containing information about the school's mission, goals, curriculum, special programs, support services, extra curricular activities, staff, class size, test scores, and so on.

5. Make sure realtors have accurate information and can answer questions about school offerings and accomplishments.

6. Refer questioning parents to the education editor of the local newspaper for unbiased impression of the school.

7. Make handbooks and school newsletters readily available to interested parents.

8. Use current students and parents as ambassadors for the school. Urge interested parties to talk to those who know the school best to learn how they feel about it.

Good marketing means seizing every opportunity to be proactive in promoting the positive aspects of the school. Unfortunately, not all communication efforts can be proactive and positive. An important part of managing communication in and out of the school is to know how to handle citizen criticism and complaints.

HINTS ON HANDLING COMPLAINTS

A frequently neglected piece of the school's communication plan is the effective handling of community feedback, criticism, and complaints. Many schools excel at disseminating positive information, internally and externally, but do a terrible job of receiving, interpreting, and responding to negative communications received by the school. Unfortunately, not all good communication can be positive and proactive. Some has to be reactive.

In most secondary schools, the principal's office is the "complaint department" where students, staff, parents, and community members register their frustrations and dissatisfaction with any facet of the operation. No one likes to be criticized, but every complaint offers an opportunity to learn something about the organization and how it works and, sometimes, contains some worthwhile suggestions for improvement.

How the principal and staff handle objections and criticism from both the inside and outside has a lot to do with maintaining a positive image throughout the community. Many businesses find that the successful handling of complaints usually results in even greater customer loyalty and support. The same thing works in schools.

The best way to respond to criticism is to meet them head-on and try to resolve the issue face to face with the dissatisfied party. When possible, principals or other staff members should meet personally with complainants. Face-to-face meetings have the advantage of providing opportunities to get insight into opinions, gauge understanding, observe nonverbal cues, and provide immediate counters to adverse reactions. Unfortunately, the face-to-face approach is too time consuming and/or too difficult to schedule to be feasible in all instances.

Often, the telephone is the first conduit for complaints. Switchboard operators and clerical personnel who receive incoming phone calls are often the first person to deal with angry or upset constituents. Their response is critical in determining how well the school is perceived to respond to negative communication. All such personnel should receive specific training in techniques for handling phone calls and, particularly, in dealing with complaints. This training should include:

- How to "speak with a smile"
- Techniques for focusing on the caller
- Proper use of voice, pitch, and tone under pressure
- How to refer complaining parties to someone who can do something about the issue or problem

Since the telephone is the school's "early warning system," all calls and callers must be taken seriously. Many principals insist on a 24-hour response time. (All calls—positive or negative—should be returned within a 24-hour period.) Whenever the school receives several calls with the same complaint, someone (usually the principal) needs to take action. The worst thing principals can do in fielding negative calls is to train their secretaries to be "pit bulls" who intimidate callers, scare off critics, and buffer the boss from unpleasant conversations. Whoever is assigned to take calls from irate callers should be part of the solution—not part of the problem.

Other effective ways that principals and others can respond to complaints include the following:

- Accept the complainant's feelings and hear their ideas.
- Get all the facts you can. Don't commit to a course of action prematurely.
- Don't ridicule or downplay any criticism. Don't tell people who are complaining that they are wrong or out of bounds.
- Don't attempt to bluff or lie to blunt criticism.
- Avoid using any form of abusive or sexist language with anyone complaining about the school.
- Rephrase what you have heard to verify understanding.
- Try to build understanding and/or provide straight answers or find someone who can.
- Commit to look into the matter. Don't hesitate to investigate any complaint.
- Support good suggestions even when they are presented in anger.
- If you cannot agree with or act on the complaint, tell the aggrieved party what other avenues are open to them (talk to your supervisor, write the school board, etc.)
- If there's nothing else to do, respectfully agree to disagree with the complaining party.

Handling adverse criticism isn't fun. Not handling it is unacceptable. It's all part of managing the school's communications.

The previous sections have dealt with the school's communication with the outside world. Of course, the most frequent and direct communication takes place within the school itself.

TWENTY-FIVE WAYS TO IMPROVE COMMUNICATION WITH STUDENTS

It's virtually impossible for principals not to communicate with students. If you don't go to them, they'll come to you. The issue is the quality of communication between the principal and students, not the quantity of communication. An open, two-way exchange of information with the student body is critical to the operation of the school. If the school leader is out of touch with the students, there can be no realistic or effective leadership.

Good principal-student communication must go beyond traditional bulletin boards, public address announcements, and assembly programs. Successful principals find a variety of ways to get important information to all the students who need it and to gather valid student input regarding issues facing the school. Following are 25 means for enhancing student-principal interaction that have worked in secondary schools across the country.

Twenty-five Ways to Improve Communication with Students

1. Rethink the role that an advisor-advisee program may play in your school. Many schools (particularly middle and junior high schools) are considering or readopting such programs.

2. Hold regularly scheduled information-exchange meetings with student leaders (including gang leaders where appropriate).

3. Develop an effective student handbook (see sample outline).

4. Include students on staff committees.

5. Provide students with folders or notebook-binders containing school facts, schedules, and so on.

6. Welcome new students personally to establish a communication channel from the very beginning.

7. Develop special brochures for specific subgroups within the student body (information for seniors only, student athlete's handbook, etc.)

8. Make sure the school's student grievance procedure is well publicized and taken seriously.

9. Run student information and announcements during the day over closed-circuit TV monitors throughout the school.

10. Hold an activity fair to help students learn about extracurricular opportunities. Include a "Name-Your-Own-Activity" booth to solicit suggestions for new extracurricular offerings.

11. Take time to sit in on and participate actively in classroom discussions on topics of student concern. Try to find out what students worry about, believe, and care about.

12. Check regularly on the kinds of complaints students make to secretaries, custodians, counselors, attendance clerks, and so on.

13. Host student leaders at an informal backyard barbeque.

14. Use coaches and activity advisors to convey important messages or policy changes when appropriate. They usually command more credibility than administrators. When the coach speaks, students listen.

15. Release selected teachers from regular supervisory assignments to have time to monitor and mentor individual students who are at risk.

16. Hold a school improvement contest to generate student ideas for making a better school.

17. Ride the school bus a few times each year and listen to what students are talking about.

18. Don't be afraid to use the student newspaper to inform and advise. It's not inappropriate for the principal to write a letter to the editor for publication in the school newspaper.

19. Develop a series of informational audio- and videotapes available for check out by students and parents.

20. Request permission to review student journals from which pupil names have been removed.

21. Make it a point to listen to the school radio station and to watch student produced cable TV shows or videos.

22. Help chaperone student activities and field trips.

23. Eat lunch in the student cafeteria on a regular basis.

24. Conduct exit interviews with students who are moving, transferring, or planning to drop out of schools.

25. Let students evaluate the administration at the end of the school year.

Student Handbook Outline

Athletics	Lost/found
Attendance	Makeup work
Chemical health	Marking system
Class load	Parking
Clubs	Recognition
Cocurricular activities	School buses
Counseling services	Sexual harassment
Dress	Special education
Examinations	Student records
Graduation requirements	Support services
Grievance procedure	Telephone messages
Library, media center	Tobacco
Lockers	Transfers

It takes extra effort for the principal to maintain close communication with the student body, but it pays off by keeping the school's leadership grounded in reality. The same effect and the same payoff applies to fostering effective internal communication channels with the staff.

ORGANIZING FOR EFFECTIVE INTERNAL STAFF COMMUNICATION

Good school communication starts with the staff. No team can function effectively unless all players know the rule book and the game plan: everyone has to be invited to the huddle. Successful internal communication means making sure that the staff is informed first about all important school issues and that no one is left out of the loop. Staff members seldom support initiatives or policies that take them by surprise.

On the surface, maintaining open, two-way communication with the staff seems easy. You work with them every day and can see them almost at will. In reality, it takes a creative and varied mix of communication channels to assure adequate give and take with the entire staff.

Some principals rely too heavily on regular faculty meetings as the mainstay of internal communications. Most staff meetings are too short to accomplish meaningful exchanges. Traditional faculty meetings are also hampered because they are usually scheduled before school when teachers are anxious to get going for the day or at school's end, when they want and deserve a break. A better approach is to hold small-group minimeetings throughout the day during teacher's prep periods.

No matter how staff meetings are scheduled or how effective they may be, they need to be supplemented with different forms of written and oral information. Many principals use a weekly bulletin to keep staff members abreast of school events and developments (see sample). Other examples of effective in-house written communication include staff handbooks, curriculum ideas exchange newsletters and staff wellness notes.

No amount of written material, however, can substitute for frequent face-to-face contacts with all staff members.

This doesn't happen accidentally. It takes a certain amount of structure and organization to guarantee optimum principal-staff interaction. Principals should try out a variety of formal communication models such as monthly department head meetings, staff forums, a faculty senate, regular meeting with union leaders, weekly breakfast meetings, staff retreats, and so on before settling on the system best suited to their particular school. In addition to structured communication channels, excellent schools are tied together by a network of informal information systems. Many principals find that an hour "hanging out" in the staff lounge is worth more than any formal faculty meeting.

St. Louis Park
Junior High School
Weekly Bulletin

SUCCESSFUL LEARNING TODAY...
PRODUCTIVE LIVING TOMORROW
S.L.T... P.L.T.

JANUARY 14-18, 1991
WEEK 1

SUPERVISION DUTY	1st Floor	R. Bergman
	Front Foyer	P. Carollo
	Fr. Foyer 2	J. Anderson/E. Adolpson
	Sec. Floor 218	G. Jenson/L. Wangen
	Sec. Floor 217	M. Buehler
	Cafe Act. Area	P. Geller/J. Richter
	Bus Sup.	J. Bemis/P. Geller

MONDAY   7:30   Short briefing for teachers involved in SRA testing
1/14   Pledge of Allegiance
                Notebook/Assignment Sheet check day
                   A—English (assignment sheet)
                   B—Math (notebook organization)
          2:45   Short briefing for teachers involved in SRA testing
          3:30   "Special help" bus
          3:45   Girls BB., SLP at Northview
          7:30 P.M.   Pilot Program Parents Meeting, Media Center

TUESDAY   **SRA Testing**
1/15   7:30 P.M.   Pilot program parents meeting, Media Center

WEDNESDAY   **SRA Testing**
1/16   1:00   Administrative/counselor meeting
          3:00   Department meetings: L. Mgt Skills, Ind. Tech., Spec. Ed.,
                 Science
          3:45   Girls BB., Wayzata West at SLP
          7:30 P.M.   Pilot program parents meeting, Media Center

THURSDAY   **SRA Testing**
1/17

FRIDAY   **SRA Testing**
1/18   6:15 A.M.   Staff breakfast (Embers, Highway #394/Pennsylvania)

COMING EVENTS

JANUARY	21	Staff development, no school
	22	Begin Winter II (Boys' Swim and Boys' Basketball)
	24	End of 2nd quarter
	25	Workshop, No school
	28	Student of the month due to Mark Haskins
	31	Concert, 8th Band and 7/8 Orchestra
FEBRUARY	5	Parent information night
	8	Issue 2nd quarter report cards
	18	Presidents' Day, no school

It's up to each principal to design an internal communication plan that keeps information flowing freely among all segments of the staff. Whatever it takes, it's worth it. No principal can afford to be cut off from staff concerns, ideas, and suggestions. A leader who is insulated or isolated is no leader at all.

Handling school communications represents the human side of leadership. Well-rounded principals also need to know how to manage a number of nonhuman resources vital to the school's operation, as detailed in Chapter 7.

Managing the Nonhuman Resources of the School

Managing people and programs are the most important things a principal does. To get this job done, however, means managing all the forces and factors that contribute to how people work and learn. The principal has to be ready and able to assemble and use all of the ingredients it takes to make a winning school.

Although human resources come first, effective leaders must also know how to manage a host of nonhuman resources so that they support and facilitate successful teaching and learning. Besides students and staff, the most critical resources available to the school are *time, money* and *space*.

This chapter focuses on the fundamentals of marshaling those nonhuman resources so that they boost the school's chances for success. The first section explains what it takes to handle the principal's budget and business responsibilities.

GUIDELINES FOR SUCCESSFUL SCHOOL BUSINESS AND BUDGET MANAGEMENT

Some principals take great pride in their business sense and recordkeeping know-how. Many others, however, are very uncomfortable with the business side of running a school. Both can succeed. Most principals are hired for their leadership skills, not their ledger books. The nuts and bolts of commanding the school's fiscal and business affairs can be learned. This section explains how it's done.

A modern secondary school budget is complicated and, sometimes, ambiguous—but it need not be threatening or mysterious. Managing the school's financial resources starts with understanding what the budget is and is not. The first thing the principal needs to know is that no budget is ironclad. The budget isn't a law. No principal will serve jail time for over- or underspending or for moving funds around within accounts. Basically, the school's budget is a process, a predictive mechanism, and a planning document. Budgets are intended to be organic. They are living documents designed to *guide* the allocation of resources and the school's pattern of expenditure. Budgets can be changed at any time. Every school's budget includes both "fixed" (locked-in) and "variable" (subject-to-change) components. The principal must learn which is which in order to know where there is flexibility.

The principal's basic budget responsibilities include:

1. Developing a reasonable, responsible and responsive building-level budget

2. Justifying (selling) the school's budget to the district office

3. Administering expenditures

4. Maintaining up-to-date records and information so that those in and outside the school can readily track where the money has gone and what is left

5. Maintaining and adjusting the budget to meet changing circumstances and unexpected developments

Half the battle is won once a budget is developed and adopted. Budgets are made up of both essentials and discretionary items that reflect the wishes of lots of people. The person responsible for budget development (principal or other designated administrator) should start by working with the total staff to identify current (short-term) and future (long-range) needs. When choices and compromises have to be made, the principal should make them based on the best interests of the school and the best ways to achieve the organization's overall goals. Budget decisions by the principal may require an explanation, but no apologies are necessary.

Building the budget is primarily a matter of discipline and timing. The process should begin early enough to permit broad-based input and proper planning. Many principals find it helpful to establish a budget development calendar similar to the sample timetable provided.

School Budget Development Calendar*

September	Adjust current year's budget as result of summer evaluation/planning.
October	Make preliminary enrollment projection and staff count as basis of projected budget estimates for coming year.
November / December	Gather staff input and budget suggestions for coming year.
January	Develop tentative budget for coming year.
February	Hold staff forum(s) to review tentative budget for coming year.
March	Finalize registration/enrollment for following year and complete budget proposal.

April	Submit proposed budget and rationale for coming year to district office.
May	School board adopts district budget for coming year (including secondary budget plans).
	Conduct year-end program evaluations to determine necessary budget changes for coming year.
June–August	Plan and effect program changes and budget adjustments for coming year.

*Exact dates will vary depending on local situations and district fiscal calendars.

After a financial plan is in place, these guiding principles can help the principal carry out a sound program of business management and budget administration within the school:

School Budget Management Principles

- Understand your own budget! If any areas are unclear, ask for help. Don't fake it.

- Review monthly budget reports and printouts carefully. Ask for clarification if necessary, and "red flag" any trends that may trigger trouble in the future.

- Be conservative in planning and approving expenditures. Don't spend money just because you have it.

- Have a reason for allocating funds and approving expenditures among departments and programs. (Past history may not be sufficient reason for continuing expenditure patterns. Resources should be allocated on the basis of real needs and school goals—not merely because of tradition and past practice.)

- Make periodic checks of variances between budgeted amounts and actual costs. Insist on reliable and realistic information. Use records to track what's going on.

- Establish a system of checks and balances. More than one person should be involved in allocating funds, authorizing expenditures, and monitoring the budget. Welcome audit opportunities.

- Pay enough attention to monthly budget activity to avoid surprises.

- Hire a good bookkeeper and use up-to-date technology to assure accurate recordkeeping.

- Stress precision and accuracy in accounting. Emphasize the importance of "doing it right the first time."

- Allow for a margin of error. Always maintain a "rainy day" fund tucked away somewhere in the school's budget.

- Get to know vendors to help staff members find the best buys and stretch limited budget dollars.

- Don't be afraid to reallocate resources as new needs arise.

- Help subordinates to handle their budgets. Department heads and program managers may need advice and assistance to monitor and administer their share of the school budget. Keep responsible parties informed of the status of their portion of the budget.

- Be honest. Never cut corners or violate legal requirements.

- Own up to mistakes and problems promptly and openly.

- Know when and how to complain about the building budget. There may be times when the principal needs to lobby district personnel for extra funds to do the job expected of the school.

No matter how carefully the budget is planned and managed, there never seems to be enough money. Creative leaders, however, can often give their school an edge by capitalizing on resources that may be available outside the regular budget. Many secondary schools augment their established budgets by getting additional monies from sources such as civic club donations, PTA funds, booster clubs, fundraisers, vending machine proceeds, and so on. Good principals are not only prudent stewards of the school's money, but are also scavengers for additional resources to support important programs and goals.

In a growing number of school situations, the principal's role in budget development and operation has been intensified by moves toward decentralized budget decision-making programs such as PPBES, (program planning, budgeting and evaluation system), which is described in detail in the next section.

WHAT THE PRINCIPAL NEEDS TO KNOW ABOUT "PPBES"

Two common threads running through current educational reform movements are *accountability* and *decentralized decision making*. The result has been widespread adoption of some form of program-based budgeting (often labeled PPBES). In short, PPBES is bottom-up budget-building based on identification of program goals and evaluation of results. Under this approach, financial plans are developed by school staffs and building program managers rather than by district personnel who are one-step removed from the daily action of teaching and learning.

PPBES places the principal at the heart of budget development. It puts a premium on building programs and priorities. This is the kind of budgeting the building leaders can get excited about. Principals who understand program-based budgeting are positioned to maximize their impact on allocating resources to support the programs they believe in.

A textbook definition of PPBES might read like this: "A systematic approach to the allocation of resources for the accomplishment of priority objectives." In layperson's terms, this means "putting your money where your mouth is." The basic premise is that goals and results should define the budget, not vice versa. PPBES starts with pinpointing goals and measuring how well programs are succeeding and ends up by allocating funds to sustain and improve the programs that work. Under a PPBES program, the budget is only the tip of the iceberg in sound educational and financial planning as illustrated:

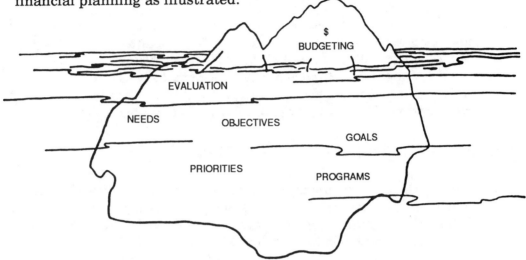

The goals of PPBES include the following:

1. Put money where it counts for excellence.
2. Demonstrate that resources are used to support effective programs.
3. Track costs on a building-level program-by-program basis.
4. Use evaluation to make annual program and budget decisions.
5. Gather data to determine goals as the basis for budgeting.
6. Use results to improve instruction—not just to prove it.
7. Identify program/performance goals and spend money where it is needed to produce desired results.
8. Make the budget a by-product of program objectives.
9. Link evaluation, curriculum, and instruction directly to budgeting.
10. Provide financial reporting that more people can understand.

Some principals are intimidated by the responsibility of program-based budgeting and would prefer that another authority decide how much money the school gets and how it should be spent. This is the wrong arena, however, for timidity or tentativeness. A bigger say in budgeting can help the school achieve its dream.

What the principal does in a PPBES model is:

- Lead the staff in identifying school goals and objectives.
- Coordinate a building-level assessment program to evaluate current program results measured against the school's identified goals.

- Use what evaluation results tell the staff to plan program adjustments that will better meet building goals.

- Develop a budget that supports the school's plans and goals.

Principals don't have to be financial wizards to manage a building-level/program-based budget program. They do, however, have to be leaders and planners. After all, that's what principals do for a living.

No matter what kind of budget a principal works under, there are going to be times of financial constraint, belt-tightening, and retrenchment. The next section offers tips on handling periods of cost containment.

WHAT TO DO IN TIMES OF COST CONTAINMENT

Hard times hit all organizations. Schools, however, seem particularly vulnerable to budget reversals because of their dependency on economy-driven tax dollars and the mood swings of fickle elected bodies. Sooner or later, every principal will probably have to deal with some kind of budget reductions.

Budget cuts are hard on everyone. The leader's responsibility is to help maintain perspective and prevent fiscal setbacks from devastating the entire institution. No matter how bad the budget news is, the business of the school must go on, and students must continue to receive the best possible educational program within available resources.

Cost containment can't be allowed to become all consuming. The best approach is to be as creative and positive as possible. Sometimes good things can come out of troubled economic conditions. Just because reductions are necessary, doesn't mean that some things can't be improved at the same time. The first steps are to search for new ways of doing things and to look for efficiencies as well as cuts. Money saved through economies means fewer outright cutbacks in the long run.

A workable cost containment process that can be applied in any school setting includes the following components:

1. Work with district personnel to identify the level of reductions needed.
2. Gather complete information to give all parties involved a realistic picture of the situation. It is important that everyone has the same facts.
3. Hold staff meetings to explain what has to be done and why and to map out a budget reduction process and timetable.
4. Develop agreed-upon criteria for determining budget reductions (see the criteria that follow).
5. Collect suggestions for possible reductions and economics from all parties involved (see Cost-Containment-Suggestion Form). Collaboration is crucial. Opportunities for input should be extended to as many stakeholders as possible. Don't leave out unions and other collective bargaining groups.

6. Meet with staff and community groups to prioritize the list of suggested cost savings.
7. Finalize the list of cost-containment measures.
8. Effect economies and implement reductions.

Values / Criteria for Determining Reductions

- Reductions will not be across the board. Decisions will be based on student and program needs.
- Any cuts should be as far away from instruction as possible.
- There will be no "sacred cows." All areas and programs will be subject to scrutiny with survival dependent on merit.
- The school's vision, mission, belief statements, and goals should determine budget priorities.

Cost Containment Suggestion Form

Name of Program of Service: _____

1. Circle the type of cost-containment measure this is:

             Program Reduction   Efficiency/Effectiveness
                                                 Measure

2. Describe the suggested cost containment measure: _____

_____

3. Project annual savings from this suggestion:

             Type of Savings   Dollars

_____   _____

_____   _____

4. Who would be responsible for implementation? _____

5. Projected offsetting costs (Do we have to spend money to save money)?

        Type of Offsetting Costs   Dollars

_____   _____

_____   _____

6. Positive implications of implementation: _____

_____

7. Negative implications of implementation: _____

_____

                (Name)   (Date)

In implementing any cost containment process, it is helpful to develop alternative scenarios of the ramifications of suggested cutbacks. Be realistic. Don't propose cuts that can't really be made because of existing mandates, contractual commitments, or legal requirements.

In most cases, the sooner that cuts can be made, the better, because of the greater cumulative impact over time ($1,000 saved this year amounts to $2000 in savings in the second year.) However, programmatic, political, or morale considerations may dictate that reductions be phased in.

School leaders are also cautioned to avoid cutting too much out of communications or public relations budgets. Understanding and support are crucial to surviving periods of retrenchment. If anything, effective communications are more important in hard times than when things are going well.

In good times and bad times, one thing never changes in running the business side of the school—*paperwork.*

WORK ORDERS, REQUISITIONS, PURCHASE ORDERS, AND INVOICES

Nobody like paperwork. Some observers believe that paperwork drives more educators out of the principalship than rowdy students and demanding parents combined. Nevertheless, managing the budget and business of the school means managing the paperwork that goes with it. This is part of the bargain the principal makes in taking the job as leader of the school.

A certain amount of paperwork is essential:

- to document budget activities
- to maintain effective financial records
- to generate required fiscal reports
- to provide supporting data for solid budget and business decision making

Work orders, requisitions, purchase orders, and invoices are all necessary to sound business. Without a proper paper trail, people inside the organization have difficulty in determining what has happened, what is happening, and what is likely to happen regarding the budget and business affairs of the school. All these documents are basic to charting the history and health of the organization. They represent accountability in black and white.

Regardless of how vast or limited the principal's business background may be, the following guidelines can help in keeping budget paperwork on track and the school's business affairs in order:

- Look for ways to reduce or combine paperwork whenever possible. (See the section "Practical Ways to Reduce Paperwork" later in this chapter.)
- Make it a habit to strive for efficiency and to avoid duplication.

- Use technology wherever possible to save time and diminish the drudgery of recordkeeping and reporting.

- Don't neglect or ignore necessary paperwork. When administrators fall behind in handling work orders, requisitions, purchase orders, and invoices, they are susceptible to a variety of embarrassing and unpleasant surprises.

- Maintain backup records of all transactions.

- Don't let one person do it all. Provide double-checks and balances for every step of the process.

- Keep all forms as simple as possible (see sample forms later in this section).

- Train staff to fill out all required forms and records completely and to adhere to established procedures.

- If mistakes occur or questions can't be answered, get help quickly. District business personnel can usually help unravel mysteries in budgeting, accounting, recordkeeping, and reporting.

- Don't let paperwork pile up in the absence of regular office staff members. Don't hesitate to hire substitutes or bring in temporary help to keep current in processing requisitions, purchase orders, and so on.

- Direct office personnel to segregate all requisitions, purchase orders, invoices, and work orders into priorities and to deal with *all* top-priority items first.

- Track the differences between purchase orders and invoices. Actual costs may vary dramatically from quoted prices because of price changes, mailing/shipping charges, quantity discounts, and so on. All such variances have some positive or negative impact on the school's budget.

- Keep staff members informed of the status of all work and purchase orders. Some principals provide monthly status reports so that the staff can anticipate when items will be received or requested work orders completed.

- To the extent possible, insist that bills be paid promptly. A reputation for slow payment can come back to haunt the school in the form of disgruntled vendors, poor service, and slow shipment. It can also result in the school being left out of special offers and other "good deals" from suppliers.

Part of managing the nonhuman resources of the school is understanding that when the paperwork part of the budgeting process is right, the whole system works better. Principals don't have to like paperwork, but they do have to see that it gets done. Experienced administrators have learned that it doesn't pay to get sloppy. If the paperwork is complete, accurate, and up to date, business operations run smoothly and people have greater confidence in the school.

Combined Claim and Claim Verification Form

_____   Date _____
(Claimant Name)

_____
(Claimant Address)

_____

I declare under the penalties of law that this account, claim, or demand is just and correct and that no part of it has been paid.

Date _____   Signed _____
                              (Claimant or Agent of the Claimant)

Requisition Sheet

Department _____ Date Wanted _____ Date _____

Teacher _____ Approved By_____

Order From: Ship To:

_____

_____

_____

Phone No. _____ Attention _____ P.O. Order No._____

Qty.	Cat.No.	Description	R—Repairs N—New Equipment S—Supplies NR—New Replacement	Each	Total

As indicated earlier, financial resources vary from time to time. But one resource remains constant—*time*. There is only a finite amount of time available to the principal and staff to achieve the goals of the school. The next section points out ways to get the most out of the time available.

MANAGING TIME AS THE MOST PRECIOUS RESOURCE OF THE SCHOOL

There are lots of things you can do in schools without much money, but you can't do anything if you run out of time. Some administrators are frugal with the school's budget, supplies, and other assets, while squandering its most precious resource and allowing others to do the same. Time is the real currency of learning. It should be consciously budgeted and managed like other nonhuman resources at the school's disposal. Efficient use of time can make the difference between a winning school and the rest of the pack.

Principals should take the lead in showing the entire organization how to make the most of the limited time available. It starts with the chief administrator modeling effective time use in order to teach the whole staff how to master the learning clock. By using the "Time Help Tips" outlined in Chapter 1, the principal can provide an example of successful time management.

The best thing the leader can do to guide the school in conserving and economizing this limited resource is to focus on how the organization actually uses its time. It takes time to save it. Hours spent in analyzing how time is lost or wasted can result in finding ways to work better, faster, and smarter to improve learning. The first step is to focus staff attention on the subtle time wasters that rob staff and students of the time it takes for all students to learn:

- Procrastination
- Waiting
- Lost Stuff
- Socializing
- Mistakes
- Understaffing
- Useless meetings
- Interruptions
- Poor organization
- Paperwork
- Confusion
- Too many goals

One effective means of measuring how well the school uses its time is for the principal to ask the staff the following questions:

1. What routine jobs/meetings take too long?
2. What are we doing that we should stop doing?
3. What jobs could be done more simply?
4. Do we have too many people doing the same thing?
5. How do we waste time each day?
6. What tasks take up more time than they're worth?

7. What time takers do people complain about most?

8. What are we doing on a regular basis that makes us mad/frustrated?

9. What do we do that is just plain dumb?

10. Do we actually realize (know) what we're doing with our time?

11. Do we have a reason for what we do?

Answering these questions can go a long way in making everyone in the school more time conscious and sensitive to making the most of every instructional moment in the school day.

Other common ways that principals have found to help the school stretch teaching and learning time include the following:

- Set and enforce deadlines. Things happen when people know there's a cutoff point at which the time is up for accomplishing specific ends. Some staff members may need to be taught that cutoff times are "real" and that deadlines are more than "guidelines."

- Stress individual and collective goal setting. Goals focus attention on action and serve as a means for gauging progress. Goals are most effective when they are written and broken down into step-by-step activities.

- Model and encourage daily planning for *all* staff members including clerical and custodial personnel.

- Eliminate, combine, or simplify as much paperwork as possible (see section on "Practical Ways to Reduce Paperwork" later in the chapter).

- Review time spent in meetings. Every meeting that doesn't accomplish something specific and/or move the school toward its goals is a multiple time waster (meeting minutes × number of participants = amount of wasted time).

- Minimize classroom announcements and interruptions. Many time-conscious administrators have begun to use written weekly bulletins, electronic message boards, video announcements, and voice mail messages as substitutes for the traditional daily intercom intrusions on instructional time.

- Show teachers and other staff members how to handle intrusive vendors (take their literature and run, don't encourage callbacks, minimize small talk, etc.)

- Examine flexible working time for staff members. Often more can be accomplished if some staff members start and end earlier, while others come later and work beyond the regular duty day.

- Ask the staff for ideas on ways to do things faster and better. (Some of the best suggestions come from the "wisdom of the ant hill.")

In addition to these measures and techniques, two of the principal's most valuable tools for managing the school's time are the master student schedule and the school calendar. The next two sections suggest ways to use these tools to carve out maximum time for instructional use.

SUGGESTIONS FOR EFFICIENT PUPIL SCHEDULING

The master schedule has always been a bugaboo for principals. Developing a daily schedule of classes in a comprehensive junior or senior high school is a highly complex operation. Fortunately, modern technology has made pupil scheduling easier, faster, and more manageable. (Now you can let your computer do the walking.)

The goal of the master schedule is to provide students with the widest possible opportunities to build individual academic programs that meet their specific needs. The master schedule is a primary tool for managing school time to promote maximum learning and productivity.

The difficulty of pupil scheduling is determined by a number of factors including:

- *School size.* Extremely small schools can usually afford only limited offerings and choices. Larger schools can support a much broader base of course offerings and greater flexibility in accommodating student choices. If schools become too large, however, students and parents only become confounded by the proliferation of choices and alternative program packages available to them. Some experts believe that secondary schools with enrollments of between 750 and 1,200 students lend themselves to the most effective pupil scheduling.

- *Number of electives.* The greater the number of elective course offerings, the greater the likelihood of scheduling conflicts and class sizes too small to be cost effective.

- *Number of "singletons."* When a large number of courses or class sections is offered only once a day, flexibility is impaired and scheduling conflicts increase.

- *Length of the school day.* The number of class periods in the day defines the amount of flexibility in pupil scheduling. A five-period day offers little opportunity for choice or straying beyond a narrow band of required subject offerings. Most modern secondary schools find a six- or seven-period day essential to providing a schedule that can meet varied students' interests and needs.

- *Number of part-time teachers.* The larger the number of part time staff members or teachers shared with other schools, the less elbow room the principal has in constructing the school's master schedule. When the daily schedule has to be planned around itinerant teacher assignments, there is less opportunity to build in flexibility for students.

Since time can be carved up in many ways, principals should examine all options for extending the daily schedule to make every minute count for learning. The easiest variables to manipulate are (1) the length of class periods, (2) the number of periods per day, (3) the length and timing of lunch periods, and (4) the time before and after school, which can be converted as a means for offering optional courses to interested students. Additional flexibility can also be gained by negotiating with individual teachers and departments to trade retaining more classes with small enrollments for accepting other classes with larger than normal enrollments.

In addition to managing the time spent in class, veteran administrators consider better ways to use student and staff unscheduled time during the school day. How students and staff members spend their time outside of class has a lot to do with school productivity. Learning doesn't have to be confined to formal class periods. There are lots of ways to help students learn before, after and between classes and during unscheduled periods. These bits of time shouldn't just be lost and go unnoticed. If properly used, they can provide new-found opportunities to stretch the amount of learning time each day.

Some schools have addressed the issue of unscheduled time by adopting an "open-campus" model that permits students to be entirely on their own when not assigned to a formal class. Under this plan, students may use available school facilities or leave the school grounds for their own purposes when not in class. Open-campus advocates argue that this program recognizes the maturing of students, prepares them for college life and adulthood, and helps teach them responsibility, accountability, and decision making. Such a format leaves the use of pupil unscheduled time essentially up to chance. In contrast to the open-campus approach, other schools try to run a tight ship whereby students are assigned somewhere every period of the school day.

In the interest of productivity and effective time use, the best approach seems to be to give students choices of where to spend their unscheduled time, along with a commitment to stick with their choice. Under this model, students may elect to spend "off" periods in the media center, in supervised study areas or labs, working with teachers who are free to help them, or relaxing/studying in the cafeteria or commons areas. Whatever their choice, the students are held accountable for being where they are committed to be. The point is that students are expected to stay in school once they arrive until their final period is over. This does not deny them the flexibility of arriving at school late if their first period is open or of leaving the campus early when all their classes have been completed. This kind of modified "closed campus" plan supports maximum use of school time for school purposes.

How productive student scheduled time may be rests heavily on the way the teachers are deployed when they are not actually teaching an assigned class. Most secondary teachers have a block of unscheduled time each day that can be and is used for a variety of purposes, including:

- Preparation time
- Break time (coffee breaks, socializing, etc.)
- Supervisory assignments
- Time for providing students extra help
- "Dead time"

Within the limits of reason and contractual obligations, the principal should structure the daily schedule to promote optimum use of teacher unscheduled time for lesson preparation, helping students, and supervising study areas and to eliminate or minimize "dead time" as much as possible. Some of every teacher's time out of class should be spent (assigned if necessary) in activities that directly support the instructional program and assist students to catch up, keep up, or move ahead in their academic program.

Once a workable master schedule and a plan for unscheduled time are in place, school personnel can help students and parents to make the best use of the time available by defining expectations for a "normal class load" and stressing the number and nature of courses/credits that colleges and prospective employers look for in evaluating student transcripts.

Just as the master schedule structures the use of time on a daily basis, the school calendar provides a blueprint for how the school uses its time over the entire year.

BASICS FOR PLANNING THE SCHOOL CALENDAR

School years have a way of rushing past. How many principals and teachers have you heard complain, "I don't know where the year has gone"? Without a conscious plan, an academic year can slip by with no rhyme or reason, resulting in activities being hurriedly scheduled at the last minute, too many events piling up at the end of the year, some events conflicting with each other, and others never being worked into the calendar at all.

At best, the American school year comes up short in comparison with the school years in most other modern nations. The traditional nine- or ten-month calendar is no longer relevant or competitive in an age of information glut and exploding technological advancement. Wherever possible, school leaders should press for some extension of our antiquated, agrarian-based school year. Short of this, however, principals and staffs must work with what they have—approximately 170 to 200 student contact days per year.

The annual calendar is the principal's guide to organizing and scheduling key events and activities to get the most efficient use of the total school year. Care spent in mapping out school activities on a year-long basis saves both time and frustration later in resolving conflicts, rescheduling, and/or squeezing in last-minute events. A well-organized school calendar helps everyone plan better for the year.

To put together a logical and workable calendar for the year, the principal needs all the pieces of the puzzle. The best way to begin is to solicit input from all staff members, parent leaders, and community representatives. The goal is to identify early on as many of the major activities that will take place during the year as possible. This can be done by providing all parties involved with a skeleton calendar for the year with certain basic dates and activities listed and asking them to submit any additional activities or events that should be included in the year-long plan.

Once all the components are known, you can structure an agenda for the year that flows smoothly, makes sense, minimizes conflicts, and gives every important event its proper time and attention. The guidelines that follow help make a functional year-long calendar:

- *Mesh the school's calendar with that of other schools and organizations within the community.* You make no friends when an important school activity is in conflict with other events outside the school that may involve students, staff, or parents.

- *Balance the marking periods.* The instructional program is enhanced when there is an equal number of student contact days during each marking period.

- *Avoid chopping up the school year.* Some school calendars schedule non-student activities (holidays, vacations, conferences, staff development programs, teacher workdays, etc.) so that there are almost no sustained periods for instruction. No one likes a stop and go schedule with numerous two-, three- or four-day weeks throughout the year.

- *Respect local taboos.* Don't schedule school activities that conflict with such events as:
  - Traditional "church nights"
  - Elections
  - School board meetings
  - Political caucus nights
  - Town meetings
  - Community celebrations
  - Religious or ethnic holidays

- *Stay away from the days/nights before or after holidays and vacation periods.* Some principals generate unnecessary resentment by scheduling major school events immediately preceding or following holidays or vacations when many students or parents are more interested in stretching their furloughs by leaving a little early or returning a day late. Special air fares and other tourist cut rates provide significant inducement for people to "take an extra day."

- *Lighten up during peak periods.* There are certain times of the year when stress runs high and everyone feels overtaxed (end of marking periods, conference time, etc.) Often the months of October, February, and May are times when teachers feel stretched to the limit. The school calendar should be designed to ease up and stay clear of those natural pressure points during the year.

- *Don't compete with yourself.* The school calendar works against itself when student and staff activities conflict with each other (e.g., scheduling a scholarship information meeting at the same time as a musical concert).

- *Schedule parent conferences at the convenience of parents.* More and more secondary schools are scheduling parent-teacher conference during evening hours when more parents are available. In most schools, it is also important to conduct conferences at least twice a year since many students change courses and/or teachers at midterm. Some schools have also had success in scheduling conferences the same week that some other break occurs (e.g., the days prior to Thanksgiving). This, then, cuts into only one week of instructional time rather than two.

- *Schedule final examinations carefully.* In some situations, the school unravels and simply falls apart at the end of the semester or year. Some classes give final exams and some don't. Some students are required to attend classes while others are excused or dismissed. Anytime that instruction ceases a few days before the term ends, problems are more likely to arise, time is wasted, and things go sour—not a pretty way to end the school term or year.

One way to make the most of the closing days of the school year is to require all courses to give final examinations, to direct that final exams last for the full class period, to excuse students when they have no scheduled class or examination, and to hold final exams for seniors as close to the end of the term as possible.

By following these suggestions, you can construct a school calendar that is a first step toward effectively managing limited school time over the course of the entire year.

Once the annual calendar and the daily master schedule are in place, it is up to the staff to make the most of all the time that has been carefully planned for getting the work of the school done.

As mentioned earlier in the section on budget management, one of the greatest threats to efficient time use and productivity is the mushrooming load of paperwork that relentlessly erodes vital teaching and learning time. As a final note on conserving the school's resource of time, the next section offers new ways to tame the paper tiger.

PRACTICAL WAYS TO REDUCE PAPERWORK

Schools are aflood with paper. Secondary schools seem particularly prone to proliferating an endless series of records and reports. As described earlier, the budget alone necessitates a sizable amount of documentation. In addition, a great deal of paperwork is generated externally by outside agencies such as accrediting organizations, state education departments and state and federal governmental agencies. Last, the school often makes more work for itself by instituting procedures that require more records, more copies, and more files of almost everything. Principals are often astonished when they add up how many pieces of paper it takes to perform routine functions (ordering basic office supplies, changing a student's schedule, keeping attendance, maintaining student records, etc.).

The introduction of new technologies has both eased and aggravated the problem. Computers have obviously reduced or eliminated the need for some records and files. On the other hand, desk-top printers and modern copy machines have made it tempting and easy to produce more and more documents of all kinds. You can now fax anything to anyone and get "faxed" in return.

Increasingly, managing school time to achieve optimum efficiency has become a matter of containing and reducing paperwork at all levels.

The way to gain control of paper overload is to analyze What's going on? Where's the paperwork coming from? Who's doing it? Is it worth it?. When paperwork piles up, the following four-point test can help determine how best to handle it:

Four-Point Paperwork Test

1. Who has the needed information?
2. Who has time to collect and organize the needed information?
3. Who has the people power to get the job done?
4. Who has the best technology for getting the work accomplished in the prescribed manner?

Based on the answers to these questions, the principal can often revise the work flow to increase efficiency and productivity.

Other ways for saving time and cutting down on paperwork are:

• Develop form letters for responding to common inquiries and repeated types of correspondence.
• Don't send or retain needless copies of anything.
• Crack down on the overuse of worksheets by classroom teachers.
• Clean out all files on an annual basis.
• Have secretaries sort out and/or dispose of junk mail.
• Ignore nonsense. Don't spend time responding to trivial and irrelevant requests.
• Train office personnel to compose routine correspondence and memos.
• Put one person in charge of access to copies and fax machines.

- Save copies of key reports as guides for future similar reports.
- Say "no" to redundant surveys. Not all surveys and questionnaires deserve a response. Complete only those that serve your purposes.
- When possible, make one report serve multiple needs. If several information requests require the same or similar data, draft a report that satisfies more than one purpose.
- Don't elaborate when responding to information requests. Limit answers to basic facts. Additional background or qualifying material will usually be lost in the summation process, and, probably, no one cares anyway.
- Highlight salient points in routed printed material to speed up reading time.
- Obey copyright laws. Don't let staff members get in the habit of copying promiscuously everything they see of interest.
- Be strict on use of school time, supplies, and equipment for personal paperwork (correspondence, personal business, etc.).
- Charge back copying costs to appropriate departments.
- Use a key-access system for copying machines.
- Identify a single grants writer on staff. It is better to have one skilled person prepare all grant proposals for the school, than to have several people struggling to complete standard proposal forms of applications.
- Let the people who are good at paperwork do it. Some people have a flair for writing, note taking, and processing paperwork. Others waste time agonizing over simple writing tasks. Build on strengths and organize so that people do what they're good at.

Like these measures, anything that saves paperwork saves time for the real-world work of the school. Managing the paper flow goes hand in hand with managing the school's overall time resources.

The next section provides equally effective tips for managing the third major nonhuman resource: space.

MAKING THE MOST OF YOUR SPACE: EFFECTIVE BUILDING MAINTENANCE

The bricks and mortar of the schools define where and how the learning process takes place. Like all resources, space can be misused, squandered, or wasted. Learning flourishes when ample, adequate, and appropriate space is available and used effectively.

Principals aren't architects or building engineers, but they are accountable for protecting and maintaining the community's substantial investment in the physical plant and for making the best use of existing facilities to achieve educational goals. As chief administrator, the principal's specific responsibilities include:

1. Preserving and maintaining the infrastructure of the school
2. Ensuring that all facilities are safe
3. Providing adequate security throughout the school plant
4. Satisfying relevant building codes and legal requirements
5. Assuring suitable handicapped accessibility
6. Promoting all necessary capital improvements
7. Upgrading facilities and equipment as new and better products become available
8. Continuously adapting the physical plant to changing program and student needs
9. Using facilities efficiently to accommodate both school and community needs
10. Respecting and protecting the building and grounds as the most tangible image of the school and the most obvious symbol of education in the community

Whether or not the principal is familiar with construction and plant operations, the best ways to fulfill these obligations are to hire the best possible custodial and maintenance personnel, to rely on their professional expertise, and to treat them as an integral part of the school team. Job descriptions and work assignments for the custodial staff should be specific and detailed (see the accompanying description). It is easier for the principal to stay on top of what's happening with the physical plant if custodial staff members are assigned to designated areas of the building and held accountable for the total cleaning and maintenance of their assigned areas.

Custodian Job Description

Immediate Supervisor: Head Custodian
Responsibilities:

1. Perform basic mechanical maintenance (lubricating hinges, minor desk repair, locker repair, etc.).
2. Perform basic maintenance on plumbing systems.
3. Assist in building security.
4. Assist in implementing preventative maintenance schedules on building equipment (cleaning univents, lubricating motors, etc.).
5. Follow established procedures in all assigned areas.
6. Maintain standards of building/site cleanliness that provide a healthy, safe, and attractive physical environment.
7. Follow all established safety procedures.

Close communication between the principal and the head custodian is essential to effective building maintenance. Many principals find it beneficial to conduct regular weekly meetings and building walk-throughs with their head custodians. Frequent meetings between the administrators and the entire maintenance staff also keeps the school leaders in touch with physical plant needs and boosts morale and a sense of belonging among the custodial force. Another way to capitalize on staff skills and knowledge is to use custodial personnel as a product quality control council to test and review cleaning products for possible purchase.

The appearance of the building sets the tone for what happens inside. An unkempt building inspires disrespectful behavior and sloppy performance. School facilities get hard use (and, sometimes, abuse) so it is critical to keep up to date on building cleaning, maintenance and repair. Preventative maintenance is not only cost effective, but essential to preserving the school's physical facilities.

Some of the best means for staying ahead of building deterioration and decay are to insist on high standards of cleanliness throughout the physical plant, to conduct frequent checks on all operational systems, to use tickler files to avoid neglecting important work to be done, and to call on outside experts (architects, engineers, building inspectors, etc.) to perform thorough building assessments on a regular basis (every two to five years).

As in all aspects of running the school, the principal and staff need a long range plan for capital improvements and facility use. Part of the planning process must be to constantly look for ways to convert unused, under-used or misused space to accommodate changing programs (e.g., converting an out-dated metal shop to a modern computer-graphics lab). Some schools establish an advisory council made up of staff and community members to project future space needs and suggest ways to make the best use of all school facilities.

Caring for the physical plant now and in the future is only part of the space management equation. The other half is making the best possible use of all existing facilities to promote school and community goals.

HOW TO SCHEDULE FACILITIES EFFICIENTLY AND EFFECTIVELY

Secondary schools contain a variety of specialized facilities (classrooms, gymnasiums, shops, conference rooms, computer labs, swimming pools, athletic fields, etc.) that are constantly in high demand by school and community groups of all kinds. The school belongs to the entire community, so it is the principal's job to allocate space in the most efficient manner possible to enhance lifelong learning for all citizens.

The staff can most easily control use of facilities during the school day. Extending effective use of the physical plant and grounds during nonschool time requires a focused policy on community use (see the accompanying sample), a system for prioritizing building requests, and some carefully developed rules and regulations for the use of school facilities.

Policy on Community Use of School Facilities

_____ Senior High School subscribes to the principles that public schools are owned and operated by and for its patrons and that the school encourages public use of school facilities and participation in community educational opportunities.

Authorization for use of school facilities shall not be considered an endorsement or approval of the activity, group, or organization or the purposes they may represent.

The following guidelines below can assist in assigning priorities for facility use:

- Consider all activities that must take place in the school before scheduling any event.
- Schedule school and parent activities first, district events second and consider other requests based on established priorities and/or a first-come, first-served basis.
- Schedule for maximum flexibility and minimum conflict.
- Provide special rooms for special purposes first.
- Follow district guidelines for assigning building use fees where applicable.
- Don't schedule meetings that may be prejudicial to the best interest of the school or the district.
- Don't hesitate to provide access for religious groups as required by federal regulations.
- Where necessary to avoid or resolve conflicts, negotiate space use by trading off better facilities for less desirable hours.

Some schools have expedited facility scheduling for nonschool purposes by determining priority categories as illustrated:

Priority Groups I

Local public agencies
Civic/charitable groups
Neighborhood associations
Youth serving organizations
City agencies/activities
Local religious groups
  (excluding fund raising events)
Federal, state and municipal
  agencies conducting meetings
  of local interest
Political Organizations

Priority Groups II

Groups I organizations that restrict
  participation
Religious groups for worship, religious
  instruction or fundraising
Business or commercial groups

Processing and prioritizing requests for use of facilities is expedited if school personnel have complete information about the nature and requirements of each proposed activity. Most schools use a standard building use permit form to collect needed information for consistent and equitable space allocation (see example).

Permit for Use of School Facilities

Organization/Group: _____

Adult Responsible: _____ Phone: _____

Address: _____

Describe Activity: _____

_____

Space(s) to Be Used: _____

Space	Hours	Dates
_____	_____	_____
_____	_____	_____
_____	_____	_____

Items to Be Bought into Building: _____

Special Services Needed: _____

Equipment Needed: _____

_____
(Applicant's Signature)

The principal is responsible for making facilities accessible for community use and is also accountable for protecting school property and limiting school and district liability. A set of specific guidelines governing proper care and use of school facilities or equipment is essential (see example).

Sample Rules and Regulations for Use of School Facilities

1. Use of facilities is restricted to spaces, times, and places listed on the permit.

2. A school representative (usually a custodian) must be present in the building at all times.

3. When necessary, organizations using school facilities will be required to furnish a certificate confirming appropriate liability insurance.

4. All groups using school premises are required to provide an adult supervisor who shall remain with the group during all activities.

5. Fire and safety regulations must be observed at all times.

6. Use of alcohol or drugs is prohibited on school premises. No smoking is allowed in any school facility.

7. Equipment and furniture shall not be moved from one area to another unless specifically noted on the permit.

8. Any accident requiring medical attention occurring while using school facilities must be reported to the custodian on duty or other authorized school personnel.

9. The individual and group named on the permit shall be held jointly responsible for any damage to school property.

10. The school will not be responsible for loss of personal property by individuals or groups when facilities are used for permit activities.

The tools and techniques just outlined can help the principal manage both time and space through effective scheduling of school facilities to achieve the greatest use for the greatest good.

Regardless of whether the physical plant is used for school or nonschool purposes, energy management has become an increasing concern for all school leaders.

HOW TO USE TECHNOLOGY TO MONITOR ENERGY SYSTEMS

Part of being a good steward of the physical plant is to champion energy efficiency. Schools are notorious energy sieves. This is particularly true of secondary schools, where students have a propensity for turning on lights, leaving doors ajar, and opening and closing windows.

All school leaders are becoming increasingly energy sensitive. Taking the lead in reducing energy cost and consumption pays big dividends because:

- It curtails escalating operating costs (savings that may be translated into added funds for other programmatic needs).

- It models environmental awareness and social concern for preserving natural resources.

- It creates positive public relations throughout the community.

Where energy efficiency is a problem or concern, more and more schools are finding the answer in installing automatic systems for monitoring and controlling energy equipment. Use of such systems can produce both energy and dollar savings.

Following are the steps needed to evaluate the potential of using technology to handle energy usage in the school:

1. Start with an energy audit to determine the need. (Most local utility companies will perform such audits free or for a nominal charge.)

2. Be cautious and conservative. Don't rush into any quick decisions. It sometimes pays to let someone else be on the cutting edge in trying new technologies and to let others work out the bugs. There's no particular glory in being the "first kid on the block" with a new system.

3. Check on the experience of other schools that have tried similar systems.

4. If the decision is "go," get skilled, professional consultation to determine the kind of energy management system best suited to your particular school's needs.

5. Base decisions, in part, on how great potential economies (rebates from utility companies, energy savings, etc.) may be and on the length of the payback periods. (Most good systems should return out-of-pocket costs within one to one-and-a-half years.)

6. Choose the simplest system that meets the school's needs.

7. Ask the right questions about any system or provider under consideration (see the criteria that follows).

Criteria for Selecting an Energy Management System

- What are the installation and operation costs?
- Are the equipment and system state of the art?
- Which features does the system include:
  - Optimum start/stop
  - Malfunction alarms
  - Independent equipment programming
  - Night setback
  - Energy usage reporting
  - Utility meter monitoring
  - Day/night cycles based on occupancy schedules
- How flexible is the system? Can it be customized to meet individual building needs?
- What are the track records of the manufacturer and the vendor?
- What support services are provided? What is the average repair response time?
- How much training is required to use the system?

Once an appropriate system is in place, ensure that maintenance personnel are properly trained in the use of the system and insist on responsive service from the supplier. Most administrators are astonished at the amount of consumption reduction and cost savings that results from converting to an automatic energy management and monitoring system.

Throughout this chapter there are tested techniques for successfully managing the non-human resources of the school, but no matter how carefully operations are planned and managed, things sometimes go wrong and emergencies arise. Chapter 8 spells out exactly what to do in times of crisis.

Managing Crises

"There cannot be a crisis next week. My schedule is already full."

—Henry Kissinger

Most of this guide is designed to help you avoid "crisis management"—by showing you how to plan ahead, anticipate and avoid problems, skirt potential pitfalls and focus on success. Nevertheless, disasters can and do happen. A crisis or emergency situation can strike your school at any time.

The most common crisis situations that may confront school personnel are: *natural disasters* (tornados, blizzards, earthquakes, etc.), *man-made emergencies* (bomb threats, violence, walkouts, etc.), or *accidental events* (fire, utility outages, accidental injuries, etc.) For the school leader, a crisis is any situation that threatens the safety and order of the school.

In any school crisis the principal is extremely visible and sets the pattern of response and resolution that will be followed by students, staff and others involved. In emergencies, you must call on all the skills and resources at your command and then some. The primary goal in any crisis is to protect, maintain, and/or restore the school as a safe and secure environment for learning as quickly as possible. Fortunately, the unpredictable and pressure-ridden daily routine of the principalship serve as good training for dealing with full-blown emergencies.

This chapter provides the basis of successful crisis management in any kind of emergency situations within the school.

GUIDELINES FOR CRISIS MANAGEMENT

Every emergency situation takes on its own unique character as circumstances change and events unfold. Nevertheless, there are certain fundamental responses that are applicable to almost every crisis.

When a crisis occurs in the school, it is critical that students, staff and the public are fully protected and that school activities are continued or resumed with the least amount of disruption possible. Regardless of the nature of the emergency, your priorities are:

- People first.
- Property second.
- Image third.

Handling emergencies requires the ability to weigh options, make decisions, respond quickly, and *pay attention to details despite distractions*. If there is ever a time for the leaders of the school to mind all their "Ps" and "Qs", it is in a time of crisis. In those situations, the "P" equals preparedness and the "Q" equals quickness. These are the watchwords for diffusing crises and reestablishing normalcy as soon as possible.

The following general guidelines for crisis management can help you deal successfully with any kind of disaster while minimizing disruption and maximizing damage control.

General Guidelines For Managing Emergencies

1. *Have an advance plan for handling emergency situations.* A crisis condition is no time for knee-jerk responses or the "wet finger" approach to leadership. Every school should have a well developed crisis management manual outlining resources, response procedures, and specific responsibilities for handling emergencies. The building guide should be coordinated with a district emergency plan whenever possible. Your first act in an emergency situation should be to refer to and review the predetermined plan. The best plan ever devised is useless if it isn't followed.

2. *Remain calm and use common sense.* The first rule of crisis response is to refuse to panic. No emergency lasts forever. There will be a resolution. Your attitude and demeanor under stress set the standard of action and reaction by others. A controlled and reasoned response by the person-in-charge goes a long way in eliminating confusion and avoiding mass hysteria.

3. *Be realistic about what you're facing.* Through misunderstanding, false bravado, or fear of losing face, leaders sometimes belittle the urgency or importance of a crisis situation. Serious matters must be taken seriously. In emergencies, it is the principal's responsibility to make a realistic assessment of the circumstances, acknowledge the seriousness of the situation, and make responses that match the requirements of the conditions at hand.

5. *Keep communications open and up front.* When dealing with a crisis in the school, you must not only handle events as they happen, but also keep all interested parties apprised of developments, actions, and reactions as they occur. It is essential that staff, students, parents, the superintendent, and the school board receive timely information as needed during emergencies.

In a crisis, the principal has the dual responsibilities of solving the problem at hand and of informing others of what's wrong and what's being done to make it right. The school's crisis management manual should include a well-defined communication plan, as well as an emergency action plan. (See "How to Handle Communications in times of Emergency" later in this chapter.)

6. *Don't be afraid to call for help.* Leaders seldom solve emergency situations single-handedly. When a crisis strikes, you must be open and astute enough to marshal any and all resources necessary to restore safety, sanity, and security. A good leader knows his or her staff well enough to anticipate their responses under pressure and to use their professional expertise and personal strengths as needed to help resolve tough situations.

7. *Follow up every crisis.* Emergencies aren't necessarily over just because the fire is extinguished, the riot quelled, or calm restored. It is often necessary for school leaders to provide appropriate follow-up activities such as grief counseling, policy adjustments, emergency procedure review, further staff training, and so on.

   Even if no other follow-up action is called for, a detailed written summary of emergency action and outcomes should be prepared as the basis for critiquing how well the situation was handled. By reviewing the lessons learned from each emergency, you can pick up clues and directions for dealing with future crises.

In addition to applying the commonsense suggestions just outlined, there are a number of specific anticipatory action steps that school leaders can take to prepare better for possible future emergencies.

GAME PLAN FOR MANAGING THE UNMANAGEABLE

To place the school in the best possible position for handling crisis circumstances when they arise, prudent principals pay attention to three major areas:

1. Developing a comprehensive emergency management plan
2. Establishing and enforcing reasonable preventative measures
3. Providing relevant staff training

Having an advance crisis management plan is essential. If no such plan exists, the principal has not exercised proper forethought, is more accountable for any harm to persons or property that may occur as the result of an emergency, and may be subject to legal liability charges.

Once developed, all staff members should become familiar with the contents of the plan. It is no good if it comes as a surprise when a crisis hits the school. Characteristics of an effective crisis management plan include the following:

- The plan must be in writing.
- The manual should be easily identifiable (red cover, bold captions, etc.)
- The manual should be loose-leaf to allow updates and additions.
- The plan should be brief and readable.
- The manual should be widely distributed (usually in all offices and classrooms and next to all telephones.)
- The manual should include detailed floor plans.
- The plan must be revised annually.

Obviously, such a plan can only do so much. It can never answer all questions or anticipate all contingencies. Individual judgment will always be necessary. Nevertheless, a well-thought-out plan can guide the staff's response to any emergency.

In addition to having a predetermined emergency action plan ready to go when a crisis occurs, you should take pains to implement and enforce reasonable preventative measures. Such efforts can help avoid or at least contain many emergency situations. It can also reduce your liability for negligence.

A third component in the school's approach to preparedness is appropriate staff training. Counselors in particular need to have special training in dealing with individuals involved in crisis situations. Every school staff should always have a number of key personnel who have received specific instruction in such areas as:

- Cardiac-pulmonary resuscitation (CPR)
- First aid
- Safety measures
- Handling athletic injuries
- Nonviolent crisis intervention
- Grief and trauma counseling
- Conflict resolution

Such training should not only be provided for appropriate staff members but should be updated at regular intervals. Having key people on hand who know what to do in a variety of crisis conditions is the best insurance the principal can obtain.

Local agencies such as fire, police, and civil defense departments, as well as national organizations, such as the Red Cross and the National

Crisis Intervention Institute, can be valuable resources in providing the necessary training.

A final preventive measure that many schools have found to be a virtual lifesaver in time of crisis is to have in place appropriate organizational machinery that can be activated immediately to handle certain kinds of emergency situations.

The most well-organized and well-prepared secondary schools have established the following mechanisms for managing crises such as:

- Special teams for specific purposes (Blue Alert Team, Crisis Communication Team, Suicide Crisis Team, etc.)
- Child abuse reporting procedures
- Emergency school closure procedure

The remainder of this section describes how to organize internally to be a step ahead in handling common crisis conditions.

The Blue Alert Team

Medical emergencies can and do strike individuals of all ages (students and staff) at any time. Obviously, schools cannot have immediate access to a physician and often do not even have a full-time nurse. This makes it important to have on board at all times a cadre of staff members who can serve as a medical emergency response team trained and capable to handle basic medical problems and situations (bleeding, shock, choking, breathing stoppage, seizures, etc.).

Many schools have established a "Blue Alert" Team to provide initial medical care while waiting for paramedics or other medical help to arrive. Most commonly, these teams are made up of specialized school personnel, such as

- School nurse or health aide
- Health instructors
- Chemical health specialist
- Police liaison officer or security personnel
- Other staff members with special skills or interest.

Blue Alert Team members should be fully trained in basic first aid, CPR techniques, and the Heimlich maneuver and know how to handle allergy victims and diabetes cases.

All staff members should know who serves on the school's Blue Alert Team and how to use the team in an emergency situation. Here are some simple guidelines for employing the Blue Alert Team when a medical emergency arises:

1. The school office should be notified immediately of any medical emergency.

2. The office will put out an "all call" announcement.

3. Blue Alert Team members will respond to the scene of the victim while office personnel call 911.

4. The victim's condition will be assessed by the Blue Alert Team to determine if CPR or other first aid is necessary.

5. If CPR is required, the Blue Alert Team will initiate the intervention and continue until paramedics arrive and take over.

6. Blue Alert Team members should prearrange for classroom backup on occasions when they may be called to handle an emergency.

7. Team members not directly involved in providing resuscitation or other first aid should clear the area by removing obstacles and furniture and directing student traffic away from the scene of the emergency.

8. The Blue Alert Team should meet with the principal following *every* emergency to evaluate the team's performance.

When properly trained and equipped (see suggested list of supplies), the Blue Alert Team can provide a sense of comfort and safety throughout the school and can actually save lives in emergency situations.

Suggested Blue Alert Team Supply List

- Towels/washcloths
- Cold packs
- Scissors (blunt end)
- Assorted bandages/Band-aids
- Adhesive tape
- Sterile gauze pads
- Disposable plastic gloves
- Allergy kits
- Sweet candy or juice
- Updated list of student medical conditions and medications (provided by the school nurse)

The formation of some kind of medical emergency response team is basic to the preparedness of the school. The checklist that follows provides a sequenced action plan for handling medical emergencies that can be followed by the Blue Alert Team until professional help is available:

Medical Emergency Checklist Procedures

____ At the first indication of a medical emergency, the Blue Alert Team should be contacted and 911 called for professional assistance.

____ Do not move a seriously injured person unless necessary for safety reasons.

____ Follow a standard first aid line of authority:

- First person on the scene directs operations and administers first aid.
- Second person goes for help.
- Third person directs traffic and assists with first aid as needed.

____ The first person on the scene should evaluate the situation and assess the victim's condition, paying special attention to:

- Hazards in the area.
- Patient's level of consciousness/responsiveness
- Patient's vital signs, general appearance, and emotional state

____ Specific first aid procedures should be administered as follows:

- *For bleeding:*
  Apply pressure to wound (or pressure point in the case of a large wound.)
  Elevate wounded area above the heart.
  Treat for shock.

- *For cessation of breathing:*
  Administer mouth-to-mouth resuscitation or CPR as needed.

- *For choking:*
  Do not interfere if victim can cough, speak, or breathe.
  If victim cannot perform these functions, apply Heimlich maneuver.

- *For convulsions / seizures:*
  Clear hazards from around the victim.
  Protect victim, but do not overly restrain.
  Do not force any blunt object between victim's teeth.
  Do not give fluids.

- *For chemical burns to the eye:*
  Flush gently with lukewarm water.

- *For shock:*
  Have victim lie down.
  Cover victim to prevent loss of body heat.
  Elevate feet unless a head injury is involved.

____ While waiting for an ambulance, recheck key diagnostic signs every five minutes, including:

- Respiratory rate

- Pulse
- Blood pressure
- Level of consciousness

_____ When professional medical personnel arrive, provide as much of the following information as possible:

- Name, age, and approximate weight of victim
- Patient's level of consciousness
- Chief complaint or symptoms
- Medical history of patient, including allergies and current medications
- Victim's vital signs
- Treatment initiated
- Family physician

_____ When necessary, a staff member should accompany the patient in the ambulance and remain until the parent/guardian or spouse/next of kin arrive.

_____ Parents/guardians of student or spouse/next of kin of a staff member should be notified as soon as possible.

_____ A student or staff member experiencing *any* of the medical emergencies above should receive follow-up evaluation by medical professionals.

The procedures just spelled out can guide school leaders in managing almost any medical emergency affecting a single individual student or staff member.

The Crisis Communication Team

Clear, complete, and timely communication is essential in times of emergency. The school can have an edge in crisis management if arrangements have been made in advance to handle necessary communications to staff, the student body, parents, the district office, and the media.

The responsibility of the school's Crisis Communication Team should be to keep all affected parties accurately informed of developments, to prevent or counteract rumors, to limit overreaction, and to instill a sense of confidence that the school is on top of the situation and capable of handling the emergency at hand.

In emergencies, time is precious and pressure is great. Thus, the Crisis Communication Team should be large enough to get the job done, but small enough to be tightly organized and capable of quick action. To be effective, the team should include both building and district personnel. Membership for such a team often includes:

- Principal or designee
- Police liaison officer
- Superintendent of schools or designee
- District communications/public relations officer
- School board chair

To avoid possible confusion, the *same* team should be responsible for official communications in *all* emergency situations regardless of the nature of the crisis.

The Suicide Crisis Team

A relatively new crisis concern in schools is the escalating incidence of teenage suicide. This serious development has prompted many school leaders to set in place a ready-made team and an advance plan for dealing with threatened, attempted or actual suicide situations. The composition of the suicide crisis team will vary depending on the size and organizational structure of the school staff, but should include such specialized personnel as

- Principal or assistant principal
- Counselor(s)
- Social worker
- School nurse or health aide
- Chemical health specialist
- School psychologist

Many suicide situations are volatile and require immediate response with little or no time for calling in outside help or expertise. Proper preplanning and the presence of a properly prepared Suicide Crisis Team can literally spell the difference between life and death for a student at risk. Following are model procedures which can be followed once a Suicide Crisis Team has been formed:

Model Suicide Crisis Procedures

All Staff Responsibilities

- Any staff member should inform the principal and/or building Suicide Crisis Team if they witness a remark, see a written message or observe behavior that indicates suicide.
- Avoid any panic reaction—stay calm and listen.
- Inform the student that information *must* be shared with appropriate Suicide Crisis Team members.

- Report all information to the building Suicide Crisis Team.
- Respect confidentiality—personal information must be handled discreetly and sensitively among staff.

Suicide Crisis Team Procedures

- Team members should not try to work alone.
- The principal should be kept informed at all times.
- The team should decide among members involved those best in a position to be supportive, effective, and caring.
- Information must be documented.
- A release of information form from parents or a judicial order must be secured before staff can share information with a treatment agency.

What to Do When a Student Talks of Suicide

- Give emotional support ("You did the right thing by coming to talk.")
- Evaluate the risk ("How do you feel right now? Do you have a plan? Have you ever tried to commit suicide?")
- Ask straightforward questions.
- Remember that hopelessness, anger, and revenge are serious suicide indicators.
- Make parental contact.
- Consult with "experts" as appropriate.

What to Do in an Imminent Life-Threatening Situation

- Call 911 and/or police liaison officer
- Contact building Suicide Crisis Team
- Follow guidelines for parent contact
- Stay with the student. (A student judged to be at risk should be accompanied by a team member and not permitted to return home without parent notification.)

Techniques for Interviewing A Suicide Student

- Focus the interview on increasing comfort and diminishing isolation.
- Allow the student to share thoughts and feelings.
- Try to offer hope and options.
- Insist that the suicidal concern be shared with those necessary to get help for the student and change whatever has precipitated the crisis.
- Listen more than you talk.

- Avoid being judgmental and critical. Don't sermonize.
- Don't jump to conclusions and overly easy solutions.
- Avoid being overly intellectual or diagnosing causes.
- Try to find out what might be viewed as a reason or force to keep living for and who is a positive influence or support person in the life of the student.

How to Follow Up a Suicide Crisis

- Identify a case manager to handle follow-up.
- Always keep the focus on the student.
- Install a monitoring system for as long as necessary.
- The crisis team should review its actions after all suicide crisis situations.

What to Do When a Student Who Has Attempted Suicide Returns to School

- Arrange a meeting with the parents and any outside counselors or therapists involved prior to reentry.
- If the student reenters unexpectedly, conduct a staff meeting as soon as possible.
- Share information with staff discreetly on an as-needed basis.

Flow Chart for Handling Concerns About a Suicidal Student —

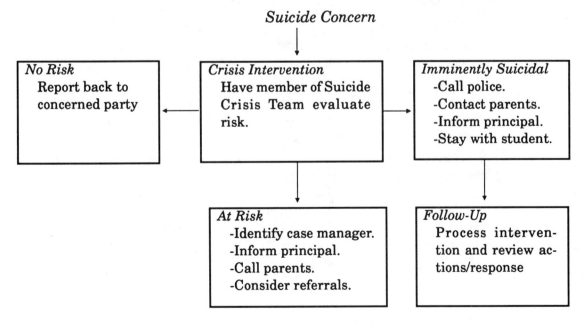

Student Abuse Reporting Procedure

Across the country, there are increasing reports of incidents involving the physical, emotional, or sexual abuse or neglect of students. The naivete and the code of silence that characterized the past have given way to reveal that abuse is a disturbingly common occurrence in American society. Whether they occur inside or outside the school, acts of abuse or neglect are emergency situations that school leaders cannot ignore.

Whenever the physical, emotional, or sexual abuse or neglect of a student is discovered or suspected, the school is obligated by law to respond and report. Since timing is often critical in an abuse situation, it is in the best interest of the students and the school to have well-defined procedures for reporting incidents swiftly and accurately to the proper authorities. The following guidelines illustrate how the school can be prepared to deal with abuse situations:

Student Abuse/Neglect Reporting Guidelines

1. Any staff member who knows of or suspects the physical or sexual abuse or neglect of a student should make an immediate report to child protection or police officials. (Such reporting is mandated by statute in Minnesota and a growing number of other states.)

2. The reporting staff member should report as much of the following information as possible:
    *   Student's name, birth date, address, phone number, and parents' names
    *   Any person(s) believed to be responsible for the abuse/neglect of the student
    *   The nature and extent of the abuse/neglect

3. An oral report should be made to an appropriate agency after the necessary information has been obtained, followed by a detailed written report to the notified agency.

4. If the reporting staff member believes that the student is abandoned, subject to imminent or real threat or in need of medical care, the police should be called immediately.

5. Staff members should be informed in writing of applicable mandatory reporting requirements, appropriate reporting, contacts (including phone numbers), and their guarantee of privacy, if any.

Having an advance plan for informing authorities of abusive/neglectful behavior can protect students from further mistreatment and protect the school from liability claims of negligence or neglect.

The Emergency Closing

One final precautionary measure that schools should take is to have a specific action plan in place in the event that an emergency situation unexpectedly closes the school down.

Emergency closures may affect a single school as in the case of a broken water main or an entire school district in such situations as a major storm. An emergency may make it necessary for the school to remain unopened, to delay opening, or to close down in midday. Closing the school once it has opened for the day should be considered only as a last resort because of the increasing number of students who may have no place to go on short notice.

In any event, the school should be prepared with a ready-to-use plan that spells out specific procedures for emergency closure with special emphasis on a chain of communication (e.g., telephone tree) that assures that all affected parties learn of the closing as quickly as necessary. The school's closure procedures should be simple, specific, and well publicized in advance.

Emergency School Closure Procedures

In the event that emergency conditions make it necessary to close the school(s) or delay the opening of school:

1. The superintendent or designee or building principal will notify the school community via communications media.

2. Specific closing information will be provided to and broadcast by the following TV and radio stations: _____

3. The superintendent will inform district office administrators, the bus company, the substitute teacher caller, and the school board of the closure.

4. Designated district personnel will personally notify each affected principal, who, in turn, shall be responsible for notifying or effecting a notification network for subordinate personnel as appropriate.

5. During pending or immediate emergency conditions, all students, staff, and other interested parties should keep tuned to designated media sources for the latest information.

6. Staff members should keep a copy of these emergency procedures at home in the event that notification occurs outside the normal working hours.

All the precautionary measures presented in this section can help place the principal and staff in a positive and proactive position to deal with any kind of crisis situation.

ADDITIONAL PREVENTATIVE MEASURES YOU CAN TAKE

In a safety-conscious school, continuing and meaningful efforts to prevent incidents that lead to emergency situations are an area of primary concern. Some additional preventative measures that you can take to avert or minimize occurrences are outlined here:

Basic Emergency Prevention Measures for Schools

- Insist on a continuous and consistent program of quality maintenance throughout the building.
- Assure that a custodian holding a current boiler operator's license is available or on call at all times.
- Keep a complete and up-to-date collection of safety manuals readily available within the school.
- Instruct the custodial staff to keep emergency exits and routes clear at all times.
- Comply with all fire, tornado, earthquake, and civil defense drill requirements.
- Install effective security systems in key areas of the building.
- Reduce, remove, or upgrade "attractive nuisances" that might precipitate trouble (e.g., unlighted parking lots).
- Provide safety awareness training programs for all staff members.
- Review accident reports and reports of all fire, insurance, and Occupational Safety and Health Administration (OSHA) inspections. Comply with any recommended corrective measures.
- Consistently discipline all safety violators.
- Provide an emergency radio in strategic locations throughout the building.
- Test all emergency power sources at regular intervals.
- Post procedures for calling 911 in a prominent place by all telephones.

What to Do When Calling 911

1. Stay calm.
2. State the problem accurately and completely.
3. State the exact location of the emergency; include direction indicators as necessary.
4. Answer all questions asked by the 911 telecommunicator.
5. Do not hang up! Stay on the phone until emergency units have arrived or the 911 operator terminates the call.
6. Let the 911 telecommunicator control the conversation.

These preventative steps will go a long way to reduce risk within the school. In those instances where prevention is not enough and a bona fide emergency strikes, however, someone must take charge to handle the crisis and restore educational equilibrium.

WHO'S IN CHARGE? HOW TO SET UP AN EMERGENCY CHAIN OF COMMAND

Since emergencies can strike any time of the day or night, every school must have a predetermined, around-the-clock chain of command. Every principal should establish a clearly delineated line of authority so that students, staff, the district office and the community know who is in charge during any crisis situation, whether or not the principal is physically present during the emergency.

The principal should designate a list of staff members to be in charge of the building and to make decisions during a crisis in his or her absence. Copies of the designated chain of command should be kept with the school's crisis management information as well as in other accessible locations. A copy should also be filed with the superintendent's office.

All building staff need to be informed as to who is in charge when the principal is absent. Likewise, the staff members responsible for the building during the principal's absence need to be thoroughly familiar with what to do during emergency situations and how to use the school's crisis management plan.

Here is a typical emergency chain of command:

School Emergency Line of Authority

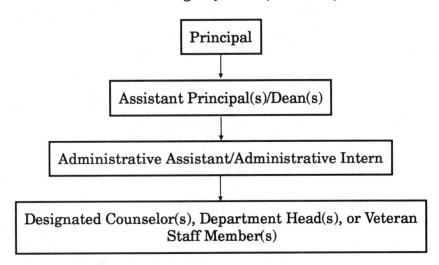

In certain situations, district administrators or specialized personnel within the building (school nurse, police liaison officer, chemical health specialist, head custodian, etc.) may also be incorporated into the crisis chain of command. You are well advised to consider personalities as well as titles or positions in identifying the school's backup order of command.

To test the effectiveness of the crisis charts of command, as well as other emergency plans and procedures, the school should religiously engage in a systematic program of announced and unannounced drills (practice exercises and simulations) under a variety of conditions.

THE IMPORTANCE OF DRILL AND PRACTICE IN MANAGING SCHOOL EMERGENCIES

Sometimes, emergency procedures that appear sound on paper contain hidden flaws, oversights, or glitches that can be detected only by putting the plans into practice. It is essential that all schools carry out a thorough program of emergency drills, including fire, civil defense, and natural disaster (tornado, earthquakes, etc.) drills throughout the year. Such drills provide a reality check for the school's state of preparedness.

All staff and students should receive complete instructions regarding the school's emergency procedures well in advance of any practice exercise. Drills should be conducted at various times throughout the day and spaced over the entire year—not batched on a few warm days in the fall and spring for convenience.

All emergency drills should be taken seriously be the school's leaders and staff. Secondary students, in particular, tend to view such drills as a lark. If the staff treats them as a nuisance or imposition, the student body will also, and the purpose will be lost.

In some parts of the country, schools have found it beneficial to tie building drills to community or statewide emergency preparedness exercises. (See statewide tornado drill schedule provided.)

Tornado Awareness Week Drill Schedule
April ___, 19___

9 A.M.
- National Weather Service will issue a mock tornado *watch*.
- National Weather Service will activate the national warning system.
- A mock tornado *watch* message will be sent over the weather wire system.

1:15 P.M.
- National Weather Service will send a mock tornado *warning* message over the weather wire system.
- All public buildings and governmental subunits (including schools) will implement emergency drill procedures.

1:30 P.M.
- "An End of Test" message will be sent over the weather wire and radio systems.

Such state or regional practice sessions underscore the importance of emergency preparedness and the seriousness of practicing drill procedures.

To dramatize the power of preparedness, a few schools have also found it helpful to stage full-blown simulated disaster drills (i.e. explosion, natural disaster, etc.), complete with special effects, sound tracks, public address systems, victim's screams, burning hair, rubble, and artificial blood. Such realistic drills can reinforce the need for crisis planning and help school authorities evaluate how well staff and students can handle panic, leadership, delegation, and overall organization under stress. A video playback can help officials assess how well emergency plans might really work. Such simulations can be educational for the entire school community.

After every drill or emergency simulation, the school's leadership team should conduct a critique to evaluate what worked and what didn't. Answers to the following questions can help hone the staff's crisis plan and its ability to carry it out efficiently and effectively:

---

1. Did the building population actually go to the designated shelter area(s)?
   ____ yes ____ no
   If yes, approximately, what percentage evacuated? ____
   How long did it take? ____

2. Was there adequate warning?   ____ yes ____ no

   If "no," why not? _____

3. On a scale of 1 to 5 (1 being lowest), rate the overall effectiveness of the drill in improving the level of preparedness.   1 2 3 4 5

4. What suggestions can be made to improve future drills?

   _____

   _____

One lesson often learned from emergency drills is the paramount importance of clear communication during a crisis situation.

HOW TO HANDLE COMMUNICATIONS IN TIMES OF EMERGENCY

Communication is never more important or more difficult than in a period of crisis. Panic and confusion affect focus, concentration, and comprehension. In an emergency situation, communication must be clear, short, and direct.

Effective communication is essential to successful crisis management and resolution. Accurate information and clear-cut communication help people handle the emergency at hand, while maintaining the school's credibility and minimizing over reaction or distortion. Information experts offer the following suggestions for school leaders in managing communication before, during, and after a crisis:

Before a Crisis

- Have a current and complete set of address labels with phone numbers for parents and staff on hand at all times.
- Communicate with parents on a regular basis. Let them know what information systems are in place in event of an emergency.
- Maintain a list of *key communicators* in the community who can help disseminate information through a telephone tree in times of emergency.

During a Crisis

- Gather facts carefully, quickly, and thoroughly. Be willing to admit you don't have all the answers, but are committed to work for solutions.
- Establish methods for getting the facts to all the following audiences:
  - Students
  - Staff (building and district)
  - Parents
  - Administrators
  - Fire, police, and government officials
  - Bus personnel
  - Media
  - Community members
  - Neighboring schools (where appropriate)
- Prepare release statements carefully, with assistance of the district communications office if possible.
- Avoid impromptu ad libs that may be embarrassing later.
- Limit statements to facts. Avoid overexplanation, speculation or inflammatory language.
- Be positive and candid.
- Establish means for the public to get answers to questions.
- Prepare any written information to be sent to parents as soon as possible.
- Mobilize a "key communicators" network.

After a Crisis

- Evaluate the total crisis communication plan.
- Extend appreciation to news representatives and staff for cooperation during the crisis.
- Follow up on parent concerns.
- Communicate preventative measures being taken.

Mismanaged crisis communication can snarl relief efforts and even make matters worse. The greatest risk of lasting harm resulting from poor emergency communication lies in the area of media relations.

DEALING WITH THE MEDIA WHEN A CRISIS HITS

In times of emergency, many school leaders resent the intrusion of the media. Nevertheless, their presence may be helpful and certainly is inevitable. Any crisis in the school is *news*. Skilled administrators learn to deal with the media in ways that accurately inform the public, put matters in proper perspective and bolster confidence in the school's ability to manage adverse situations. Basic guidelines for successfully working with the news media in crises include the following:

- The principal's goal must be to inform the public concerning the crisis while maintaining student privacy and assuring as little disruption to the educational process as possible.
- Use the services of the district communication coordinator in preparing basic facts and news releases.
- If reporters appear while school is in session, try to guide their activities to minimize distractions. If necessary, solicit police assistance.
- Hold a press conference if appropriate.
- Designate a specific spokesperson to accept and respond to reporter's calls.
- Don't presume to tell reporters what is or is not newsworthy.
- Answer questions factually without embellishment or editorializing. (Don't feel compelled to fill time on the six o'clock news.)
- Never lie to the media.
- Tell bad news quickly and get it over with.
- Guard students against intrusion or harassment when genuine grief is involved.
- Get parent permission before allowing interviews.
- Don't put reporters off. They have deadlines.
- Don't expect or request to approve articles before publication.
- Don't complain if you feel the media treats you unfairly. If major inaccuracies are publicized, *request* a correction or retraction.
- Don't guess.
- Remember that school reports and surveys are public information. You can't withhold such data.
- Avoid jargon.
- Keep promises to call reporters back.

- Remember that nothing is "off the record."
- Don't assume you can pick your own time for publicity.
- Keep in mind that news people want to know: who, what, when, where, why, how, and who or what was the cause.
- Try to establish the school as the best source of information on the crisis.
- Don't back away from microphones.
- Avoid letting reporters get you off track.
- Call on the district's professional communications staff to handle interviews and coordinate the flow of information.
- If possible, "don't screw up on a slow news day."

Although there's no formula for guaranteeing positive press coverage, the crisis-tested tips given here will help you convey an image of responsibility, credibility, and professionalism. That's about all you can expect as a public official caught up in a period of stress, pressure, and emergency.

Most of this chapter has offered proven principles and practices for dealing with crises of any kind. The remaining sections focus on techniques for handling specific emergency situations such as the threat of fire within the school.

FOOL-PROOF FIRE EMERGENCY PROCEDURES

Fear of fire overshadows concern for any other type of emergency that might strike a school. All schools have some procedure for responding to a fire emergency, even though they may have no plan for any other kind of crisis. By the time students reach junior high or senior high school, they are veterans of countless fire drills and fire prevention programs and assemblies. Students and staff almost universally know what to do in case of fire. This does *not*, however, diminish the need for an up-to-date fire evacuation plan and continuous drills to ensure that the plan works.

The following factors should be considered and included in any modern fire emergency strategy:

- The building fire alarm system must be operable and easily activated.
- Emergency battery-operated lights should be brought into play whenever necessary.
- Emergency routes, roads, and driveways must be kept open for use by firefighters.
- When evacuation is necessary, occupants should be removed at least 500 feet from the building.
- Special arrangements must be made for handicapped and disabled students/staff.

- Evacuees need to be sheltered in severe weather.
- Elevators should not be used in a fire emergency.
- Evacuation protocol should emphasize these points:
  - Movement should be rapid and orderly.
  - Unnecessary noise should be avoided.
  - All room exits should be used.
  - The last people out should close classroom doors.
  - Double columns should be formed where possible.
- Following evacuation, all fire doors should be closed.
- All the following parties should be informed as soon as possible:
  - Fire Department
  - Utility companies
  - Bus officials
  - Superintendent
  - Supervisor of buildings and grounds
- Evacuees should not return to the building until fire department officials give the "all clear."

In many situations, the school's fire emergency procedures serve as the centerpiece for an overall, comprehensive crisis management plan. The same basic steps can be adapted to a variety of other emergency conditions such as a civil defense alert.

WHAT TO DO IN A CIVIL DEFENSE ALERT

In the frightening, but unlikely, event of a national emergency necessitating a real-life civil defense alert, the school should have a plan for responding as follows:

- Community warning systems, as well as radio and television, should be monitored closely.
- Information on dismissal will be released by the superintendent (or designee) to predetermined communications media.
- If case conditions do not allow time for students to be dismissed, all building occupants should be assembled in designated shelter areas within the school or in other shelters established by the city or county emergency operations plan.
- Plans for student dismissal or removal to shelter areas should parallel the school's fire evacuation procedures.

Although on a smaller scale, an emergency involving a bomb threat to the school can be as chilling as a national civil defense alert. The next section defines a proper response plan in case of a bomb warning.

BOMB THREAT/WARNING PROCEDURES

Most bomb threats to schools are hoaxes. Nevertheless, bombs are serious and no threat can be ignored by school officials. From the moment a phone threat first reaches your office until the matter is totally resolved, the school needs a step-by-step procedure for dealing with all aspects of a bona fide bomb scare.

Office personnel should be instructed to take all threatening calls seriously. The person receiving a bomb threat should try to keep the caller on the line as long as possible while trying to attract someone's attention to trace the call. (All office staff members should be familiar with the process for tracing a call.) The staff member handling the phone should also obtain as much information as possible from the caller. More and more schools are using a phone service that shows the phone number of all callers.

It is important that all the information extracted from the caller be recorded accurately, (see recording form provided). Notes should include the specific time and date of the call, exact language used by the caller, an estimate of the caller's sex and age, and any background noises.

Bomb Threat Recording Form

Date: _____ Time: _____

Person receiving call: _____

Phone number on which call was received: _____

Caller's message (exact words): _____

_____

_____

Caller's voice characteristics/mannerisms: _____

_____

Caller's accent: _____

Other identifying characteristics: _____

_____

Background noise: _____

Other comments: _____

_____

Obviously, the police and the superintendent must be notified immediately of all bomb threats. The decision whether to evacuate the building must be made by the principal only after consultation with police specialists. If the decision is made to evacuate the premises, the procedures usually follow those for a fire emergency drill. Teachers should be instructed beforehand to make a visual check of their classroom during the evacuation and to report anything unusual. They should refrain, however, from touching anything suspicious. Radios and walkie-talkies should never be used in the bomb threat area as they may trigger the bomb.

If a bomb is discovered in the school, only specially trained police personnel should move or handle it . Following evacuation, no one should return to the school until police officials declare the building safe for occupancy.

Executing a successful response to a bomb scare requires an incredible amount of teamwork by a variety of staff members. This same kind of coordinated effort is necessary to defuse the explosive potential when a severe natural disaster threatens the operation of the school.

WHAT TO DO IN A NATURAL DISASTER

Unlike many man-made crises, school officials usually have some period of warning of a pending natural emergency or crisis (i.e. blizzard, tornado, severe thunderstorm, hurricane, etc.). Specific emergency procedures should be geared toward the kind(s) of natural emergencies most common in the geographic area of the school. However, the following guidelines are applicable to most natural phenomena that may disrupt school operations.

Natural Disaster Guidelines

- As conditions warrant, the principal or designee should continuously monitor all National Weather Service warnings and radio/TV advisories.

- Normal school activities should be continued until conditions require implementation of emergency procedures.

- The superintendent will determine if and when the school(s) will close. If the superintendent is not available, the principal has ultimate authority to close the school if necessary.

- Students should be reminded of emergency procedures, evacuation routes, and/or personal safety measures as appropriate.

- When necessary, students, staff, and other occupants of the building should evacuate the building or proceed immediately to predesignated shelter areas as directed by the principal.

- The school's crisis communication plan should be activated as directed by the principal or superintendent.

- Extracurricular activities should be canceled as appropriate.

- Special provision may need to be made for handicapped students and personnel.

- Specific personnel should be assigned to close the school vault and secure files containing records.

- If conditions at dismissal time are threatening, consideration should be given to retaining students at school until the threatening period is over.

During any kind of natural emergency, utility services to the school are extremely vulnerable. Power outages and gas line or water main breaks often compound problems caused by natural disasters. The next section offers specific suggestions for responding to utility emergencies that occur in isolation or in conjunction with a storm or other natural crisis.

HOW TO HANDLE A UTILITY EMERGENCY

In utility emergencies, school officials are almost certainly dependent on others to remedy the situation. If there is immediate danger due to fallen live wires or leaking gas, it may be necessary to evacuate the building, following routine fire drill procedures. When conditions dictate that the school be closed or students dismissed early, alternative transportation arrangements may have to be made. In electrical power emergencies, staff members should avoid using electrical switches and exercise care so that computers and other equipment are not damaged by a power surge when service is restored. Similarly, all water should be shut off in the event of a broken water main. Other than these simple precautions, the principal's primary responsibility in a utility emergency is to notify all appropriate parties, including:

- Appropriate utility company
- Fire and/or police departments as necessary
- Superintendent of schools
- Supervisor of building and grounds
- Bus company (if transportation is affected)
- Media (if closure or early dismissal is required)

Once proper officials have been informed, the building staff can do little else but attempt to maintain calm and wait for help.

PROCEDURES FOR MANAGING DISTURBANCES AND DEMONSTRATIONS

Much of what we know about handling student disturbances and demonstrations we learned during the 1960s and 1970s. The lessons derived from dealing with civil rights clashes during early desegregation efforts and antiwar protests during the Vietnam era can be applicable in subduing walkouts, protests, and other student demonstrations today.

When tensions or emotions among the student body signal the potential for a disruptive demonstration, the principal and staff should do everything possible to prevent or quell the disturbance in the making. It is sometimes possible to negotiate a settlement or alternative process with key student leaders. Often verbal intervention by school leaders can be effective before a volatile situation becomes physical. Such intervention works when student participants are looking for a face-saving way out of a tense situation.

If and when a full-blown emergency erupts, you must assess the situation to determine its seriousness and its effect on the safety of students and staff before taking any action. Such assessment should take into consideration the number of participants, the energy level of the situation, the presence of weapons, the potential audience, and what assistance may be available.

In any kind of student demonstration situation, the superintendent and the district communications coordinator should be constantly kept abreast of developments. They can assist you in notifying outside authorities as appropriate. Any decision to use uniformed police in a crisis situation must be handled with extreme care and should be made in consultation with the superintendent.

If conditions permit, normal classroom operations should be maintained as much as possible and all students encouraged to remain in the building. It is essential that the staff and students be kept informed of the situation as events develop. Conferences with representatives of key student groups are often helpful in dispelling rumors and calming fears. Parents, community organizations and leaders and the media should likewise be kept informed of developments and of all decisions made by the school administration.

There needs to be specific prearranged understandings that the custodial staff will have primary responsibility for building security throughout the emergency period and that clerical personnel are to be responsible for the security of all files and records.

If the situation becomes ugly enough that safety is jeopardized and real danger exists, the only resource is to close the school. Only the principal (in consultation with the superintendent) should determine when the time is right to shut down the operation of the school until order can be restored. Once a decision is made to close the building, students, staff, parents, transportation officials, the police and the media should be informed as soon as possible (see "Emergency Closing Plan").

Any incident of student demonstration or disturbance should be followed up by efforts to reduce tension and allow everyone involved to regain composure and rationality and to establish expectations and consequences that may prevent future crisis.

One of the best buffers against any continuation or recurrence of student disturbances is careful management of all crowd-related situations involving the student body.

CRITERIA FOR CROWD CONTROL

Whenever and wherever large numbers of students congregate for a period of time, there is always some risk of behavior getting out of hand, mob psychology taking over, and/or some kind of disturbance erupting. The most volatile situations are athletic contests, school social events, large group assemblies, and the always interesting daily lunch period(s). These situations can readily result in just the right mix of numbers, time, space, and energy to produce disruptive behavior.

The following steps can help neutralize potentially explosive crowd situations in the school and help the school staff head off problems before they start:

1. *Identify situations where trouble is most likely to start.* A record of discipline incidents over a period of time can provide the basis for analyzing the kinds of situations in which crowd situations are most likely to cause problems.

2. *Minimize congestion wherever possible.* Helpful techniques for easing congestion include staggering starting and dismissal times and spreading out bus pick-up points so that the number of students congregated in any one place at any given time is minimal.

3. *Provide adult presence whenever crowds congregate in or around the school.* It is crucial that key adults on the staff be present and visible to provide needed supervision in any crowd situation. The principal should not be exempt from this responsibility and can provide a meaningful model for the entire staff.

4. *Prohibit certain articles from school premises.* As a preventative measure, some schools have adopted a policy of prohibiting students from bringing certain articles to school that sometimes serve as a catalyst for calamity. Examples include inflammatory signs or banners, lighters, weapons, (including toy guns, sling shots, and knives), boom boxes, and so on.

5. *Vary the mix of students.* One effective way to short-circuit explosive crowd conditions is to manipulate the mix of students who are clustered

together in situations that tend to be particularly troublesome. Some schools have had success in reducing crowd problems by varying seating arrangements in assembly programs so that different grade levels are interspersed and selectively scheduling lunch periods to break up certain groups, cliques, or gangs. It pays for administrators to be students of the chemistry of the student body and to avoid creating undesirable combinations of individuals and groups whenever possible.

6. *Arrange for adults to eat with students.* This can be done by assigning staff members to mingle with students during the lunch period and by inviting parents, senior citizens, civic clubs and other adults in the community to sample the school lunch. Adult presence tends to have a stabilizing effect on the cafeteria scene.

7. *Exercise strict parking lot control and supervision.* Large numbers of students and cars gathered together in a limited space can create physically hazardous conditions and a combustible situation. Many schools have taken the following measures below to minimize crowded conditions and other parking lot problems:
   • Require registration of vehicles parked on school grounds.
   • Control access to student parking lots.
   • Separate student, staff, and visitor parking areas.
   • Limit and/or discourage students driving to school.
   • Establish parking fees.
   • Reduce speeds. (Install speed bumps.)
   • Provide ample lighting.
   • Provide adequate supervision. If necessary, assign a security aide to patrol all parking areas during peak periods throughout the day.

8. Provide an overall plan for crowd control at athletic events.
   • Conduct "fan education" programs for sporting events by holding miniclinics prior to each sports season and distributing guidelines for spectator sportsmanship at all athletic events.
   • Insist on noninflammatory behavior on the part of all coaches and teams representing the school.
   • Institute a program recognizing good sportsmanship at athletic events. Many schools and athletic leagues have established sportsmanship awards and trophies to encourage positive fan behavior at athletic contests.
   • "Stack the stands" at athletic contests where rivalry and emotions run especially high. Security personnel, off-duty police officers, aides, and other staff members can be interspersed throughout the crowd to squelch disruptive behavior in its embryonic state.

- Overload security and surveillance in controlling access to playing and spectator areas at popular athletic events, parties, concerts, and so on.

- Vary the time of athletic contests when trouble seems imminent. Some systems have gone entirely to late afternoon and midweek games.

- Limit attendance at athletic events to students and family. Some schools have found it necessary to ban junior high students from attending senior high games.

All these easy-to-follow measures can go a long way in handling crowds in or on school grounds and avoiding potentially disruptive situations that can grow to crisis proportions.

In addition to the more traditional emergency conditions that can cause havoc among students and staff dealt with in this chapter, one relative new menace requires attention: the threat of an armed person in or around the school.

FACING A NEW THREAT: MANIAC ON THE SCHOOL GROUNDS

In a society where guns are accessible, drugs are commonplace, street gangs are prevalent, and violence is a daily occurrence, schools (as well as other public institutions) now face the possible threat of acts of terrorism, murder, and even massacre. Recent years have witnessed an increase in incidents where crazed individuals, armed and dangerous, threaten individuals or groups for no apparent reason. Isolated schools across the nation have experienced such unprecedented emergency situations as inexplicable rampages of vandalism, random outbursts of violence, the holding of hostages, and so on. Fortunately, such senseless acts of brutality in schools are rare. Nevertheless, no principal in tune with the times would permit the school to be totally unprepared for such a crisis.

Most educators have no training or experience to equip them to know how to react if a deranged or drug-driven person suddenly turns the safe haven of the school into a battle ground. There are, however, measures that school leaders can take to reduce the possibility of sudden violent acts or to deal with a crisis of violence should it occur.

The first step is to do everything possible to make the school off-limits for guns and weapons of any kind. Every school should have a tough, no-nonsense policy prohibiting the presence of weapons (see the school weapon policy provided). In certain high risk schools, it may be necessary to enforce such policies through the use of metal detector screenings and weapon searches of both persons and lockers.

School Weapon Policy

Students are prohibited from possessing or using articles that are dangerous, illegal, or a nuisance at school, on school grounds, or at school-sponsored activities.

All students are particularly prohibited from having a weapon of any kind on their person, in their locker or among their belongings at school, on school property, or at a school-sponsored activity.

Possession of a weapon may result in
  1. suspension for five days
  2. confiscation of the weapon
  3. a recommendation of expulsion or a police referral

The principal may also recommend a police referral.

Some schools have taken an even tougher stance by making the possession of a weapon at school automatic grounds for permanent expulsion.

A second precautionary step that administrators can take is to heighten awareness of strangers in the building. Although it is important to maintain an atmosphere of openness for students, parents, and the public, it pays to be wary of suspicious intruders who have no legitimate business on the premises. The simple measures that follow can make it more difficult for persons posing any kind of threat to gain access to the school:

- Limit the number of unlocked entrances to the school (in accordance with fire marshal requirements).

- Establish a predetermined coded announcement to alert teachers to lock their doors and retain their students.

- Post notices requiring all visitors to check in at the principal's office.

- Maintain a visitor's sign-in book.

- Use name tags to identify volunteers and visitors.

- Have visitors routinely accompanied by a staff member.

- Enforce trespassing ordinances when necessary.

- Elicit parent and neighborhood support in reporting suspicious individuals in the area of the school.

- Arrange for routine police patrols of the area to help spot the presence of unwanted visitors or intruders.

If all precautions fail and a dangerous person is suddenly at large in the building, the principal must get outside help immediately. This is not the time for theatrics or heedless heroism. Negotiations with an armed and dangerous person in the school should always be left to the experts (police, psychologists, etc.). It should also be remembered that any incident of violence in the school may need to be followed up by considerable debriefing and counseling for students directly affected by the situation.

This chapter has provided tools to handle emergencies that may strike any school. Some schools out of control are crisis driven on a daily basis. Others operate smoothly, preventing and avoiding most emergencies and handling those that occur infrequently with dispatch and minimum disruption. The difference lies in proper preparation and effective leadership on the part of the principal.

To be able to control day-to-day operations, as well as occasional crisis situations, you must first be in control of yourself as a professional and as a person. The next chapter focuses on the fundamentals of self-management for school leaders.

Chapter 9

Managing Yourself as a School Leader

Some principals (particularly beginners) attack their leadership role with a vengeance—trying to be all things to all parties, to do everything, to attend to every detail, and to cover every base—while neglecting themselves in the process. In the long run, this won't work. It is a mistake to believe that leaders shouldn't think of themselves or that it is selfish to take care of yourself first.

In every school, the whole organization looks to the leader for hope and health. As principal, if you don't have your own act together, personally and professionally, the whole institution suffers. You have to be able to manage yourself, your personal life, and your career before you can successfully manage anything else. The smartest and most effective principals learn quickly and early on that their first order of business must be to cultivate, nurture, and care for themselves as leaders, as professionals, and as human beings. One way to handle your professional role as principal is to pattern your career after the success of others.

SECRETS OF SUCCESS FOR SCHOOL PRINCIPALS

Most individuals who achieve the principalship usually succeed in terms of keeping their job, maintaining an adequate school operation, staying out of trouble, and avoiding disaster. But there are some principals who seem to be a cut above the ordinary. Their success is defined by widespread professional recognition, unusual staff loyalty, and long-lasting community respect. They are the stars in the field. What makes the difference between run-of-the-mill principals and the best of the profession? Many veteran observers among teachers and administrators point to a dozen distinguishing factors that account for the special success of some principals:

1. The most successful principals find a way to take care of the little leadership things that count. They pay attention to details, meet deadlines, and stick to established policies and procedures. Their secret

often lies in selecting competent assistants and secretaries and in delegating details effectively.

2. The best principals keep a vision of where their career and the school are headed. This vision is their promise to themselves and gives them an edge over others. By visualizing where they want to end up, they continually bring their vision a step closer to reality.

3. They are authentic. They avoid adopting any false "leadership persona" and their leadership is grounded in what they care about.

4. They take the leadership of the school one day at a time. They realize that if they deal successfully with today, they'll be ready for tomorrow.

5. Outstanding principals know they're good, but they don't let their egos get in the way. They make having a great school a team effort. They give credit and share victories.

6. The best principals remain ethical and principle centered. They resist any temptation to play petty politics, cut corners, or sacrifice values.

7. They claim territory and carve out a niche for themselves. They have a platform and stick to it. They become known for something (innovation, student-centered learning, staff development, etc.)

8. Principals who rise to the top aren't afraid to take credit for successes. They share the glory, but they also refuse to be buried or become obscure through false humility.

9. Winners associate with winners, not whiners. They align themselves with successful fellow professionals and distance themselves from chronic complainers and losers who don't care.

10. The best leaders make continuous improvement a way of life. They don't waste time fixing blame, but constantly work to fix and improve the system.

11. They avoid focusing on "control." To be successful doesn't mean demanding blind obedience or being in charge of all aspects of the school's operation.

12. The most successful principals consciously concentrate on success. They are aware of the power of the "Walenda factor"—focusing on walking the tight rope rather than on avoiding the fall.

Principals who incorporate these features into their leadership stand the best chance of success. Every principal needs to work on these elements of their management/leadership style. Of course, another major secret of success is to stick around long enough for it to happen.

JOB SURVIVAL TIPS

In education, as in other professions, success can be transitory. We all know principals who experience quick success and gain almost instant recognition, but can't make it last. Within three to four years after they've introduced some glitzy innovations or turned a school around, they can't hold it together and must move on. Flash-in-the-pans leave little legacy.

Long-lasting differences require continuity of leadership. Part of successfully managing your career as a principal is to learn what it takes to survive over time and stay effective. Endurance is essential to endearment. If you want to be in the principalship for the long haul, here are some of the lessons passed on from practicing and retired veterans who have managed to succeed and survive:

- Don't hold an unreasonable, unrealistic, or undoable model of leadership for yourself. Accept and respect yourself as you are. Recognize your shortcomings, but maintain faith in what you can do. Hang on to an "I'm enough" attitude.

- Keep setting new goals. One trick to surviving is to always have something significant yet to do.

- Reconcile yourself to "the system." Both you and the system have flaws and limitations. Keep trying to stretch or bend the system where possible. Otherwise, accept things as they are and do the best to achieve all you can within existing realities.

- Conduct periodic "reality checks." Confront yourself honestly and keep making decisions based on who you are and what you believe in. Know how you feel about things and accept and act on your feelings.

- Keep your sense of perspective and humor. If you take yourself or your job too seriously, the system will chew you up, and you'll become a phony in the process.

- Take care of yourself physically and emotionally and work as hard on managing your important personal relationships as you do on managing your job (see the discussion on dealing with health and stress later.)

- Stay renewed and keep learning (see the discussion on professional growth activities later). Keeping up with technology is a classic example. Principals today who have not achieved computer literacy have forfeited a good deal of their leadership capability.

- Remember where you come from and where you want to go. Sometimes, the only way to keep going is to recall why you set out to be principal in the first place.

- Know when to walk away. If you're going to last in the job, you need to avoid wasting time on things that will never work and can't be changed. Drop ideas and projects that aren't going anywhere.

- Learn when to lay low. When the proverbial manure hits the fan, it is not dispersed equally. There are times when it is best to be low key, to stand on the sidelines, and to stay out of the line of fire. You'll last longer if you don't jump on short-term bandwagons or feel compelled to commit to lost causes.

- Adjust your leadership style over time. There are things a beginning principal can do that a 20-year veteran can't and vice versa. The newcomer may be able to achieve some things through sheer energy. A seasoned administrator, may, however, accomplish the same results by working smarter and applying experience. Don't be afraid to let your leadership mature as you do.

These measures are what it takes to last in the job as principal. One other essential element of longevity is to master the politics of the principalship.

HOW TO BECOME "POLITICALLY SAVVY"

Like most human institutions, schools and school systems are permeated by politics. Smart principals don't get caught up in playing petty political games, but they must learn how to work with and around the politics of the situation. To be successful, every principal needs to develop a degree of political savvy (i.e., "street smarts" for getting things done in the organization). To strive to remain above political infighting is one thing. To be so naive that you deny the existence of politics is another. No principal can afford the latter.

The goal of good principals should be to place professionalism over politics. (Ethical behavior beats political behavior in the long run.) The most appropriate form of political leadership by school leaders involves emphasizing collaboration, forming coalitions, building partnerships, influencing decisions, taking risks, and sharing power.

To use the positive side of politics, while avoiding being tainted by the "dirt" associated with some political activity, there are certain realities that every principal needs to know or find out, including:

- Who are the policymakers and who are the power brokers in the system?

- Who are your friends?

- Who are your enemies? (Sometimes, it pays to cultivate a good enemy if you don't have one. Then, at least, you have one person who will quickly and directly point out your shortcomings.)

- What are your supervisor's hot buttons and career objectives?

- Who is successful in the system and why?

- Who has the real power and where do they get their clout?
- Who are potential back-stabbers and/or staff members most likely to go over your head?
- What political factions exist and how do they work?
- Who are the political phonies in the organization? (See what to watch for next).

How To Spot Political Phonies

The most dangerous political phonies:
- Focus on appearances.
- Steal ideas.
- Specialize in double talk.
- Make promises they don't intend to keep.
- Put personal gain over organizational goals.
- Deal in disloyalty.
- Use sex appeal for political advantage if they can.
- Take undeserved credit.
- Spread rumors and gossip.
- Attack personalities and exploit others' weaknesses.
- Cheat if it serves their purpose.
- Shirk blame.
- Lie about performance and distort their successes.
- Disregard confidentiality.
- Try to build a career on "brownie points."

Based on a good feel for the organization, savvy principals use politics to their advantage by:

- Developing negotiating skills.
- Making concessions when the results are worthwhile.
- Cultivating as many mentors as possible.
- Listening to and respecting the rumor mill while not feeding it.
- Letting people become indebted to you so you can call in your marker later on. (Examples include loaning employees to help out in tight situations and offering to handle new elementary registrations during summer months when K–6 schools are closed.)
- Avoiding being linked with individual board members or aligned with any specific political factions in the system.
- Getting an edge an adversaries by looking at them from different perspectives (renaming the opposition).
- Taking smart chances—being bold when the risk is reasonable and the reward worthwhile.
- Exercising some "enlightened paranoia" to avoid being blind-sided.

- Practicing amnesty. (Don't let grudges get in the way of forging more productive relationships.)

Handling the political dimensions of the organization without engaging in dirty politics is part of managing your role as principal. The next section deals with managing and maintaining your health as the school's leader.

HANDLING YOUR HEALTH AS A SCHOOL EXECUTIVE

Healthy organizations require healthy individuals to run them. Good health is critical to peak performance. Through neglect or self-destructive lifestyles, some promising leaders undermine both their health and their careers.

Without self-care and self awareness, a host of health problems (high blood pressure, heart trouble, ulcers, chemical dependency, etc.) can short circuit a successful career in the making. As principal, your first job is to take care of yourself on and off the job.

The best way to start managing your own health is to put physical well-being at the top of your priorities and to put the job in proper perspective. Leaders who last understand that no job is worth sacrificing your health. Even leaders should work to live, not live for work and work alone.

Being full-time head of the school is a demanding, stressful, and draining role. To survive and succeed, every principal must operate from a basic "energy core." It is this energy core that provides the necessary strength, stamina, creativity, and resiliency to get the job done. One important aspect of maintaining good health is managing the forces that add or subtract from your core of energy as depicted in the fishbone diagram provided.

Health is holistic. Good health means nurturing physical and mental well-being, wholesome relationships, a positive work life, a supportive environment, and spiritual serenity.

Neglect or abuse in any one area can cause a ripple effect that does damage to all the others. The foundation for good health in all these areas is a positive, optimistic attitude. People who believe they are healthy tend to be healthy.

Although all the factors outlined are important, one has taken on special significance for today's principals. As the pressures of the principalship have intensified, job-related stress has become a major health hazard. The next section defines ways to handle stress on the job.

ENERGY CORE
(Cause and Effect Diagram)

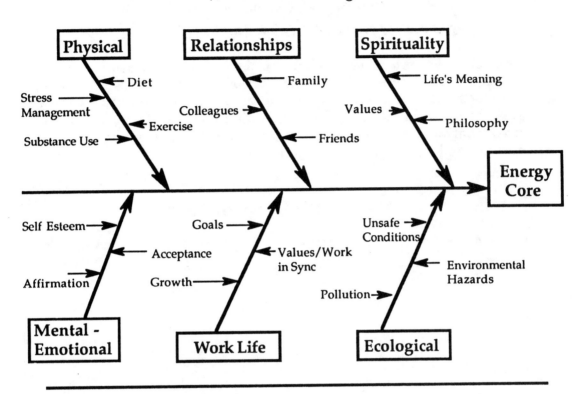

ESSENTIALS OF STRESS MANAGEMENT

Stress has both positive and negative effects. Positive stress is what makes people meet deadlines and achieve goals. The negative impact of excess stress, however, can cause all kinds of problems in the health of the individual and the harmony of an entire group. When the leader is over-stressed, it often spills over into the organization. If the principal has a "bad day," the whole school can be affected. Like most fields, school administration has its own set of stress agents, including:

- Relentless visibility
- Emotional overload (Being expected to serve as the problem solver for other people's problems takes an emotional toll.)
- Long hours (full days plus numerous evening and weekend activities)
- Lack of privacy
- Isolation and limited support (Principals are constantly surrounded by people but have limited access to peers in similar positions.)

- No set routine and a schedule that is often beyond control
- Continuous pressure to do more, better, faster, and cheaper
- Red tape and bureaucracy
- Wide variety of audiences and would-be bosses
- Heavy life/safety responsibility for others.

These elements add to the buildup of stress for all principals, but each individual reacts differently. The first step of successful stress management or reduction is stress awareness—the knowledge of what causes you the greatest stress and tension. Some administrators use a simple individual stress analysis form to understand where their stress really comes from and how they're handling it (see sample).

Individual Stress Analysis Form

List what bothers you most.	What do you do about it?	Does it help?	What might work better?

In addition to awareness of what causes your stress, it is important to be alert to signs that stress is affecting your behavior and performance. For most people, there are definite indicators that signal they've had enough and need to do something about their stress level.

Stress Signals: Sympoms of too much stress

- Becoming argumentative and irritable (short fuse)
- Shouting
- Hostility
- Indecisiveness
- Poor judgment
- Lack of concentration (inability to focus)

- Inconsistency
- Confusion
- Forgetfulness
- Desire to escape
- Avoiding people
- Sleep loss
- Loss of appetite
- Physical symptoms (headaches, neck pain, rapid pulse, irregular breathing, chest pains, excessive perspiration, etc.)

A certain amount of negative stress can be tolerated, but each individual has a threshold at which some form of stress reduction is vital. When signs point to a level of stress that is getting in the way of performance, it is time to take action. There are lots of things principals and other administrators can do to maintain or eliminate excess stress. The following coping mechanisms can help you avoid becoming overstressed:

- Develop rituals. Familiar patterns of behavior can help see you through stressful periods.
- Change your routine. If your regular routine isn't working, shake up your day by doing things differently. If you normally begin the day dealing with office matters, start off by visiting classrooms for a change.
- Have a personal retreat in the school. Some principals find solace in visiting an industrial education class or browsing in the library or dropping into the head custodian's office. Don't however, retreat to the teacher's lounge if you are looking to get away from stress.
- Exercise at your desk. Physical exertion releases stress.
- Take "minute mental vacations." Visualize doing things you enjoy in places you like to be.
- Be aware of emotional overload and give your emotions some down time. Let your mind go numb for a while.
- Don't focus too much on details. Let others sort out minutia.
- Make time every day to do something you like to do in the school.
- Be willing to live with a "wait and see" attitude.
- Don't take work home. When you carry your briefcase home it is usually filled with the stress of the office. Leave both at school.
- Try not to be judgmental. Playing judge for others adds to your own emotional stress.
- Change your attitude. See the opportunities in problems. Sometimes,

there is a semantic solution by which you can assign a new meaning to a stressful situation by renaming it.

- Build your own support group. Find ways to associate with successful principals and other administrators.

- Admit mistakes and ask for help (personally and professionally) when you need it.

- Get right with people. Make amends if necessary. Festering relationships feed negative stress.

- Use humor to break up tension.

- Disappear for a while. Eat lunch away from school or stop to enjoy the day enroute to the district office or another school. If necessary, take a day or two of personal leave to slow down and gain control of your feelings.

The causes and cures of excess negative stress are individual. Each person needs to find out what works for him or her. The worst thing you can do about stress is ignore it.

Part of managing yourself as school leader and maintaining both personal and professional health is to build in opportunities for continuous renewal and growth throughout your career.

HOW AND WHEN TO FIT IN PROFESSIONAL GROWTH ACTIVITIES

Being an effective principal doesn't happen by accident. You have to learn how to do it and keep learning to keep doing it. One of the most marked distinctions between an ordinary principal and an outstanding one is the latter's capacity and commitment for continuous professional growth. School leaders who stay at the top of their profession understand that they are responsible for their own professional development and that lifelong learning requires motivation, conviction, and action. They also realize that lethargy is the antithesis of leadership.

It's not easy to grow professionally. Some principals take the line of least resistance and adopt the position that "I don't have time to read" or "I can't afford to take any more courses." This is the shortsighted attitude of a leader who is going to "lose it" along the way. Good principals cannot afford not to keep learning, growing, and developing.

Not many of us want to go to a doctor who does not keep up with the latest medical advances or a lawyer who has not turned a page since law school. Likewise, students, staff and the community deserve more than a leader who refuses to stay fresh in his or her profession. There are six compelling reasons why you owe it to yourself and your school to continually engage in professional growth activities:

1. Continual learning helps you find out what is possible.
2. You cannot expect teachers and other staff members to improve their skills and knowledge if you don't model lifelong learning.
3. Working at continuous renewal is the only way to build vitality for the long haul.
4. Without ongoing growth, you cannot develop the organization—you can only maintain it.
5. You cannot hope to be innovative and renew the school unless you persistently renew yourself.
6. Continuous growth and development helps give you energy and keep you young.

The nation's best principals are open to new experiences, seek them out, and make learning a habit. The alternative is professional stagnation.

One of the best ways to keep up with the ever-changing world of education is to read, keep on reading, and then read some more. Our society abounds with worthwhile books and articles on schools and schooling, on adolescence and youth, on leadership, on teaching and learning, on family life, and so on, that all have direct bearing on the role of the principal. Some successful principals keep reading materials with them at all times to make the best use of downtime or wait time as they pursue their day.

Any principal who claims to have no time for reading has got to be suspect. There's too much important information out there and too many ways to get at it to use "time" an as excuse. The most avid leaders who want to keep learning often augment their reading by listening to instructional cassette tapes at home or while driving.

In addition to reading and listening to tapes, the sources and opportunities for professional growth activities for principals are extensive. A partial list includes the following:

- University courses
- Professional workshops
- Conferences/conventions
- Sabbaticals
- Professional associates/organizations
- Teaching college courses
- Visiting schools
- Using consultants
- Professional writing
- Videotapes
- Networking

All principals can find time for professional development once they commit to its importance in their professional lives. Some have gone so far as to negotiate up to five "professional growth days" into their contractual duty year.

All of us exist in a state of partial fulfillment and development. The complete principal accepts that learning should never end. This is a major piece of managing yourself as a leader and is what makes the principalship a profession and not just a job.

This chapter and all the preceding ones have offered understandings, techniques, and tools that can help any principal succeed and enjoy the role as leader of a totally unique institution—the American public secondary school.

Final Word: Managing Tomorrow

All the preceding chapters laid out the nuts and bolts of succeeding as a secondary school principal today. But no "owner's manual" can provide complete instructions for handling what the principalship will become tomorrow. The given is that schools will change and school leaders will have to retool and adapt accordingly. For the timid, this is scary, but timidity is not the stuff that leaders are made of. The best principals relish the renewal and challenge of change.

This final chapter offers hints on what paths and passages seem to lie ahead for secondary schools and what principals can do to prepare for the future.

WHAT GOES AROUND COMES AROUND (BUT NOT EXACTLY)

No matter what form the school of tomorrow assumes, it is almost certain to have some of the look of the school you manage today. Education in America tends to move forward in fits and starts and in waves and cycles. Despite all the clamor for radical reform and major restructuring, much of what changes in educational organizations is often more a matter of recycling than of total transformation.

Veteran principals sometimes feel that they've earned a doctorate in *déjà vu*. The pattern of secondary education in this country reflects a number of movements that come and go and reappear later with new twists and additional trappings (e.g., yesterday's "management by objectives" becomes today's "outcome-based education"). Back to basics, accountability, and humanizing the school are among the many recurring themes that periodically take center stage in educational discussions across the nation.

The important thing for principals is to appreciate that each time schools recapture an old idea or resurrect a past practice, they do it better. The trick is to avoid becoming cynical. How many times have you heard seasoned educators respond to suggested change with comments such as, "We've tried that before and it doesn't work" or "I'm not going to get excited;

this, too, shall pass away"? It's easy to become blasé, but it's an attitude school leaders can't afford.

It is a mistake to view the cyclical nature of educational change as an exercise of going in circles—getting nowhere. Progress in education is more like a spiral than a circle. Each time schools revisit a program or practice, it is cranked up a notch, improved, and refined. This is the way schools move onward and upward and improve. Good principals understand this and make the most of it.

The best way to manage the future is to be a student of the past and present. When an old idea resurfaces, remember and learn from what may have gone wrong in the past and stay fresh to new possibilities.

CREATING YOUR SCHOOL'S FUTURE

The future of your school will most likely be a mixture of old ideas and innovations. Whatever it contains, tomorrow is something that can be shaped and influenced today. The future doesn't just happen. It is invented. Whatever happens to the school in the years ahead will have been created, prompted or allowed by today's school leaders and staff.

Contrary to what many shortsighted administrators believe, schools can alter their own destinies. That is what the best secondary schools are doing on a daily basis. If the principal and staff do not consciously set about forging a future for the school, others (including politicians, business leaders, and special interest groups) will do it for them.

Shaping a school's future starts and ends with a vision. A clear-cut image of what the school can and should become is what separates great principals from merely adequate ones. If the principal can define, articulate and "sell" a specific image of tomorrow's school, that image will become the school's future.

Chapter 2 spells out the means and steps for developing a vision for the school and a plan for making it happen. Do not make the mistake of always being too busy to get around to visioning and strategic planning. Your choice is to either envision the future you want for your school and work toward it or become victim of a future you never intended and had no hand in designing.

WHERE DO PRINCIPALS GO FROM HERE?

Whether running the school today or shaping the school of tomorrow, principals need to be sensitive to emerging trends and future directions. This awareness of where things are headed helps root today's decisions in reality and increases the likelihood of planning effectively for the future.

Of course, it is hazardous to speculate on future developments. Nevertheless, some growing trends, such as choice, parental involvement, business partnerships, and the concept of a global community, may be here to stay. To ignore such developments is to deny yourself some essential planning and action tools.

Many current indicators point toward two interrelated directions, in particular, that certainly will have impact on schools and school leadership in the years ahead. The first is *quality management* and the second is *open systems*.

Quality Management

The principles of total quality management, which W. Edwards Deming used over 50 years ago to spark the legendary "Japanese transformation," are now being recognized and adopted by the leaders of corporate America. There are also signs that these same principles are beginning to spill over into the public sector, including schools. The 3M Company is now marketing a system for "Managing Quality Education" (MQE). To be ahead of the game, educational leaders would be well advised to study the elements of quality management for application in their own school setting (see "Buzzwords of Quality Management").

Buzzwords of Quality Management

- Customer service/satisfaction
- Value added
- Continuous improvement
- Systems improvement process
- Zero defects
- Pride and joy in work
- Customer-driven
- Constancy of purpose
- On-time delivery
- Exceeding customer expectations
- Problem prevention
- World class standards
- No fear/no barriers
- Doing the right thing right
- EOS (evidence of success)
- Doing it right the first time

The quality movement can and should be related to school restructuring. In deciding where to go from here, astute principals won't ignore this trend.

Open Systems

There appears to be little question that the management/decision-making systems of schools will continue to become more open in the future. There are lots of ways to describe the trend toward openness including:

- Flattening the hierarchy
- Turning management on its side
- Moving from top-down to bottom-up decision making
- Turning the organizational chart upside down.

All these suggest a dramatic blurring of historic distinctions in power, position, and influence. When you see a principal insisting that staff members help define their own job descriptions, letting employees criticize the boss, asking how they can help others do their job better, and managing by expectations and encouragement, you are observing an open system in action. This is the stuff visions are made of.

Opening up the system does not muzzle leaders; it multiplies them. An open system can actually make the principal's job easier. Part of creating your school's future should be finding ways to open up the system. This is one legacy you can leave to succeeding generations of school leaders and learners.

ONE PERSON CAN MAKE A DIFFERENCE: THE LEGACY YOU CAN LEAVE

There are leaders who like the freedom of not having a destiny to live up to. Most principals, however, want to leave some lasting impression on their school. Having a building or a library or even an athletic field named after you is a nice tribute and remembrance. But there are greater legacies a school leader can leave. The most significant and enduring contributions that a principal can make to any school are the *people* and the *culture*.

If you can assemble a staff of professionals and support personnel who take responsibility, see options, and take risks, you will have influenced generations to come. Likewise, if you can establish a school culture based on excellence, pride and human concern, it will tend to be self-perpetuating.

Not everyone can become a principal. But most of those who do can be successful. It is hard work, but it can be done, and it can be fun. Secondary principals, more than many other kinds of leaders in our society, can make a lasting difference. This guide is designed to help. Good luck!

Index